SANCTIONED

NICK PUREWAL

SANCTIONED

THE INSIDE STORY OF THE SALE OF CHELSEA FC

\Bᵇ\
Biteback Publishing

First published in Great Britain in 2025 by
Biteback Publishing Ltd, London
Copyright © Nick Purewal 2025

Nick Purewal has asserted his right under the Copyright, Designs and Patents Act 1988 to be
identified as the author of this work.

ISBN 978-1-78590-989-4

10 9 8 7 6 5 4 3 2 1

A CIP catalogue record for this book is available from the British Library.

Set in Minion Pro and Trade Gothic

Printed and bound in Great Britain by
CPI Group (UK) Ltd, Croydon CR0 4YY

CONTENTS

PROLOGUE

On the afternoon of 2 March 2022, Roman Abramovich stepped quietly out of a luxury office in a converted Ottoman palace in Istanbul's upmarket Besiktas district to make an urgent phone call. He had spent the day brokering meetings between Russian and Ukrainian government delegations in an ambitious bid for peace. Only six days had passed since Russian forces invaded Ukraine, but in that time Abramovich had been jet-setting across Europe on a delicate mediation mission. Russia's invasion of Ukraine was already at full-scale, but he still hoped a lengthy and gruesome campaign could be averted.

On another front, Abramovich saw only one option. After nineteen years of ownership, he had accepted he would have to sell his beloved Chelsea Football Club. That morning, two of his most trusted advisers had been dispatched back to London. By the time their plane landed at Heathrow Airport, he was ready to move.

Hardly on the London tarmac when his call came, Abramovich's aides hurried to set up a makeshift office on the floor of Heathrow's arrivals hall. With battery-drained laptop plugged into the only available power point, the pair rushed to compose a statement.

Even after the week's extraordinary events, its contents would shock the world.

Only a handful of people knew Abramovich was even considering selling Chelsea. His closest staff still expected him to find a way to retain his ownership, perhaps by ceding central control of the Stamford Bridge club. He had always had suitors trying to buy Chelsea, and before this moment, he had rejected every single one.

His instructions had stunned the team at Heathrow. He had ordered them to draft a clear, unequivocal statement confirming that Chelsea was for sale, in full, with all proceeds to be donated to all victims of the Ukraine war.

Word quickly spread among Abramovich's inner circle. Chelsea chairman Bruce Buck found himself shedding a quiet tear, struggling to reconcile the realities of war with the end of a Stamford Bridge dynasty. Abramovich had led Chelsea to nineteen major trophies since buying the club in 2003, in an unprecedented era of success. Now it was all over.

Buck would quickly turn his pragmatic mind to helping to manage the most public elite football club sale of all time. But in the moments after discovering Abramovich's decision to sell, shock, reflection and sadness all combined in an emotional flash.

Chelsea director Marina Granovskaia was at home ill, suffering from Covid-19. Precious little could surprise someone who had long since developed into one of football's most powerful decision-makers. Amid her Covid fever, however, Granovskaia had to perform a double-take on receiving word of the sale. The Russian-Canadian initially thought herself delirious through illness, until a second inspection confirmed the news.

Meanwhile, Abramovich's two aides at the airport raced against time to meet his demands for a quick turnaround of the statement, still tapping away sat on that unforgiving arrivals hall floor. In less than thirty minutes, the right words had been found and were duly double- and triple-checked. As fingers prepared to hit send on an email carrying a revelation to change the course of Premier League history, one turned to the other and asked, 'Holy shit, are we really doing this?'

A slew of expletives echoed that astonishment some thirty-four miles north, at Luton Town's Kenilworth Road stadium, where Chelsea's coaches and players were preparing for their FA Cup fifth-round tie. With no advance warning, the news was a genuine shock, breaking as it did in the hour before kick-off. Agricultural language turned the touchline and the dressing room blue, as the full Chelsea contingent broke off from warm-up routines and pre-match planning, immediately questioning their futures.

As reality dawned, text messages and emails flooded the inboxes of senior Chelsea staff, who could not keep pace with the sheer volume, let alone comprehend the content. Some employees were fearing for their livelihoods, some were reduced to floods of tears, while others were simply too stunned to speak.

Abramovich, meanwhile, had to attend to other matters. Immediately after putting the phone down to his two advisers at Heathrow, he hopped from Istanbul to Poland, via Ankara. From there came a convoy drive into Ukraine ending in Kyiv, the sole route available into the war-torn country.

The journey was treacherous, the gunfire and rocket shelling of live warfare providing a deadly backdrop, the motorcade halted at regular intervals by roadblocks and military checkpoints en route to the Ukrainian capital.

At the same time, Chelsea's stunned players took to the Kenilworth Road pitch, some 1,400 miles away in Luton. As the Blues ground out a 3–2 win, supporters, now well aware of the announcement, doggedly chanted Abramovich's name from the stands.

The very next day, a world away from the UK media's focus on the snap Chelsea sale, an attempt was made on Abramovich's life. He came to late at night, unable to see and in intense, stinging pain, the skin peeling from his face and hands. Two colleagues had suffered the same symptoms and all three had to be rushed to a hospital outside Kyiv for emergency treatment. Independent experts would later say the men had been poisoned. They all made a relatively full recovery, but the scale of the danger in Abramovich's mission was laid bare.

As doctors doused his eyes in that Ukrainian medical facility and his sight started to return, the picture was crystal clear that for both Abramovich and Chelsea nothing would ever be the same again.

CHAPTER ONE

WAR ON THE EDGE OF EUROPE

23 FEBRUARY 2022

Roman Abramovich surveyed the damage at his estate in the south of France, indulging in a wistful lament for the passing of time. High winds had felled a 200-year-old tree, loved by the Abramovich family as much for its character as for its history. As he helped clear up the wreckage, he had no idea of the events in store across the few days ahead, neither their enormity nor their rapid escalation. If he was shocked when Russia invaded Ukraine the following day, he was equally surprised to be asked to join the embryonic efforts towards seeking peace.

After the invasion, the Ukrainian government wasted no time seeking sit-downs with Russia. President Volodymyr Zelensky's closest personnel had been mining their most trusted contacts, trying to open lines of communication with Vladimir Putin's administration. More than forty prominent Russians and Ukrainians were approached and asked to help set up a link to the Kremlin that could, at the very least, float the idea of both sides breaking bread in the same room. Abramovich not only numbered among that call list: he was the only one who agreed to help.

And so, less than twelve hours after Russia invaded Ukraine, on 25 February Abramovich flew to Poland for secret peace talks, just two days before Chelsea were due to face Liverpool at Wembley Stadium in the League Cup final. In other circumstances, Abramovich would have been making plans to jet in to London to take his seat among the 90,000 supporters at Wembley that Sunday. Instead, he was preparing to broker mediation summits. Amid the myriad brutalities of war, Abramovich was en route to Warsaw.

Touching down in the Polish capital, Abramovich and several of his most trusted advisers headed straight for a conference hotel on the outskirts of the city. After a lengthy wait in a faceless conference room running into multiple hours, the Ukrainians arrived and set out their stall.

The meeting was surprisingly short. The Ukrainians only needed to state their case and hope that Abramovich could deliver their message to Moscow. He left with Ukraine's delegation agreed, and his role of unofficial go-between settled too. While willing to help, Abramovich's role was merely to pass on the Ukrainian messages, unsure how those would be received back in Russia.

Despite the intensity of the war and the escalation of aggression and rhetoric, the response from both sides appeared extremely positive. The Russians were not just willing to engage in communications but also prepared to receive the Ukrainian proposals – so prepared, in fact, that the first official meeting happened just two days later.

Having only just reached Moscow to deliver the initial Ukrainian request, on 26 February, Abramovich was on the move again straight away. This time he was headed for Belarus. Putin and Zelensky would not talk directly, but both did immediately arrange for their negotiating teams to meet.

On Sunday 27 February, with Chelsea just hours from their

League Cup final showdown with Liverpool, official delegations from Russia and Ukraine descended upon the springtime retreat of Belarusian President Alexander Lukashenko, who was to play host as well as mediator. Nestled in the Pripyat National Park, some thirty miles from the border with Ukraine, sits Lukashenko's countryside residence. Enveloped in forest, a sprawling campus boasting a helipad and a sports complex would stage the first official talks between Russia and Ukraine, with peace on the agenda.

Two days after sitting down in secret with the Ukrainians in Warsaw, Abramovich and his team found themselves on hand at the Lukashenko compound, just outside the village of Liaskavichy.

Vladimir Medinsky, a senior adviser to Putin and former culture minister, headed a group of Russian envoys also comprising representatives from the ministries of foreign affairs and defence. Ukraine's delegation was led by Davyd Arakhamia, the parliamentary leader of Zelensky's political party. The then defence minister Oleksii Reznikov, future defence minister Rustem Umerov and presidential adviser Mykhailo Podolyak were also on hand.

Russia's opening gambit was brutal in tone and content: the Moscow delegation demanded Ukraine's total capitulation. The bullish starting point could easily have ended the entire endeavour, but both parties managed to finesse discussions to the point where communication lines were left open. All and sundry departed with plans to convene again, and soon, with Belarus primed for further hosting duties.

Abramovich was retained in his role too, asked to continue back-channelling efforts. Already committed to the cause, he was not about to back out. In a conflict changing by the hour, the two sides meeting once and agreeing to do so again represented significant progress.

• • •

Joe Ravitch was on holiday with his wife in Mexico when Russia was preparing to invade Ukraine. The co-founder of renowned merchant bank Raine was refreshed and reinvigorated from just one of many days' scuba diving when he returned to his hotel with designs solely on relaxing and mulling over dinner plans. The moment he checked his mobile phone, however, the rest of that February 2022 day's itinerary took a drastic turn, because Ravitch had more than 100 missed calls and an even higher number of messages.

Abramovich was still some days away from resolving to sell Chelsea, but the turbulent situation on the Ukraine–Russia border left him on alert, making preparations to cover a raft of eventualities. The Blues owner's most senior and trusted staff were doing what they always did in times of great potential change, battling to stay ahead of that curve. And so, Abramovich's senior aides had spent a large chunk of time trying to track down Ravitch at his Mexico vacation bolthole. The fast-developing situation, with Russian troops again mobilising, left Abramovich's staff acutely aware they had to prepare for all eventualities, from testing the market on a hypothetical deal to putting Chelsea fully up for official sale.

Ravitch's instructions were clear and concise: start making early logistical plans for a potential sale process. The vastly experienced banker and broker had overseen Abramovich's last toe-dip into the potential sale market in 2018 and 2019, when Todd Boehly had seriously explored a deal for the Blues, but that had never reached the latter stages of a negotiation. At that point, as with every other time Abramovich had considered selling, eventually he decided entirely against it.

This time, though, everything would be different, and the coming sale process and public circus would turn Ravitch into something of a household name, at least in footballing terms. He and partner Colin Neville tasked ten staff with full-time work on the Chelsea sale, even from the day Russia invaded Ukraine. As Abramovich's staff were acutely aware, he would expect headway to have already been made by the time he would make the final call on the sale. That meant Raine getting the jump on the final decision, and their early tasks included sketching out a plan for the process itself and also setting up a virtual data room, the type of secure online portal that can house an investor pack through which interested parties can carry out due diligence.

A gregarious, animated character with a knowing flash in his eye and a winning smile, New York native Ravitch had spent sixteen years as a senior partner at Goldman Sachs, helping to broker deals like the sale of MGM Studios and the creation of NBA China. A Yale Law School graduate and the son of Richard Ravitch, the former lieutenant governor of New York, Joe Ravitch founded Raine with Jeff Sine in 2009. Through personal contacts and robust acumen in brokering major deals, Raine steadily built its portfolio and client base, to the extent that a sporting figure of Abramovich's calibre would turn to the US-based group as a first port of call for any kind of sale consideration.

Brokering the Chelsea sale would drive Ravitch and his colleagues to their professional limits, earn the firm millions and propel the bank to new heights in the world of sports club transactions. When Ravitch's scuba diving trip was interrupted, though, the first steps towards building a sale process had to be tentative – and discreet.

●　●　●

Just days after Ravitch's Mexico trip hit the buffers, at Chelsea's training ground in Cobham, Surrey, head coach Thomas Tuchel met the media, ostensibly to preview that Sunday's Carabao Cup final against Liverpool. The articulate German expected to be quizzed on the war in Ukraine but had not planned the emotional monologue he delivered in response. Tuchel quickly found himself fielding a glut of questions on the future: his own, the club's and that of Abramovich. He should have been talking about how to defeat Jurgen Klopp's resurgent Liverpool, and how Chelsea were fixated on adding more silverware to the Club World Cup title they had won in Abu Dhabi just thirteen days earlier, finally completing the full set of global trophies. Instead, he broke with flat-bat protocol and opened up on a host of distractions affecting the west London club. A visibly moved Tuchel admitted that he and his players had been 'clouded' by events in Ukraine.

While Abramovich was waiting patiently in that plush Warsaw hotel conference room for Zelensky's chief aides to arrive, Tuchel surprised even himself when he lamented the reality of war on the edge of Europe.

'Maybe people understand that me as a coach or the players, we don't have the insight into what is really going on,' said Tuchel, amid one of the most obscure situations ever faced by an elite football manager. 'At the moment we don't feel responsible for all this. We feel that it is horrible and there can be no doubt about it. War in Europe was unthinkable for a long period. The impact is clear and the discussions have an impact.'

Where elite sports stars would normally insist on a tunnel-vision approach in a ruthless bid for success, Tuchel admitted Chelsea had lost that luxury. For the manager of the reigning Champions League, European Super Cup and Club World Cup winners to accept such distractions was no small beer.

'It's pretty unreal, it's clouding our minds, it's clouding excitement towards the final, and it brings huge uncertainty,' said an agitated Tuchel, talking in Cobham's bespoke press conference room. 'Much more to all people and families who are actually more involved than us. And our best wishes and our regards and thoughts are obviously with them.'

Asked if he would try to switch off from those realities, Tuchel insisted that would be impossible. 'I think you can't,' he said.

I think the situation is too big and it is not an isolated situation somewhere. It concerns Europe, it's in Europe and we are part of Europe. We cannot say let's put this to the side. It's the opposite. We have to live with it right now. There is no running away from it. There is no shutting the doors and now we focus on football. We are still privileged to live in peace and freedom right here where we are right now. And we are still privileged to have a game of football, to have an emotional but peaceful environment with fans in the stadium.

This, the first of many erudite and impassioned speeches from Tuchel, struck a chord among the hushed assembled press. So animated and angular, Tuchel was all elbows and knees on the football touchline but so considered and thoughtful in front of a microphone, and when it mattered most.

Senior figures at Chelsea were doing their utmost to talk of business as usual, briefing media off the record that life had to go on as normal and that the club was not in any immediate threat of change. Tuchel's candour on Chelsea's unsettling links to the war left club communications staff uncomfortable. But this was a well-read, learned man in his fifties entirely sure of his own mind, and who had in effect paid with his job at Paris Saint-Germain for sticking to his principles when falling out with the club hierarchy.

Any such worries on Tuchel's open dissection of Chelsea's situation were not shared in the Abramovich camp. Firstly, Abramovich had far more pressing concerns, not least that sought-for peace. But secondly, Abramovich wanted coaches confident, articulate and brave enough to speak their minds in public, to communicate intimately and in detail with the club's supporters. Abramovich had always adopted a default approach of keeping his own counsel on a public front in his Chelsea tenure, never involving himself in the politics of either football or the UK.

When the political climate would allow, Abramovich had always been on hand for Chelsea's biggest triumphs. He had been in Lisbon for the 2021 Champions League final victory over Manchester City, and in Abu Dhabi earlier in February for that maiden Club World Cup success. Though the rest of English football's great and good turned out in force at Wembley on Sunday 27 February for Chelsea's Carabao Cup final clash with Liverpool, however, the Blues owner did not. A world away from his meetings with Russian and Ukrainian delegations in Belarus, Abramovich's Chelsea took to the Wembley turf with thoughts of war in Europe firmly on their minds, but also hopes of taking yet another trophy back to west London.

The League Cup was meant to have accrued an almost second-tier status in the modern era, but here were two teams in full flow, at full strength – and managed by two full-throttle German super-coaches. If ever a manager cracked a club's genetic code, it was Klopp, who had transformed Liverpool through tactical acumen and force of personality. Tuchel's counterpart was every inch his equal, in world view, intellect and bold strategy.

Both teams tore into each other, laying on a compelling and

chance-laden encounter that somehow ended goalless after extra time. The multi-billion-pound world of elite sport would grind on, regardless of whether it came to represent a cosy bubble or an important distraction from the terrors of war.

The 120-minute deadlock could only mean penalties. But after two hours without a net once rippling, suddenly neither side could miss – ten players from each team converted their spot-kicks in style. And there were moments when it appeared that the shoot-out might never end. With all the outfield players having taken and scored their penalties, the goalkeepers had to step out of the net and up to the ball. Reds goalkeeper Caoimhin Kelleher nervelessly converted his side's eleventh spot-kick, heaping the pressure on his Chelsea counterpart, Kepa Arrizabalaga.

The Spain stopper was itching for penalty redemption, after refusing to be substituted in the 2019 Carabao Cup final in a bizarre spat with then boss Maurizio Sarri. Kepa had saved one spot kick in that match, but Manchester City had still prevailed 4–3 on penalties, leaving combustible Italian coach Sarri fuming, for once not due to his trademark smoking habit. Three years on from that peculiar clash with Sarri, Kepa could not seize his chance for atonement. Desperately searching for a definitive strike, he instead blazed the ball high over the bar as the most intense of sporting pressures took its toll. As Liverpool's players hoisted the trophy high into the north London sky, Chelsea's mood was about to darken significantly – and not because of losing a penalty shoot-out.

•   •   •

Abramovich was never in the business of public statements as Chelsea owner. That he would take the rarest of steps and put his own name to a quote spoke volumes on the far-reaching consequences of the war in Ukraine. On Saturday 26 February, Abramovich broke his silence, but he chose to address Chelsea's situation rather than the conflict directly. Abramovich and staff were in Poland when they drafted a 110-word statement that proved an early, and unsuccessful, attempt to secure Chelsea's future. He wanted to pass control of the Blues to the club's foundation trustees.

> During my nearly 20-year ownership of Chelsea FC, I have always viewed my role as a custodian of the club, whose job it is ensuring that we are as successful as we can be today, as well as build for the future, while also playing a positive role in our communities. I have always taken decisions with the club's best interest at heart. I remain committed to these values. That is why I am today giving trustees of Chelsea's charitable foundation the stewardship and care of Chelsea FC. I believe that currently they are in the best position to look after the interests of the club, players, staff, and fans.

As the statement reverberated around the world, a raft of questions was quickly raised, quietly from some of the Chelsea foundation trustees themselves but noisily from football's punditry machine. Chelsea chairman Bruce Buck and women's team manager Emma Hayes were among the trustees nominated to shoulder the 'stewardship and care' of the club, alongside Paul Ramos, John Devine, Piara Powar and Hugh Robertson.

While several of the six-strong group of trustees aired concerns behind the scenes, Abramovich would come under fire from ex-players like Gary Neville and Jamie Carragher, who criticised Abramovich for not condemning Russia's war. Some also questioned whether handing control of Chelsea to the club's charitable foundation trustees would represent a sufficient break from Abramovich's regime. Abramovich adopted a holding pattern, seeking to understand his Chelsea position in more detail. No one outside his inner circle had any idea of his peace mission, robbing his statement of crucial context. Critics chided Abramovich's lack of comment on the war, but he was not interested in public statements and instead focused on his back-channelling. Any such equivocation was clearly unsustainable, however well-intentioned.

And so, the very next day, while Chelsea's players were locked into that Carabao Cup final with Liverpool on 27 February, the club issued a far shorter follow-up statement. 'The situation in Ukraine is horrific and devastating,' read the second statement. 'Chelsea FC's thoughts are with everyone in Ukraine. Everyone at the club is praying for peace.'

And in just twenty-four words, a postscript was added to Abramovich's statement. Abramovich again had his peace mission in mind when choosing not to put his own name to the addition. Once again, however, much of the public reaction was to question why there was no condemnation of the Russian aggression. Try as he might, Abramovich was struggling to uphold his rule of not mixing Chelsea with politics.

• • •

Todd Boehly fielded a call from long-time associate Joe Ravitch that moved quickly from catch-up pleasantries to a proposition that, in a flash, commanded both imagination and attention. Bringing Boehly up to full speed on the events that looked to have precipitated Chelsea's sale, Ravitch asked whether the American financier and keen sports investor was still as interested in buying the Blues as he had been back in 2019. The answer was an overwhelming, immediate yes – at which point, before he was even off the phone, Boehly was already planning a bid in his mind.

If this was the spark to ignite an all-out bid to buy Chelsea, then the fuse had been set not just in 2018 and 2019, when Boehly first explored a potential deal for the Stamford Bridge club, but also at various points throughout the American billionaire's life. A two-time conference champion wrestler in high school, Boehly then competed for a further two years in college – but football had actually been his first sporting love. Between the ages of five and fourteen he had featured in midfield for the McLean Lancers and the McLean Ambassadors, two travel teams in his hometown on the outskirts of Washington DC, before continuing when at Landon School in Maryland.

Boehly would even be pressed into emergency stints in goal, and only stopped playing football when the time came to focus exclusively on one sport, and his talents dictated that sport became wrestling. A business administration degree focusing on finance followed at the College of William & Mary in Williamsburg, in the final year of which he opted to head overseas. London was calling, and Boehly duly finished his degree at LSE, where he was also able to launch his finance career by working at Citibank.

That year in London saw his fixation for football revived, but it was when he co-founded the real estate platform Cain International in 2014, alongside British business magnate Jonathan Goldstein, that his passion for England's national game was fully reignited. Prominent Tottenham fan Goldstein took Boehly to the old White Hart Lane, and rumblings about a potential sale of Spurs had piqued interest. Several exploratory conversations were had, but when they failed to develop into anything tangible, Boehly was still left with the overriding feeling that he wanted to invest in football – and in London.

After Sergei Skripal and his daughter Yulia were poisoned in Salisbury in March 2018, the UK expelled record numbers of Russian diplomats amid increasingly tense geopolitical relations. A former Russian intelligence operative and UK double agent, Skripal had been the victim of foul play. The magnitude of the incident and its fallout left Abramovich and his team carrying out due diligence checks on the market as regards parties interested in potentially buying Chelsea. Boehly was asked by Raine to be a part of that review, and he had no hesitation in agreeing, highly prizing the allure of west London. As the groundwork progressed, Boehly started attending matches at Stamford Bridge, relishing the full experience and gaining valuable insight into the club's workings. The more Boehly learned about Chelsea, the more he came to appreciate what Abramovich had achieved, in what he came to regard as a club-wide renaissance, across everything from the set-up at Cobham to what the modern iteration of the Blues stood for.

Boehly's exposure to English football broadened even further across the same timeframe, through a loan he made to Sunderland. Ellis Short, who owned the Black Cats, was looking to sell the club and approached Boehly about a potential sale. Boehly explored the opportunity, but the more he examined the details, the more convinced he became of the power of London. As he considered England's capital, he crystallised his opinion that Chelsea was London's club, from its geography in the historic and fashionable west of the city to the club colours, the badge and even the gritty determination exuded by the team itself. Through his ownership share in MLB side the LA Dodgers, Boehly was experiencing first-hand how a big city can support a team, and this only served to boost his inclination to hold Chelsea in the highest esteem.

Boehly's discussions with Raine and Chelsea ownership representatives in 2018 and 2019 never reached the stage of an official bid, with the talks taking place in a relaxed, low-stakes manner. It was always understood that Abramovich and his advisers were exploring all options and testing the market, in order to be prepared in case a sale would ultimately be desired. Comfortable with what proved a learning experience for both sides, especially with the lack of pressure and the high levels of growing mutual respect, Boehly was able to build relationships with Abramovich's camp to sit alongside his already robust working partnership with Ravitch and Raine. In the fullness of time, Boehly would consider this a dress rehearsal for the 2022 sale process, but across 2018 and 2019, the discussions only served to raise his interest in the club and his ambitions for future Premier League ownership.

So when Boehly took Ravitch's snap call at the tail-end of February 2022, there was no hesitation or doubt: he would be bidding for Chelsea, and he would go all-out to win. Boehly had spoken excitedly about Chelsea three years earlier to Mark Walter, the chief executive of Guggenheim Partners and one of his fellow Dodgers investors. His mind then turned to Hansjörg Wyss, remembering the Swiss billionaire's passion for football, how he had grown up playing the sport and that his apartment had overlooked a football pitch. Both men were quickly as energised as Boehly about forming a consortium, so much so that by early March they were already building a partnership. So even when the sale was yet to be confirmed fully in public by Abramovich himself, Boehly, Walter, Wyss and Goldstein were already starting to circle the capital they felt would be required to pull off what would become a world-record sports franchise sale.

• • •

In the meantime, politics was coming for Abramovich. The Chelsea owner had felt UK authorities breathing down his neck to varying extents ever since the Skripal poisoning affair of 2018. But in Russia's edge towards war with Ukraine, all subtlety evaporated on the winds of political change. In announcing a raft of sanctions to Parliament on Tuesday 22 February 2022, Prime Minister Boris Johnson falsely claimed that Abramovich had already fallen under such restrictive measures. Labour MP Chris Bryant then told Parliament on 24 February that he had obtained a leaked Home Office document from 2019 detailing alleged links between Abramovich and the Russian state, and alluding to 'corrupt activity and practices'. Bryant suggested the government should freeze Abramovich's UK assets, bar him from owning a British football club and even block him from basing himself in the country.

Spokespeople for Abramovich questioned Bryant's actions, stating, 'This document was never published, and nobody has been able to verify the content or context of this alleged document.' Abramovich's staff also added further background to Bryant's Commons address. 'The document which is referenced is named "HMG's Russia strategy aimed at targeting illicit finance and malign activity". This is not a document specifically aimed at Mr Abramovich. He has not been accused of anything and in fact has been able to visit the UK after the document was allegedly created.'

The outbreak of war had lowered the threshold for imposing sanctions, and British public support was overwhelmingly with

Ukraine and their courageous leader Zelensky in the face of Russia's aggression under the feared and erratic Putin.

The Tory government wanted to cripple the Russian war machine through economic constriction, manifesting as sanctions, but Johnson also craved any possible public approval boost. For all his bombast, Johnson was still weighed down greatly by the political after-effects of the Covid-19 pandemic and the lasting impacts of various lockdown stints – not to mention the ongoing Partygate scandal, which had engulfed his regime. A sequence of parties breaking the government's own social distancing rules had threatened to floor Johnson and his leadership group. The Prime Minister was characterised by many close to him as determined to gain ground in the court of public opinion when it came to handling Britain's response to the war in Ukraine.

The Ukrainian government saw the tides and trends turning against Abramovich too, just when they were hoping to rely on his support in their greatest hour of need. The Ukrainian leadership was understood to have called Johnson to explain Abramovich's efforts, requesting that the UK refrain from raising sanctions, suggesting these could prove counterproductive to the peace process.

The request was met with scepticism in Downing Street, especially as to the scope of Abramovich's role. The Ukraine government insisted, though, that Abramovich was viewed as neutral and reliable in both Moscow and Kyiv, hence the two sides remaining agreeable to his involvement.

Seeing the writing on the wall from a UK government perspective, and through some back channels of their own, the Ukrainians ensured that news began to break on Abramovich's early efforts towards peace talks.

Abramovich considered his mission would be best carried out

in the shadows. But Ukraine's leadership feared he could not maximise his impact without wider knowledge of his work. Alexander
Rodnyansky had stepped back from his usual pursuit of directing
Oscar-nominated documentaries to help Ukraine's government
secure high-profile go-betweens with Putin's regime. It was Rodnyansky who broke the hushed silence on the negotiations, confirming on 28 February that Abramovich was indeed involved in the
process. Rodnyansky spoke of President Zelensky's relief and hopes
that meaningful talks might achieve an early resolution.

In Ukraine, Abramovich was viewed through a new lens of respect for shouldering great personal risk in his attempts to broker
talks. In London, the reception ran the full spectrum. At Stamford
Bridge, loyal Chelsea fans still had club colours in mind when
praising the owner who had transformed their entire footballing
experience. At Westminster, politicians had angled the prism a full
180 degrees. Labour MPs Chris Bryant and Dame Margaret Hodge
took to Twitter to question the sourcing and veracity of reports providing basic details of Abramovich's new role.

Battle lines were being drawn in every arena, from the court of
public opinion to football's global contests, via the House of Commons and the halls of both the Kremlin and the Rada. Arching
above it all, however, were very real and deadly fronts of actual war.
As Russia had breached the lines of international diplomacy and security with its invasion, so too had the UK's boundaries of football
and politics been blurred like never before. As February turned to
March, all parties involved crossed a line in the sand.

CHAPTER TWO

KENILWORTH ROAD

Minutes after Abramovich's shock announcement that Chelsea was for sale, Petr Čech walked into the boardroom at Luton Town's ageing Kenilworth Road stadium. Oblivious to the throwback surroundings and cramped facilities, Chelsea's technical director was struck instead by the reception from his executive counterparts in the Luton hierarchy. Čech led the Chelsea delegation into Luton's directors' facilities on the evening of Wednesday 2 March 2022, in the final build-up to the Blues' fifth-round FA Cup encounter, against a Championship club battling to match their lengthy past with a buoyant future.

As Čech entered the room, all eyes locked immediately onto his giant frame, all gazes fixed intently on the Stamford Bridge board member and his colleagues. The former Chelsea and Czech Republic goalkeeper had grown accustomed to being stared at, his 6ft 5in frame and footballing renown making him instantly recognisable to fans and the wider public alike. This was a man who had won the Champions League and four Premier League titles in a glittering eleven-year playing stint at Chelsea that also included winning the Europa League and three League Cups. He was a mainstay of the Chelsea side that set a Premier League record low of fifteen goals conceded in the 2004–05 campaign. He was entirely used to receiving attention, and just as adept at dealing with it. But in the immediate aftermath of Abramovich's revelation that he would sell the Blues, Chelsea were suddenly the world's biggest sporting story, bar absolutely none.

So for anyone in that room of a Luton persuasion, it was impossible not to let their gaze linger a beat too long as a minimum – and in some cases to downright gawk. At least, that is how that boardroom entrance felt to Čech and company, who were stepping into the unknown in so many more ways than simply embarking on Chelsea's first competitive trip to Luton since 1991. The game's global foundations were still shaking as Čech and the rest of the Chelsea cohort met their Luton counterparts, whereupon they had no choice but to field a slew of questions about the future.

'So what happens now? What is the process? How long will a sale take? What's next for you all personally?' All these enquiries and more had to be batted away, deftly and gently, for at that point, there were precious few answers.

Abramovich's statement that Chelsea was for sale had been posted to the club's website and social media channels at the very point that the Blues' players were warming up for their last-sixteen FA Cup clash at Luton. Supporters filing into the ground stopped in their tracks as notifications landed on their phones. The assembled media, packing out a set of Luton facilities not so often accustomed to such numbers, were sent into a frenzy of filing words, recording new audio reports, and ripping up any existing plans on how to cover the night's events.

Abramovich, for his part, had issued an unprecedented and deeply personal statement that laid bare his plans for Chelsea and his own hopes, even signing off his message solely with his given name.

I would like to address the speculation in media over the past few days in relation to my ownership of Chelsea FC. As I have stated before, I have always taken decisions with the club's best interest at heart. In the current situation, I have therefore taken the decision to sell the club, as I believe this is in the best interest of the club, the fans, the employees, as well as the club's sponsors and partners.

The sale of the club will not be fast-tracked but will follow due process. I will not be asking for any loans to be repaid. This has never been about business nor money for me, but about pure passion for the game and club. Moreover, I have instructed my team to set up a charitable foundation where all net proceeds from the sale will be donated. The foundation will be for the benefit of all victims of the war in Ukraine. This includes providing critical funds towards the urgent and immediate needs of victims, as well as supporting the long-term work of recovery.

Please know that this has been an incredibly difficult decision to make, and it pains me to part with the club in this manner. However, I do believe this is in the best interest of the club. I hope that I will be able to visit Stamford Bridge one last time to say goodbye to all of you in person. It has been a privilege of a lifetime to be part of Chelsea FC and I am proud of all our joint achievements. Chelsea Football Club and its supporters will always be in my heart. Thank you, Roman.

Čech and Chelsea's other directors at Kenilworth Road could tell their Luton peers and anyone else they would meet that night that

Abramovich meant every word of a statement that many considered bittersweet. They could talk of a determination that the sale should not be rushed, that all proceeds would be aimed to benefit all victims of Russia's war in Ukraine. They could talk of Abramovich's groundbreaking ownership, how he had transformed Chelsea, and the Premier League, in his nineteen years at the Stamford Bridge helm. They could not, however, talk with any certainty about how any further events would unfold.

The UK government and the European Union were both busily examining how to sanction Abramovich, aiming to prove his ability to influence President Putin in order to impose asset freezes and travel bans that could aid Ukraine's war effort.

The sale of any major business, but especially a Premier League club, would only usually be announced on, or at least close to, completion. Geopolitics had conspired to remove any chance of following accepted protocol, and certainly any confidentiality: the sale was public knowledge before any process had even begun. This total inversion left staff at every level of Chelsea's organisation in a spin.

If Čech and his fellow directors were swimming in uncertain seas then, the players, coaches and staff could have been forgiven for struggling to tread water amid an announcement that created a storm the like of which none of them had ever seen. The players had been particularly stunned by the news, and left in a state of confusion. Athletes crave the certainty of structure, the security of routine, and elite performance finds its bedrock in both.

The large contingent of homegrown Chelsea players, the highly prized and accomplished academy graduates, were among the most distressed. Senior stars and England internationals like Mason Mount had been connected to Chelsea for almost their whole lives. Talented forward Mount, born in 1999, had joined Chelsea aged seven and not only had he never looked back – he had never even known a Chelsea that had not been owned by Abramovich. Even Čech, who had already made his name with Sparta Prague and Rennes before joining Chelsea in 2004, had never had any first-hand experience of a Stamford Bridge set-up not operated by Abramovich.

Now, in the bowels of Luton's cramped stadium, Čech seized a vital opportunity to address the team's questions as best he could, delivering one straightforward message: for tonight, keep it simple.

One thing was certain: the Luton match would go ahead. Win this game, and everything – the uncertainty, the drama, the shock, the sadness – would feel instantly better. The reigning champions of Europe would be expected to roll over second-tier Luton without issue, and no quarter would be given if they failed. Čech told the Chelsea squad to control what they could and put the rest aside, certainly for the duration of the evening. Coaches, players and support staff were asked to do what they loved doing, what they did best, and to do that to the best of their ability.

There were no tears in the dressing room that night, perhaps mainly because of the collective shock. There was an immediate frustration and anger, however, and an overt feeling of discontent that both Čech and Chelsea's coaches, led by the shrewd and savvy Tuchel, quickly looked to shape into a driving force.

As the minutes until kick-off ticked by, preparations became ever more match-focused, but many of those in the Kenilworth Road dressing room and on the pitch for the pre-match warm-ups recall a heady mix of autopilot preparation and latent, building indignation. The final messages before Chelsea took to the field to contest a place in the FA Cup quarter-finals echoed Čech's initial advice: win the match, and everything will feel that little bit better.

• • •

Abramovich's move to sell Chelsea had been every inch the lightning bolt that had struck the Blues players mere hours later in Luton, his decisiveness catching everyone involved unawares. The billionaire was already well ensconced in early attempts at back-channelling, aimed to try to create a platform for peace talks between Russia and Ukraine. On the ground and on the move in Istanbul, he had spent the bulk of 2 March shuttling between luxury hotels in the swish Besiktas district, as well as offices of the Turkish government, all of which were housed in varying converted Ottoman palaces.

He had stepped away from those high-level and high-stakes concerns just long enough to act on his decision to sell Chelsea, by picking up the phone and ordering two of his closest aides to get to work drafting a statement.

After almost a week's worth of delicate, nigh-on dangerous discussions with representatives of all the key players in this deadly Russia-Ukraine conflict, the advancing global, geopolitical and footballing events made it abundantly clear he could not extend his nineteen-year tenure of his beloved Chelsea. Never a man to waste time, he stuck to type, made the call and tasked his staff with a statement that would change so much so markedly, and forever; for himself, his family and friends, for Chelsea, for the Premier League and even for the wider world of football too.

In just half an hour, Abramovich's aides had drafted that statement, the Chelsea owner had approved it personally, and then it was prepped for imminent publication.

While Cech had been dealing with many of the issues immediately arising from Abramovich's seismic revelation at the Blues' match in Luton, another Chelsea director was conspicuous by her absence, albeit entirely unwittingly. Senior director Granovskaia was ill, at home in west London suffering from Covid-19, and had spent the day in bed and battling to shake off a nasty sickness arising from the still-raging global pandemic.

Missing a match through illness would be nothing to relate in normal circumstances, but by the time the shock statement on the club sale had pinged around the world, her absence suddenly sat in an entirely new context. Immediately, Granovskaia worried that idle talk would suggest she had stayed away from Kenilworth Road on purpose and because of the planned club sale. But in fact, she had learned of the statement on Chelsea's sale only in the final run-up to its public release.

Amid the flu-like symptoms of Covid, Granovskaia did a double take when checking her phone and reading the statement. While she had been all too aware that the mood music was potentially inching towards Abramovich making this decision, the speed of his final snap call meant she had not expected this move so quickly.

On first reading, she feared her illness was playing tricks on her, so she straightened herself out and looked at the statement again. No matter how many times she read it, the words and their meaning remained the same. This was the end of an era to end all eras.

Granovskaia gathered herself enough to speak to Abramovich on the phone, telling her long-time boss that not only did she agree with his decision, she also considered his aims to donate all proceeds to all victims of the conflict as an act of ultimate kindness. Even from her sick bed, one of the hardest working and shrewdest football administrators and negotiators was already mapping out a potential sale process, despite a slew of unknowns and amid a constantly changing wider geopolitical landscape.

Uncertainty had been building among staff at Chelsea, from the ticket office to the executive suites, ever since Russia's invasion of Ukraine. Abramovich's statement answered several questions, but posed countless more, and the initial reaction to the shock news had left many staff members in tears. Chairman Buck had numbered among those who did indeed shed a tear for the end of Abramovich's glittering tenure, with no more trophies to add to the Club World Cup title, that had been claimed less than a month previously in Abu Dhabi.

The shock and immediate grief at Chelsea, whether from wider club employees at home, players, coaches and other staff at Luton, and even those connected to Abramovich and his family, gave way to a sense of immediate high alert in other realms. From the UK political scene to the global banking fraternity, via a coterie of already eager suitors, who had long since harboured aspirations and ambitions of owning the Blues, decision and policy makers across the world were all watching.

• • •

Kenilworth Road is a living, immersive museum piece, a still-beating homage to football's hyper-local and community-focused past. Luton moved to the ground, in the Bury Park area of the Bedfordshire town, in 1905. To say that the club is intimately linked to the local area would be an understatement. Parts of the stadium are physically connected to the traditional homes that surround it, so much so that the away end's Oak Stand entrance has been carved into a row of Victorian terraces, leading fans into the ground via a narrow alleyway passing directly under several flats.

Chelsea's fifth-round FA Cup tie at Luton was littered with proverbial banana skins well before Abramovich's staggering sale statement. But as supporters filed in through that retro Oak Stand gate, trudging up steps overlooked at distances of a few feet by bathroom or bedroom windows, their phones were dinging and pinging non-stop with notifications of the greatest impending change at Chelsea in more than a generation.

Rain earlier in the day had given way to glowering mist, swirling and catching the beams from the old-fashioned tower-style floodlights encircling the field. As the night air grew colder, so did the pre-match Chelsea mood – that is, until passionate, focused and driven boss Tuchel told his players to turn the frustration, uncertainty and upset on its head and channel it into a performance that could stand as a statement all of its own.

Čech, meanwhile, had invoked the spirit of Chelsea's 2012 Champions League-winning side, of which he had been a key part, in asserting that the Blues have always been at their very best when written off. Just as interim boss Roberto Di Matteo had faced down low expectations when he led Chelsea to their maiden top-tier European triumph a decade earlier, so too would rivals, detractors and naysayers now line up, excitedly rubbing their hands in the hope that the Blues would fall hard, flat and fast.

As Tuchel's team took to the field, lining up for kick-off, they did so with messages swirling in their heads: keep it simple, vent some frustration within professional boundaries if necessary, win and everything will feel better. However, nowhere in any of those pre-match speeches, which ranged from the Churchillian to the prosaic, did anyone talk about Luton taking an early lead. But when the unmarked Reece Burke thumped in a header just two minutes into the tie to put the hosts 1–0 up, Chelsea's night somehow became even tougher.

A rotated Blues line-up looked disjointed and almost dispirited from the off – perhaps understandably given the off-field context, though they would be shown no mercy for underperformance, such are the ruthless demands of elite competition. Burke took full advantage to land that early blow for the hosts, and Chelsea needed time to find both their bearings and anything approaching rhythm either on or off the ball.

Chelsea's ever-present travelling support were frustrated by the early setback but refused to be cowed by the day's biggest news regarding owner Abramovich. In fact, a large contingent of the Blues faithful quickly struck up chants in support of the owner, singing his name as much in hope that his tenure could somehow continue as in defiance at the impending end of an era.

Those chants were branded controversial immediately, by sections of the media urging caution amid a developing military conflict, by Luton fans just happy to jeer their Premier League visitors in classic football pantomime – and by some Chelsea supporters, who appeared to voice their displeasure in the Kenilworth Road stands by urging their fellow Blues to hold their tongues.

Football match atmospheres are never more menacing than when a fanbase is split, and this was no exception, with an air thicker than the lingering mist. Burke's early goal for Luton represented the worst possible Chelsea start, threatening to undo all those fine pre-match words about coming out fighting when backs are against the wall.

Luton's Aston Villa loanee goalkeeper Jed Steer quickly suffered a nasty knee injury, falling to the turf in a heap under no challenge, in an incident that only served to add further strain to proceedings. Luton had the lead, but no single person in the stadium seemed able to settle, least of all the home side's visibly hyped-up players, who were rightly eyeing a major giant-killing.

Spain midfielder Saúl Niguez added a vital touch of calm to the night, though, clipping home neatly from Chelsea's first attack to level the tie at 1–1, striding onto the ball after Mount had sent Timo Werner racing away from the Luton defence. Atletico Madrid loan man Saúl was then quickly presented with a gilt-edged chance to wrestle Chelsea the lead, only to fail to beat replacement goalkeeper Harry Isted from close range.

Scoreboard parity should have allowed Chelsea to settle, even despite Saúl's miss, but just when the visitors would have been looking to take control, Luton struck again. Harry Cornick stormed clear of the Chelsea cover, set himself and then slotted coolly past Blues goalkeeper Kepa. The Spain stopper had delayed coming off his line just long enough to hand Luton striker Cornick the angle to slide the ball past him and into the net.

And so Luton took a 2–1 lead into a half-time interval where again the Chelsea coaches reiterated their pre-match messaging: keep it simple, follow the gameplan, stay focused, pick Luton off for the win, and then regroup. Without any complacency or the assumption of a victory, Chelsea's players and staff were also wholly frustrated by their below-par first-half showing.

The starting XI were sent back to the field, boss Tuchel resisting any urge to make early changes and demanding that the men initially chosen to complete the job get back out there and do exactly that. The third quarter proved an uphill struggle for both teams, the varying pressures weighing down the hosts as much as the embattled visitors. Eventually, Chelsea's class and focus told, and Germany forward Werner rifled home to level the game at 2–2.

Senior replacements Christian Pulisic and Reece James added impetus and incision for the final quarter, squeezing a fading Luton side still further, before Belgium hitman Romelu Lukaku ultimately settled the tie with a neat finish from a Werner assist. At the full-time whistle, Chelsea greeted their tense 3–2 win with palpable relief: no major celebrations, no milking any adulation from the crowd. Instead, the Blues were respect personified in acknowledging the supporters before making quiet but quick exits to the changing rooms.

In contrast, a gutted but proud group of Luton players rightly spent extra time applauding their raucous supporters, having threatened a major upset that would have led to their first FA Cup quarter-final since 1994. Chasing an against-the-odds promotion from the Championship to the Premier League on a shoestring budget, Luton would use their pulsating performance as a springboard back into league ambitions, even in defeat.

For Chelsea, this was a patchy victory in a match they should have won at a canter, notwithstanding the day's unique and unsettling events. Still, the Blues had achieved their stated pre-match aim of securing a result that could ease the obvious pain of events entirely outside the control of the squad, coaching staff or executives.

Full time meant the usual raft of post-match media interviews, many straight away and on the pitch, with players and coaches, and more later in set-piece press conferences. Čech, Tuchel and Chelsea's experienced and savvy media team had all been clear with their players before kick-off that when it came to press engagement, less would have to be more, and simplicity again would be key.

Wisely, the players followed the script, sticking to football when appraising the night's events. Chelsea were in the hat for the quarter-final draw, which was perhaps more crucial than anyone could know on the day. All anyone could say in addition was to admit their hopes that a potential takeover would put an end to any instability.

Footballers, like all elite sportspeople, crave absolutes, and while they are frequently out of reach, normally the result of a match, especially a win, provides at least a modicum of certainty. Chelsea's players found themselves unnerved by the inability to talk with any assuredness in almost any aspect in their post-match interviews, but still, the win was in the bag.

For exacting German boss Tuchel, victory created a platform for him to remove some of the sting that had characterised the previous few press conferences, both before and after the Carabao Cup final, and in previewing this Luton trip itself. 'It was difficult in terms of the circumstances, a huge difference, you come from Wembley, the Carabao Cup final on Sunday, and then we gave the players a well-deserved day off,' said Tuchel. 'There was some noise around the club, of course, so it was not so easy to focus, but we did very well, I think. So full credit, we did not over-expect from us, and we played a very humble match, very seriously.'

With no extra knowledge beyond Abramovich's statement, Tuchel had nothing to add on the ownership, sale or future front and so wisely opted not to offer any embellishment. At the end of a press conference held unusually on the touchline of the pitch rather than in a purpose-built indoor facility, Tuchel was finally free to take himself out of the freezing cold, doubtless as keen to thaw out mind as body.

As the mist still clung to the biting Bedfordshire air, Tuchel trudged off sporting a wry smile and shaking his head in bemusement, encapsulating a day of ultimate change.

·   ·   ·

The day before that FA Cup victory over Luton, Čech and fellow director David Barnard had held two extended meetings at the Blues' Cobham training ground. Čech and Barnard met first the men's senior squad and staff, then their women's counterparts, attempting to allay the elite squads' concerns. Even though Abramovich was a day away from officially announcing the club sale, speculation was rife about Chelsea's future, and his attempts to pass control to the club foundation's trustees had failed to gather momentum.

Čech had asked senior director and transfers chief Marina Granovskaia if he could hold the meetings, in order to add stability and structure amid the confusion that was surrounding the club. When Čech stood before both sets of football operations, first the men and then the women, he had to take a calculated risk: he had to display a poker face of confidence that Chelsea's board would be able to ensure that day-to-day working life would remain unaffected.

Čech and Barnard stood up and vowed that they would do everything in their power to insulate the players, coaches and staff from all the wider issues, and that they would fight to keep daily operations as close to normal as possible. The message was delivered strongly and clearly that as far as goals for the season were concerned, for both club and individuals, nothing should change. What the players and staff had to do was try to stay grounded, balanced and focused.

While Chelsea's hierarchy remained confident these pledges could be upheld, Čech was still left with the nagging worry that the cliché of losing a dressing room starts when leaders fail to keep their word. As Čech and Barnard outlined what little they could of what was happening in the wake of Russia's invasion of Ukraine, Čech knew full well that Chelsea's seasons, both men's and women's, would stand or fall on the club's ability to live up to these promises.

Keep the pressure off the players, minimise or eradicate change from an elite performance and preparation perspective, and there would be no issues. Slip from these standards, and the risk was genuine that players or staff could lose heart, and perhaps commitment. Čech's extensive dressing-room experience across Chelsea's most decorated era also meant he knew squad dynamics, and specifically those at Stamford Bridge, far better than most. This intimate understanding led him to expect that Chelsea could harness the frustrations and turn them to their advantage, through a carefully composed and measured siege mentality.

Managers Tuchel and Emma Hayes proved crucial to Chelsea's club-wide ability to build even stronger internal bonds and focus on the football amid a state of Stamford Bridge limbo. Tuchel and Hayes had already started the process of reassuring players and staff in earnest by the time Čech and Barnard delivered their set-piece talks at those all-in meetings at Cobham.

Tuchel's outspoken but highly savvy approach to press conferences had already alleviated a huge amount of pressure on Chelsea's board, filling the natural void of uncertainty created both by the war and by club chiefs weighing up their options. The decorated women's boss Hayes was already at the peak of her coaching powers and possessed a press conference confidence and control to match Tuchel's.

While Čech would conduct several television interviews in the immediate build-up to live broadcast matches, Tuchel and Hayes were tasked with previewing and reviewing every match as a key tenet of their positions. Under normal circumstances, these set-piece press conferences run the full spectrum from benign to explosive, humourless to hilarious. Under the extra weight of the war and the speculation regarding the owner and club, Tuchel and Hayes were now quizzed as many as four times a week on the wider situation, which forced both to field questions on an altogether novel geopolitical level.

Both figureheads acquitted themselves admirably, mixing humility with respect and candour. Chelsea's senior management and board, and Abramovich too, were relieved and impressed. The most senior faces at the Stamford Bridge club considered it a stroke of no little fortune that in both Tuchel and Hayes they had the right people at the right time to handle some of the most testing press conferences in modern football memory.

CHAPTER THREE

FOUL PLAY

While Chelsea's players and directors were broaching unchartered territory in that 2 March FA Cup clash at Luton, owner Abramovich was navigating a real, live war zone. When Abramovich's statement that Chelsea was for sale dropped just as the Blues' men were gearing up for that fifth-round tie at Kenilworth Road, the owner himself was thousands of miles away and in another world entirely. Abramovich was headed straight for Kyiv, and key meetings with the Ukrainian government, continuing his mission to try to broker peace talks between Ukraine and Russia.

There is no such thing as air travel in an active conflict, so Abramovich had flown from Turkey to Rzeszów, from where he would continue by road convoy right through Poland and on into Ukraine. Backed by a soundtrack of gunfire and rocket shelling from the nearby front line of the conflict, every roadblock or checkpoint stop forced the travelling party to confront the deadly realities of their mission. Having travelled through the night and skirted the zones of combat, when the meeting finally came, the discussions were far more straightforward than the journey.

Abramovich's status as a go-between only extended to facilitating potential meetings between the Russian and Ukrainian delegations. He felt hopeful and confident that he possessed the trust of both sides, having asserted to everyone involved that he had neither agenda nor bias in the process, save a desire to avert a long and bloody campaign that would doubtless lead to a major loss of life on both sides.

Once the first meetings were at an end, Abramovich and two others headed to an apartment in Kyiv to have something to eat and prepare for more talks the following day. Road-worn and negotiation-weary, Abramovich was ready for pretty much any safe place to lay his head, determined to refresh body and mind before another day of tense and important duties.

The trio settled down in the Kyiv apartment, and quickly tucked in to some food that had already been prepared and left out on the dining table. The three men enjoyed the simple fare in contemplative quiet. After one of the men left, Abramovich and his other colleague settled down to remain in the apartment for the night.

Abramovich went to another room to take a phone call, only to be struck by searing pain, before losing consciousness. When he came to, some time later, he could not remember anything after moving rooms to speak on the phone and then being overcome by that intense pain. Trying to work out where he was and what had happened as he came around, his eyes were burning with pain. As he attempted to open his eyes, he realised he could not see anything at all.

Disorientated and with no idea of the time, at first he wondered if he had eaten something spicy and perhaps unwittingly rubbed his eyes with chilli remnants on his fingers. Quickly, however, he realised that the overwhelming burning sensation was like nothing he had ever experienced.

Trying with all his might not to speculate on his temporary blindness, he tried to stand to find the bathroom for a tap to wash out his eyes, only to stumble into a suitcase as he failed to navigate the unfamiliar apartment. As he desperately tried to gather his composure and bearings, he heard his colleague shout out loudly, at which point he called out in reply. Following the voice, finally Abramovich was able to locate the bathroom and douse his stinging eyes, which were also constantly watering.

Abramovich's companion was suffering some of the same symptoms, though only the Chelsea owner had lost his sight entirely. Eventually the two of them went to the kitchen and brewed the strongest and hottest possible tea, with which to clean their eyes – a common method to combat eye complaints in Russia. Abramovich hoped the traditional remedy might help ease his debilitating pain. Soon it would become clear that the third member of their trio, who had left the apartment earlier that night, had also initially faced the same symptoms.

In addition to the distressing eye problems, the three men reported peeling skin and shedding hair, with the same burning sensation from their faces extending to their limbs. As sunrise came, all three had gathered again, and the group travelled by car to hospital on the outskirts of Kyiv. Arriving safely at the hospital was tense and tricky enough, but the group then had to identify themselves as civilians genuinely seeking medical help. Once they had managed to convince the soldiers guarding the facility that they were seeking legitimate treatment, they were taken through a sparsely populated hospital to be examined by a doctor.

As the three men had their eyes washed out more thoroughly and their other symptoms addressed, Abramovich's sight was beginning to return, but only barely.

The ageing facilities and equipment at the crumbling hospital left the doctor informing his patients that they would need to seek further treatment elsewhere, as soon as they were practicably able. Instead, the group sought clearance to head straight back to the talks. And so, with strict orders to seek more detailed and specialist attention after leaving Ukraine, and fast, Abramovich returned to his chief mission, and to the peace talks scheduled for that day, 3 March, in Kyiv.

• • •

Having acted on instinct to seek emergency aid, it was only when Abramovich and his two colleagues arrived at the venue for their further meetings that the reality of the episode started to sink in. Up until that juncture, Abramovich had not even considered the merest notion of foul play or conspiracy. In fact, he had approached the entire incident with a mixture of his typically unruffled practicality and an overwhelming need to first fight and then end the searing pain.

The day's meetings had been delayed by several late arrivals, and it was in that downtime waiting for the events to get under way that Abramovich first started to appreciate the jeopardy of his situation. On relaying events to Ukrainian representatives, Abramovich was told how one of their delegates who should have been attending had been killed just hours earlier. Denys Kireyev had been tasked with communicating directly with Russia on Ukraine's behalf, and he had paid the ultimate price for his role in the quest for peace, shot dead by persons unknown. The proximity of the two incidents left little room for coincidence.

Sat listening to the story of Kireyev's fate, Abramovich's eyes continued to water uncontrollably from his symptoms, so much so that his face was constantly wet. Hardly able to see more than blurry shapes at this stage, forced to close one eye and squint to gain any kind of long-distance vision, Abramovich was left with no choice but to confront the overriding suspicion that this had been a deliberate attack. Another medical team was brought to the venue of the meetings, who did indeed believe he had been the victim of a deliberate poisoning attack and advised that Abramovich needed to seek medical attention at a specialist hospital in Germany.

Determined that the meetings would not descend into the chaos of some kind of inquest, Abramovich urged all concerned to stick rigidly to the plans of bidding to progress the peace talks. Having insisted he was fine to continue, Abramovich and his cohort completed the meetings, delaying further treatment until leaving Ukraine.

•　　•　　•

Abramovich's poisoning ordeal remained at its most extreme for thirty-six pain-ridden hours. Then, at last, two nights and one day after he had lost consciousness and come around to find himself suffering from temporary blindness, his symptoms finally started to recede. By this time he had been able to leave Ukraine, again negotiating that dangerous drive back towards Poland before flying to Turkey. In Ankara, Abramovich was examined by more doctors, who thoroughly washed out his eyes, carrying out a number of tests and analysis procedures, including measuring for possible radiation exposure.

Independent investigative journalism outlet Bellingcat then quickly confirmed that, according to their own comprehensive checks, Abramovich and his colleagues had been poisoned, and they too were advising him to travel to Germany for further testing. Abramovich, for his part, had no interest in pursuing the matter further: having been poisoned once despite attempting to take the most neutral stance, he had no intention of pursuing a course of action that might further antagonise any potential perpetrators.

With the war in its infancy, tensions through the roof and volatility at every turn, Abramovich felt that any thoughts of injustice had to be set aside amid the bigger, far more important picture of the work towards a solution for peace.

While his symptoms abated in the space of several days and he made a relatively good recovery, Abramovich's sight was never restored to its previous level. Straight after his recovery, Abramovich found that he required markedly stronger corrective prescriptions in his glasses. Bellingcat's experts meanwhile theorised that the poisoning was perhaps designed not to kill but to intimidate and deter.

• • •

Certain sections of the Ukraine delegation meeting with Russia, along with several prominent Ukrainian government officials, wanted to go public immediately with news of the poisoning incident. Amid the typical claim, counter-claim and propaganda of any conflict, there were those in Ukraine's ranks who saw a way to gain ground through disseminating news of an incident born of potentially fatal foul play.

Abramovich and his senior advisers, however, quickly insisted that the entire incident be kept under wraps. The Chelsea owner and his staff felt there would be no upside whatsoever in the incident finding its way into the public domain. From a pure safety point of view, Abramovich absolutely did not want any further attempts made against him. He had no intention of making anything remotely approaching accusations as to who may or may not have perpetrated the attack, and he felt the only way to limit any further fallout was by shutting down any and all talk.

Abramovich clearly needed his health in order to continue attempting to set up peace talks through facilitating dialogue between the two sides. He also needed whatever chance possible of moving around without the constant scrutiny of a running public commentary on his every move. Eventually, the Ukrainians were talked around to his way of thinking, agreeing to keep a total lid on the incident.

While discretion led Abramovich to keep a low profile in order to push for the highest possible yield in terms of progress towards peace, even beyond the poisoning incident he was still able to have a tangible impact on easing the horrors of war. Abramovich himself has always downplayed his involvement, but senior Ukrainian delegates were quick to lay a great deal of credit at his feet when humanitarian corridors were set up to allow civilians to evacuate cities and territories under siege in the war-torn state.

By mid-March, Mariupol was under relentless siege, with Russia considering the beleaguered port city a key target in its offensive. Cut off by the shelling, civilians had no exit on any side and were forced to endure several treacherous weeks until an agreement was brokered to create a safe evacuation route. On 14 March, some four days after Abramovich was officially sanctioned by the UK government, humanitarian corridors were put in place, which had been jointly agreed by delegations from both Russia and Ukraine.

Abramovich had played a key role in the brokering of the talks that would lead to the ratification and enaction of these corridors, which saved thousands of lives. By 17 March, Mariupol officials had estimated that some 6,500 cars had fled the once bustling port, carrying roughly 30,000 people, headed for the nearby city of Zaporizhzhia. As with the poisoning incident, Abramovich kept his counsel on the entire endeavour and again worked hard to keep talk of his involvement to a minimum.

It would not be until the middle of June, three months later, that anyone with first-hand knowledge of the situation would feel prepared to talk on the record about Abramovich's role in the evacuation arrangements that had spared thousands of innocent lives. As with Mariupol, Abramovich was said to have had an important hand in similar arrangements for Berdyansk and eventually Zaporizhzhia itself. The Ukrainian MP David Arakhamia, head of the country's peace negotiating team, told Voice of America in June 2022 that 'most of the agreements were reached through him' in regard to humanitarian corridors. As March continued to unfold, though, hopes were raising markedly that a peace accord could actually be within touching distance. And amid that delicate status, Abramovich was determined not to make any moves that might upset any possible equilibrium.

Abramovich's involvement in the logistics of peace talks had been established publicly for weeks by this stage, but the detail still had to remain under wraps. Abramovich's role had been confirmed by impeccable sources weeks earlier, and yet plenty of high-ranking UK politicians continued to pour scorn on such claims. Even as some of the detail of his efforts became talked about behind the scenes in Westminster, those who were determined not to give credence to Abramovich's role refused to accept that he was involved at all, let alone had held any genuine influence.

As the realities of the Ukraine war, ranging from incidental to fatal, began to bite, the contrasts could not have been greater between the end of Abramovich's Chelsea reign and the breathless thrill-ride of a takeover that had been completed in a flash some thirteen years earlier, in July 2003.

CHAPTER FOUR

THE ROMAN EMPIRE

23 APRIL 2003

At the very last minute, Abramovich let some friends twist his arm into a rare football trip. Jumping on a jet from Moscow, he raced off to Old Trafford for Manchester United's Champions League semi-final second-leg clash with Real Madrid. Taking time out of his busy schedule as Blackburn Rovers manager, Graeme Souness picked up Abramovich and his party from Manchester Airport. Abramovich could not place Souness, thinking him extremely well dressed for a driver. Quickly set straight by his companions, any awkwardness was deftly averted.

Abramovich felt like the star of his own movie as Souness whisked them straight to United's famous home ground. Arriving at Old Trafford, Abramovich fell in love. Parking the car and walking between cordons of police on horseback, filtering into the throng of fans, he felt the electricity sparking off that procession of supporters. So many people in one place, marching towards a common venue; this was the first time Abramovich could count himself among football's flock.

A mix-up at the wrong entrance slowed the group down, and

then Abramovich was asked to put on a tie to enter the directors' box. Eventually, he was in, with a little help from United's chief executive Peter Kenyon. Every football fan can recount every single second of the journey to their first match. From leaving home to walking out into the stadium, emerging from the darkness underneath the stands to the blinding lights of the terraces. As he took his seat, Abramovich realised he was now no different.

Sir Alex Ferguson's Red Devils were in their prime and beat the mighty Real 4–3 on the night in a genuine thriller. Madrid progressed to the final 6–5 on aggregate, however, thanks to Brazil striker Ronaldo Nazário's decisive hat-trick. David Beckham stepped off the bench to slot two quick goals, but to no avail. Ronaldo asserted his O Fenômeno nickname that night, in a match that immediately entered Champions League folklore.

Abramovich could not believe what he was seeing, nor the level to which he was transfixed. His night was not about to become any less surreal either. After the match and associated receptions, Abramovich and his party feared their attempts at a quick getaway were about to be halted. The car they had booked to whisk them back to the airport was parked outside the area cordoned off to allow supporters to leave, and stewards explained that they might face a thirty-minute delay. Just as Abramovich and friends geared up to wait patiently, however, Rio Ferdinand's family explained that there was space on their pre-arranged minibus, which was only moments from arrival. And so, not content with being chauffeured to the match by Graeme Souness, Abramovich left Old Trafford in the same car as England defender Ferdinand – who had just played in the match, no less. An enraptured Abramovich found himself lifted by the openness, the energy and the passion, two sets of individuals committed to the same cause, and the emotional, physical and mental maelstrom. His friends had been telling him for months how much he would love the sport, especially if he became a club owner. He had caught the football bug, and at the perfect time too.

At the tender age of thirty-six, he wanted to retire. After selling several significant shareholdings, and with other investments still performing impressively, he felt ready to ease off the gas. No one could have imagined that a multi-billionaire's version of putting your feet up meant buying into and then transforming global football – least of all Abramovich himself.

The impromptu Old Trafford trip changed everything. For a man raised in some unforgiving environments, where demands were expressed in dispassionate style, here was a novel emotive, conversational tone. Watching the highest-stakes drama at a distance from the stands, then going up close and personal with players fresh from the field, this was what Abramovich could not shake.

He was enticed by the opportunity of running the show, shaping an entire club's future and building a legacy. Abramovich's football-mad friends were finally speaking his language – and talking him into club ownership.

Abramovich flew straight back to Moscow after that Old Trafford showstopper. For the first time ever, he did not sleep all the way. In fact, he was so amped up that he did not sleep at all. As the ideas started rushing through his head, he quickly formulated a plan. Never a man known to rest on his laurels or second-guess a decision, he acted without delay. Abramovich's team of trusted advisers were called in for a crunch meeting first thing the next morning. A new top priority was declared: the project to buy a football club.

The morning after that Old Trafford night before, the protestations started to come back. Some of those close to the would-be soccer mogul warned against ploughing money into what can so easily become a bottomless pit. His advisers kept trying to talk him out of the idea, but his mind was firmly set. Without delay, Abramovich started meeting club owners and football powerbrokers, with one goal in mind: buy quick, and buy big.

Abramovich twice met with Tottenham chairman Daniel Levy, where discussions were held about buying Spurs, though Abramovich never felt Levy truly wanted a deal. Levy advised Abramovich to look at clubs and cities in eastern Europe, suggesting Prague as a good fit.

Having been at Old Trafford for that Real Madrid thriller, Abramovich asked why not Manchester United? The answer, quickly and firmly, was that it would be impossible to buy the Red Devils. While Abramovich's full focus was now owning a football club, he was still not fixed to a specific team.

He did, however, have a home in Sloane Square, and amid all the planning, he decided to take a walk down Fulham Road – all the way to Stamford Bridge. What started as a casual stroll and a quick look at the Blues' ground rapidly turned into a full-scale takeover. Several meetings with then owner Ken Bates later, and Abramovich was well on his way to buying the club. Abramovich came away from one key meeting with Bates at the Dorchester Hotel confident he could complete a brisk deal. He received widespread advice to hang fire, with many feeling a delay would reduce the purchase price.

Chelsea were flirting with insolvency, slipping towards debts of £80 million. Bates had bought the Blues for £1 in 1982, shouldering debts of £1.5 million and securing the west Londoners' future. Now, the club's stability was again in doubt – but Abramovich was in no mood to wait. For the first time in his life, he risked putting heart in front of head for a business deal, and terms were struck within weeks.

Abramovich concluded a British record £140 million deal to buy Chelsea on 2 July 2003, shocking the sporting world and arriving at Stamford Bridge as a relative unknown. The Russian-Israeli billionaire had broken character, acting on emotion and impulse. His decision to buy the Blues came like the flick of a switch. Once his mind was made up, Abramovich's commitment was total.

JULY 2003

Abramovich could not fathom the idea that he was famous. An overnight celebrity on buying the Blues, he still did not understand why people were so interested in him. His immediate renown was not universally recognised, however. On one early visit to Stamford Bridge, Abramovich was approached by a member of the public asking for a photograph.

Always happy to oblige supporters, he asked one of his team to take the picture and he posed alongside the punter, with the stadium neatly in the background. When the man smiled politely and asked for another picture, but this time on his own, Abramovich and his cohort fell about laughing. Abramovich and friends have jokingly wondered ever since how long it took that man to realise he had one of the first pictures with Chelsea's new owner.

Abramovich was ultimately as delighted as he was amused not to have been recognised. He was well aware he would have precious few chances to slip under the radar in future.

All this attention felt a world away from his humble beginnings. Born in Saratov, Russia, in October 1966, Abramovich was raised by relatives from the age of four, after the death of both his parents. His maternal grandparents came from Ukraine but were forced to flee to Saratov during World War Two. Following military service, Abramovich's lucrative business career was cemented by buying formerly state-owned industrial assets after the fall of the Soviet Union. Even though he acted as governor of Russia's Chukotka region between 2000 and 2008, gaining prominence in his home country, precious few people knew what he looked like. As soon as he bought Chelsea, his face was everywhere. An already varied life was transformed once again.

• • •

Abramovich's purchase of Chelsea moved so quickly that even on the day he bought the club, some of his senior staff still had no idea about the deal. Paul Heagren had come on board as secretary of holding company Fordstam in January 2002, helping to set up Abramovich's UK family office, with premises in Weybridge, Surrey, as a new base of operations. Initially, Heagren was not sure exactly why he and the other staff had been drafted in, but as the projects started to build, so did the excitement and satisfaction of working for Abramovich.

On 2 July 2003, the day Abramovich bought Chelesa, Heagren was at home watching the evening news. As the story that an un-known Russian had bought Chelsea was covered, Heagren turned to his wife and said, 'I bet that's us.' Just five minutes later, he received a phone call ordering him to report to Stamford Bridge the next day rather than go to the Weybridge office as usual.

Heagren recalls that the speed of developments was so fast that it was as exhilarating as it was difficult to keep pace. The next morn-ing, Heagren reported to Stamford Bridge as agreed and made a beeline for the boardroom. As he entered, Ken Bates strode straight over to him and said, 'Hello, I hear you're Roman's man and that you're very important. This is John Terry, and he would like to say hello.'

Even as a lifelong West Ham fan, Heagren could not hide his excitement both personally and professionally: suddenly he was thrust into conversation with Blues linchpin Terry, and he found himself gripped by his personal role in Chelsea's total transformation. When Heagren had started work for Abramovich eighteen months earlier, at first it was only him and one other employee, though the number quickly rose to thirty-five. By the time the purchase of Chelsea was complete, Abramovich's UK staff numbers had again risen significantly, with a nucleus transferring from Moscow and more recruited in London and Surrey.

While Heagren's projects had been growing steadily since his arrival, once Chelsea had been bought, his responsibilities were turbocharged. Abramovich was naturally spending far more time in London, so required an increased staff to ensure smooth UK operations. The buzz, the activity and the scrutiny all ratcheted up overnight.

A family office was established to help run Abramovich's physical assets outside of Russia, primarily houses, private jets, boats, cars – and one Premier League football club. Heagren's role ultimately morphed into delivering, or finding a way to deliver, whatever was required and wherever. While this extended to Chelsea, Heagren considered himself the owner's representative in the context of the football club, providing support from logistics to guidance for club staff. Without a formal role in the club, Heagren would advise, then report back to Abramovich. Among the most senior eyes and ears for an owner transforming not just Chelsea but also football, Heagren saw a focus and direction from the very top that centred on delivering the best in every facet at the Blues, from personnel to facilities, attitudes to outcomes.

Abramovich wasted no time overhauling Chelsea that July, shelling out a mammoth £120 million to transform the squad. Damien Duff arrived in a club-record £17 million deal, with superstars Juan Sebastián Verón, Hernán Crespo, Claude Makélélé and Adrian Mutu also rolling into town. Peter Kenyon was installed as chief executive – the very same Kenyon who was in situ at Manchester United when Abramovich pitched up at Old Trafford for the Real Madrid match that hooked him on the sport.

Genial manager Claudio Ranieri had duly been backed to the hilt by the new Chelsea ownership. But Abramovich's high expectations, coupled with him meeting with England manager Sven-Göran Eriksson, put the squeeze on Ranieri from the start.

Abramovich lapped up the bedlam of his first Premier League match as Chelsea owner, relishing the boisterous atmosphere against Liverpool at Anfield. Michael Owen missed a penalty only to bury the retaken spot-kick, but Chelsea still won 2–1 on 17 August, thanks to goals from new recruit Verón and Dutch striker Jimmy-Floyd Hasselbaink.

Abramovich and the Chelsea hierarchy found affable manager Ranieri endearing and frustrating in equal measure. Dubbed 'Tinkerman' for endlessly rotating players and tactics, Ranieri's incoherence eventually turned Abramovich off.

Ranieri improved Chelsea's Premier League points tally in each of his four seasons at the Stamford Bridge helm. In his fourth and final campaign, however, despite Abramovich's vast investment, city rivals Arsenal stormed to the league title, the 'Invincibles' running the whole season unbeaten. Chelsea finished second, their highest league finish in forty-nine years, but this still fell short of the new expectations.

Abramovich anticipated his manager would deliver the top trophies and without delay. Though Ranieri had fallen short in the league, Europe could still offer a life raft. Chelsea were favourites against Monaco in their Champions League semi-final, only to lose the first leg 3–1 and draw the second 2–2. Their 5–3 aggregate defeat, confirmed on 5 May 2004 at Stamford Bridge, ultimately proved Ranieri's undoing.

Abramovich watched Monaco's Champions League final with a mixture of envy and intrigue. If the new Blues owner had expected the Ligue 1 side to power to glory, the brick wall of a well-drilled Porto prevailed instead. A certain José Mourinho had whipped Porto into a gritty, abrasive unit, culminating in that 3–0 Champions League final victory in Gelsenkirchen on 26 May 2004.

If Porto had piqued Abramovich's attention, the braggadocious 41-year-old coach Mourinho entirely turned his head. And while Porto celebrated their stunning European Cup final victory at the end of May, Abramovich made his move.

Abramovich and Kenyon travelled to Portugal to meet Mourinho for exploratory talks. Mourinho's agent, Jorge Mendes, met the Chelsea duo and quickly ended up having to hold the fort. Minutes turned to hours, and the awkwardness rose as Mourinho's lateness spiralled. Eventually, a profusely apologetic Mourinho arrived several hours late, having been delayed in a meeting with Porto's owners. Mourinho need not have worried: Chelsea were already convinced he was their man.

Abramovich believed Mourinho had come as close as could be to achieving the impossible in spearheading Porto's Champions

League triumph. Even in the days after that Porto victory, the new Chelsea owner considered there to be a strong chance that no Portuguese club would ever again conquer Europe. Chelsea's new figurehead owner saw a kindred spirit in Mourinho, but beyond that a colourful character and a strong leader. Abramovich identified with Mourinho's winning mindset and wanted him to recreate that at Stamford Bridge.

Negotiations were straightforward, once Mourinho made it to the meeting. Ranieri was dismissed on 1 June 2004, compensated to the tune of almost £2 million. The very next day, Mourinho was unveiled as Chelsea's new manager in London. Abramovich wanted a decisive hand on the tiller, and Ranieri's constant rotations were interpreted as a lack of self-confidence.

There was no such shortage of belief from Mourinho. 'I don't want to sound arrogant, but I am a special one,' said the new Chelsea boss at his first Blues press conference on 2 June, coining his own nickname. 'We have top players, and we now have a top manager.' Mourinho's brash attitude received mixed early reviews in England, with as many relishing the fresh approach as warning against the folly of over-confidence.

Abramovich loved every minute of it. Looking back, more than twenty years after Mourinho's arrival in English football, he still thinks the young Portuguese manager turned Chelsea into a bulldozer of a team. Abramovich and his closest advisers used to joke that if Mourinho's Chelsea scored first, you could leave straight away, safe in the knowledge that they would go on to win, whatever happened. They never did leave early, though, entranced by the coaching and its application. Mourinho prized substance over style and brutality over beauty, and in such hyper-efficiency Abramovich discovered a certain compelling elegance.

Mourinho was forty-one when he first took to the Chelsea dugout, almost five years Abramovich's senior. They brought the competitive animal out in each other. Mourinho's impact was as stunning as it was immediate. He swiped the first trophy he could, flooring Liverpool 3–2 in the League Cup final at Wembley on 27 February 2005. The Blues then dethroned Arsenal's 'Invincibles' in brutal style, conceding a miserly fifteen goals – still a record – en route to the 2005 Premier League crown, the club's first top-flight title in fifty years. Goalkeeper Petr Čech returned a remarkable twenty-four clean sheets, as Mourinho built his team from the back, leaving all and sundry trailing in Chelsea's wake. The Blues notched a then-record final tally of ninety-five points, in a season including a run of just one defeat in twenty-eight league matches. Abramovich's inner circle felt Mourinho fully vindicated his 'Special One' hype, while Chelsea's players would have done anything for the visionary coach.

Russomania took over at 'Chelski', much to the rest of the league's chagrin and amid some worried looks from the wider game itself. The speed and power of Abramovich's investment would in time lead to a raft of new financial rules. But in the summer of 2005, no one at Stamford Bridge was particularly concerned about profit and sustainability. Abramovich's billions were bankrolling Mourinho's juggernaut, leaving Chelsea supporters donning Russian hats and rival fans waving fake roubles in stadiums across England.

Abramovich was along for the ride and then some, metaphorically no doubt, but physically too. He joined the open-top bus tour to celebrate their first Premier League triumph, on 22 May 2005, cutting a relaxed but at times nonplussed figure. Supporters were throwing celery and vodka jelly shots at the bus, much to Abramovich's bemusement. Mourinho and Abramovich were set, and the rest of English football was scrambling to keep pace.

• • •

On 19 September 2007, Abramovich jetted into London to deal with deepening fault lines in his relationship with Mourinho. The pair met for crisis talks in the wake of Chelsea's 1–1 Champions League draw with lowly Norwegians Rosenborg the previous day. Chief executive Peter Kenyon, chairman Bruce Buck and director Eugene Tenenbaum then convened a summit meeting that ran late into the night. The outcome was clear: despite consecutive Premier League titles then a domestic cup double, Abramovich and Mourinho's relationship was beyond repair.

The next day, Mourinho left Chelsea by mutual consent, shocking the football world and leaving Blues players stunned and upset. Mourinho's strained relationship with Abramovich had started when he questioned specific recruits and money available for transfers. Avram Grant's arrival as director of football in July 2007 heaped up the tension.

Mourinho's first Chelsea stint burned white-hot with success but fizzled out quickly. Champions League glory still eluded the team, though, and Abramovich still saw European dominance as the ultimate target.

Grant took over as manager and set about calming the frayed nerves of both supporters and players. The reserved Israeli dragged Chelsea all the way to the 2008 Champions League final – and in Abramovich's home city of Moscow to boot. Chelsea and Manchester United slugging it out in Moscow on 21 May was almost too good to be true for Abramovich. And in the event, that is how it proved. Frank Lampard cancelled out Cristiano Ronaldo's opener and the game stayed at 1–1 until penalties. John Terry would lose his footing on striking his penalty, sending the ball against the post and wide. Nicolas Anelka missed too, and United won 6–5 on spot kicks. Abramovich still believes Chelsea deserved to win and has never understood the criticism aimed at Terry, insisting the England star was not responsible for the loss.

Chelsea's pursuit of the Champions League would at times drive the club to distraction, and six managers came and went before that ultimate prize was finally achieved. André Villas-Boas had been drafted in, ostensibly to overhaul the Blues squad and build for the future, in June 2011, but the young Portuguese lost the trust of the dressing room and could not meet the challenge of becoming Abramovich's Mourinho Mk II. From the ashes of his March 2012 sacking, however, came the European Cup that had eluded Chelsea for so long. Just two months after Villas-Boas's departure, former Blues midfielder Roberto Di Matteo took Chelsea all the way to the Champions League final, remarkably as a caretaker manager.

The task this time was to topple Bayern Munich in their home stadium, Munich having long since been chosen to host the 2012 finale, on 19 May. Thomas Müller struck to put Bayern into the lead in the closing stages, with Chelsea looking floored. But just when all hope was about to be lost, Didier Drogba equalised with two minutes to play. Extra time again came and went, and again, penalties. Juan Mata missed Chelsea's first penalty, but Ivica Olić and Bastian Schweinsteiger both failed for Munich. Up stepped Drogba again, and the Ivory Coast hitman buried the decisive spot-kick.

Drogba raced around the field, pretending to use the Champions League trophy as a steering wheel, as Chelsea's celebrations powered into overdrive. If Abramovich did not recall too much detail about the disappointment of 2008, the triumph of 2012 is for ever etched on his mind. Caught in a cold sweat from kick-off, Abramovich could hardly speak, experiencing an almost out-of-body detachment from his words and deeds. Later when he watched the match back on TV, he could not recognise himself. When Drogba buried the winning penalty, Abramovich and friends lost all reservations, trading measured and businesslike demeanour for exuberant, expletive-laden celebrations.

If the immediate victory salutes were unrestrained, Abramovich would also take the rare step of spending extended time in the dressing room after the match. Changing-room celebrations were put on hold for some time while Drogba went through routine drug testing. When the Ivorian finally walked in, he started talking directly to the trophy.

Abramovich was just as much a spectator as the rest of the Chelsea players and coaches, as Drogba spoke to the trophy as though the coveted silverware were a long-lost friend. 'Where have you been all my life?' Drogba. 'Why have you taken so long to come to me?'

Abramovich marvelled at the air of ritual, and the tenderness of Drogba's off-the-cuff paean. That affection eventually gave way to the more traditional spraying of champagne and beer. Not even Abramovich could avoid a dousing, ending up soaked and carrying a distinct whiff of alcohol.

An element of relief washed over Abramovich and his cohort, who had put untold emotion not just into that single contest but also into the relentless pursuit of European glory. The ruthless streak in Abramovich meant there would be no let-up, however – winning one Champions League just left the Chelsea owner targeting another. In this intensely personal love story, Abramovich was every bit as besotted approaching ten years at the helm as he had been on the day he took charge.

• • •

Abramovich's total control of Chelsea meant he could arrange the club's off-field structure with a small nucleus of trusted staff, empowered as senior decision-makers. The direct chain from owner Abramovich to the Chelsea head coach could contain as few as two links, and such agility proved vital to the Blues' ability to act swiftly and decisively.

During the course of Abramovich's Stamford Bridge tenure, Marina Granovskaia developed into his footballing right hand – which duly meant she became one of the world's most powerful women in sports administration. In a game dominated by men both on and off the field, Abramovich broke new ground by gradually increasing Granovskaia's responsibilities and influence. If the Russia of outdated stereotypes might have had the west imagining a chauvinistic, hyper-masculine business culture, Abramovich certainly did not subscribe to such an outlook. Instead, he would promote on performance not reputation, and in Granovskaia he quickly identified a person whose judgement he could trust.

Granovskaia went to work for Abramovich's company Sibneft in 1997, straight after graduating from Moscow State University with a degree in modern languages. Almost eight months after joining Sibneft, Granovskaia was moved to a new role, working for Abramovich. He had been impressed with her work and specifically requested she be reassigned to his team.

Back in 1997, Abramovich's profile was so low that people who worked for him then recall newspapers in Russia even running competitions challenging the public to provide them with a picture of a man who had never courted exposure. Despite early misgivings about her new job, Granovskaia quickly flourished under Abramovich, and the two struck up a formidable professional bond. From helping with projects to save whales during Abramovich's time as governor of Chukotka to managing his personal assets, by the tender age of twenty-three, Granovskaia had already gained an integral role in the future Chelsea owner's working set-up.

By the time Abramovich took control of Chelsea, Granovskaia was already regularly in and out of London, helping to run his properties and other assets in the English capital. Granovskaia's early involvement in Chelsea was intended to be temporary, as she had not been entirely sold on moving to London lock, stock and barrel. But from dealing with correspondence to helping navigate the mechanics of everything from ticketing to administrative football paperwork, gradually Granovskaia found herself in an integral role – albeit without a specific title.

As time moved on, Abramovich started asking Granovskaia to attend board meetings when he was unable, tasking her to observe and report back. As those reports morphed into conversations, increasingly Abramovich would ask Granovskaia's opinion on even the biggest Chelsea matters. Granovskaia was always respectful but candid and forthright, and the combination found favour with a boss who demanded such qualities, especially given the purposely tight-knit executive set-up at Stamford Bridge.

Increasingly those conversations became about players and potential targets, but despite her burgeoning sphere of influence, Granovskaia still felt that her move into dealing with transfers came about accidentally. Granovskaia had become Abramovich's official representative at the club in 2010 but did not roll up her sleeves on the transfer front until the 2011 January window.

When Frank Arnesen resigned as sporting director in November

2010, Abramovich turned to Granovskaia to hold the fort on transfers, and that meant navigating the fast-approaching January window, in which the Blues were poised to make several significant squad additions. Though Arnesen would not leave Chelesa until the end of that 2010–11 season, he relinquished all transfer control, and it was the unproven Granovskaia who stepped into the breach.

Abramovich's focus on ultra-detail at the time extended to meeting with agents, holding direct conversations with all parties at all levels of Chelsea and the wider footballing world, and he would always bring his questions back to one main topic – how to make improvements across the board. Granovskaia had always found that if she ventured an idea in which she had full conviction, invariably Abramovich would tell her to act on it, putting his faith in her judgement. When she tentatively took those transfer reins in the build-up to the 2011 January window, nothing changed. Abramovich told Granovskaia, 'Well, OK, if you think you know how to do this transfer job, then do this job.'

In Granovskaia's maiden transfer window directing the Blues' plans, Chelsea duly set a new British transfer record by spending a then-mammoth £50 million to prise Spain striker Fernando Torres away from Liverpool. The dramatic deadline-day deal – the fourth most expensive signing in football history at that point – hogged all the headlines, over and above Liverpool snaring two strikers as replacement, in the shape of £35 million man Andy Carroll from Newcastle and the £22.7 million Uruguay forward Luis Suárez from Ajax. Chelsea also recruited Brazil defender David Luiz from Benfica, in a £21.3 million deal.

While both transfers were regarded internally as coups at the time, Granovskaia still felt something to prove both personally and in order to secure the handling of Chelsea's transfer business for the long term. Abramovich had long since had his pick of the world's leading sporting directors, and up against such elite company, Granovskaia knew she had to make her mark to retain the role.

Arnesen's resignation as sporting director had come amid Chelsea struggling on the pitch to replicate their 2010 Premier League win under lauded Italian boss Carlo Ancelotti. Despite capturing both Torres and Luiz in January 2011, Chelsea finished that campaign without a trophy – and Ancelotti paid the price with his job. Torres had joined Didier Drogba and Nicolas Anelka in Chelsea's forward line but immediately lost the scoring touch that had so characterised his Liverpool tenure. He ploughed through thirteen matches without a goal before his maiden Chelsea strike, finally finding the net in a 3–0 win over West Ham on 23 April 2011.

Ancelotti's unseating brought Villas-Boas to the Chelsea hotseat, tasked as he was with revamping the Blues squad and its leadership profile. Chelsea's state of flux and frustration continued until the 2012 Champions League triumph, of course, by which time Villas-Boas had already been consigned to Stamford Bridge history. But en route to that unforgettable Munich night, Granovskaia was finding her transfer business feet.

As the 2011–12 campaign started to unfold, the newly appointed Villas-Boas was struggling to get the best out of Drogba, Anelka and Torres. The investment in Torres meant the Spain striker remained a long-term project, but there were discussions behind the scenes regarding Drogba and Anelka. Something of a split emerged in the Chelsea hierarchy between those determined that Ivory Coast hitman Drogba must be kept on at Stamford Bridge and those supporting Anelka's continued west London stay. Drogba's red card for a two-footed lunge on Adel Taarabt in a dismal 1–0 loss at Queens

Park Rangers had a number of influential figures again claiming that the potent striker was becoming unmanageable.

Drogba's remarkable goal-scoring talents were never questioned, but he had courted regular controversy ever since his extra-time red card for slapping Nemanja Vidić in the 2008 Champions League final, in which Chelsea lost out to Manchester United on penalties. Now, the QPR red card reignited wider frustrations with Chelsea's otherwise talismanic striker.

Granovskaia, however, backed Drogba and staunchly defended her position to Abramovich. The Chelsea owner in turn supported Granovskaia's call, but with a word of caution that it would be her responsibility to manage Drogba and ensure he was kept in check. The not-so-subtle subtext was that failure to keep Drogba under control could well mean the end of Granovskaia's influence on Chelsea's transfer policy and planning.

Few people can have been as elated and relieved as Granovskaia, then, in the immediate aftermath of Drogba's Munich exploits in the 2012 Champions League final. If Drogba's last-ditch equaliser would have been sufficient to save Granovskaia's transfer role, his match-winning penalty effectively rubber-stamped her position.

From that moment, Granovskaia was cemented as Chelsea's most senior director, and there she stayed for the rest of the Abramovich era. The Russian-Canadian never shied away from the fact that she had no background in football, instead basing all her decisions on business acumen, people skills and trust in a core group of expert advisers. Granovskaia's assessment of Drogba was that he needed to feel loved in order to perform to his peak and give everything back in return. Chelsea could not have asked for more in return than the club's maiden Champions League triumph.

MARCH 2018

Abramovich was finally ready to break ground on his dream of a new stadium for Chelsea. Years of revising and refining planning applications had given way to the absolute green light to demolish Stamford Bridge. In its place, Abramovich was itching to construct an architectural masterpiece that would become the envy of the world. Chelsea had explored the options of outside investment, from sources as far-flung as China, but in the end, as always, Abramovich eschewed any help in favour of funding the £1 billion project himself. He wanted to deliver a new London icon, to boost tourism in the capital and provide Chelsea fans with a purpose-built stadium to maximise supporter energy, transferring it directly to his team.

But just as Abramovich was about to push the button on this transformative project, Sergei Skripal and his daughter Yulia were poisoned in Salisbury. A former Russian intelligence operative and UK double agent, Skripal was the victim of foul play. Britain accused Russia of attempted murder, as spycraft infiltrated a quaint cathedral city in the heart of middle England.

Any diplomatic equilibrium between Britain and Russia disappeared. An unprecedented 153 Russian diplomats were expelled from Britain by the end of March. Russia denied the accusations, expelling diplomats in retaliation and making counter-accusations that the UK itself had carried out the attack. Icy diplomatic relations extended towards high-profile Russians in the UK, Abramovich included. He started to experience the mission creep of subtle actions aimed at making his UK life difficult.

Only an event of paradigm-shifting magnitude, over which Abramovich could exert no control, could derail Chelsea's new stadium project. Here it was. Abramovich was waiting for what should have been a routine work visa renewal. After the Skripal incident, all dialogue with authorities over the visa stopped in its tracks. Home Office staff had previously visited his London home, offering to help him complete his forms, even suggesting he apply for an investor visa instead. Suddenly, in the place of all that collegiate bonhomie, radio silence.

Abramovich took the hint and withdrew the visa application. Begrudgingly, he also shelved Chelsea's new stadium project. He was not about to create his magnum opus in a city where he suddenly felt so alien. By that point he had an Israeli passport, so he was still able to come into the UK via that route. Those close to Abramovich felt he was being scapegoated. Abramovich himself received varying advice on how to proceed with the officials but saw no merit in confrontation.

For the next three years, Abramovich stayed away from London. He felt uncomfortable and unwelcome in the capital. Speculation was rife that he would look to sell Chelsea, and several suitors showed the Blues their wares. Abramovich's associates would put any interest to their boss, mainly out of diligence. Every time, he would respond in the same way: why would I sell Chelsea?

NOVEMBER 2021

Out of the blue, Abramovich was invited to an interview with UK officials in Istanbul, to talk about visas. In this unofficial meeting, he was told he would be fine to travel to England. And so, on Sunday 21 November, Abramovich's three-year UK exile was over. Jetting into London, he landed at Biggin Hill Airport, to be met by an unusual 45-minute wait to clear immigration checks. Arrivals on private jets would normally be ushered through with little delay, but here Abramovich had to be patient. His advisor Rola Brentlin, who had organised the visit, was waiting to greet him at the airport and could see him in discussions with officials through a glass partition. While it looked as though Abramovich and those officials had been laughing, the wait went on. When Abramovich was finally admitted, he revealed the conversation had been simply about football.

Abramovich was in London as part of Chelsea's award-winning and long-running Say No To Antisemitism campaign. The Blues chief had backed the initiative with both funds and time, for a cause close to his heart. He visited London's Imperial War Museums Holocaust Galleries, where he had sponsored an exhibition, and was taken particularly with elements regarding the Kindertransport. The name Abramovich was spotted several times amid the horrors of that history, and while these were not relatives, the impact upon him was profound.

The next stop was Stamford Bridge itself, for his first visit since 2018. This was not to attend a match, however – at least not yet. Instead, he received guest of honour Israel's President Isaac Herzog for lunch, amid the 49 Flames art exhibition, another project to combat antisemitism. Abramovich was humbled by the presence of Holocaust survivor Sir Ben Helfgott, the former British Olympic weightlifter, the day before his ninety-second birthday.

Abramovich had to travel to Moscow for a charity event, so missed Chelsea's 4–0 home win over Juventus on Tuesday 23 November. But he did return to London to attend Chelsea's 1–1 draw with Manchester United the following Sunday. His first in-person match at Stamford Bridge in more than four years – and what would prove to be his last.

Abramovich felt reinvigorated by his long-awaited Stamford Bridge return, but that boost quickly subsided. Returning to his London house for the first time in more than two years left him with a level of disquiet he has not been able to shake since. Feeling uncomfortable in London had been a strange enough experience, but now he found himself out of place at his own home in the English capital. As he entered the house, he felt as though he was going into a place where someone had died.

Abramovich felt backed into a corner: he considered the political climate between the UK and Russia left him unable to give his best to the Blues. Allegations were resurfacing that he had bought Chelsea to gain influence in British life and perhaps even politics, a premise that he had always rejected.

In the 2020 book *Putin's People*, journalist Catherine Belton had repeated claims that Abramovich had bought Chelsea on President Vladimir Putin's political orders, without including sufficient denial from the Russian billionaire or his staff. The issue would prove central to a high-profile legal action from Abramovich against publishers HarperCollins. Abramovich would accept a settlement almost a month later, in December 2021, when the publishers apologised, amended the text and agreed to a charitable donation in lieu of damages.

The return of the issue put him in mind of his governorship of Russia's Chukotka region, between 2000 and 2008, where he had been accused of using the post as a political stepping-stone. Abramovich might have seen the argument had he been mayor of Moscow or London, but he viewed the duty of running one of Russia's most remote communities, and all its challenges, as a world apart from the kind of role that might launch a political career.

Abramovich has always maintained that he bought Chelsea purely as a passion project, though he quickly became immersed in the overwhelming drive for sporting success. He had always dealt with any Chelsea crisis by parachuting himself into London summits with coaches, staff and players. He needed to see the whites of people's eyes to direct club operations. Less than four months after his last visit to Stamford Bridge, he would be barred from operating the club at all.

CHAPTER FIVE

SANCTIONED

Boris Johnson stood at the dispatch box, under attack on all sides and desperately searching for a way to quell the House of Commons inquisition. In a chamber with perhaps higher demands for truth and accuracy than even a court of law, in response the Prime Minister 'misspoke', as the explanation of his official spokesman would later have it.

This was 22 February 2022, two days before Russia would invade Ukraine. To understand the eventual sanctioning of Abramovich by the UK government in the round, it is important to return to this episode and examine the events in Parliament in further detail.

Russian troops had been mobilising at the Ukraine border, for the umpteenth time in months. Johnson's Tory government was finally able to announce a new round of UK sanctions against high-profile Russian individuals and companies, the first to capitalise on strengthened legislation that lowered the threshold for imposing such penalties. As the Conservative leader, battling the peak of the Partygate scandal amid the continued fallout from the Covid-19 pandemic, attempted to herald this breakthrough, his rivals immediately argued that the measures did not extend nearly far enough.

Three individuals and five banks would face UK asset freezes and travel bans, amid financial measures aimed at crippling Russia's economy. One name conspicuous by its absence in that sanctions announcement was that of Roman Abramovich, and Johnson appeared to lurch onto the back foot when quizzed on that fact.

Challenged directly by Labour MP Margaret Hodge on why the Chelsea owner had not been targeted, Johnson said, 'Abramovich is already facing sanctions.' Another Labour MP, Chris Bryant, immediately jumped on Johnson's assertion, pointing out that the Prime Minister's claim was untrue, calling on him to 'correct the record'. Even Johnson's own MPs felt frustrated that the initial round of sanctions did not hit Russia nearly hard enough, with Foreign Affairs Select Committee chair Tom Tugendhat one of the highest-profile detractors to break Tory ranks.

The Prime Minister moved quickly to admit his error in claiming Abramovich was already subject to sanctions, with his spokesman issuing that official statement about Johnson 'misspeaking' later the same afternoon. Misleading the House, even unwittingly, remains a point of embarrassment even though it appears to have become more commonplace in modern times. Johnson's mistake carried far deeper frustration and shame behind the scenes in both Westminster and Whitehall, however, for a government struggling to match the pace or impact of the European Union's own sanctions suite.

Legal experts have characterised the EU sanctions enterprise as far more sophisticated, agile, organised and effective than its UK equivalent, especially in the build-up to Russia's Ukraine invasion. Johnson and his Cabinet were feeling the pinch to exude strength publicly against Russia's might and also to show solidarity and support for Ukraine. No one in the Tory administration had any designs to be seen as lagging behind European counterparts either, following the UK's fraught departure from the European bloc in January 2020.

A vast number of specialists, from lawyers to civil servants right up to the most senior ministers, had spent years framing and focusing sanctions legislation and were now finally enacting those powers. Many of those who had worked tirelessly and with ultimate expertise and precision were said to have been shocked by the ease of Johnson's false claim about Abramovich. Those same frustrated parties then considered his spokesman's tame and muted admission as not nearly atoning for the size or significance of the mistake.

Scores of staff in Westminster and Whitehall working all hours on UK sanctions against Russia were said to have been stunned that Johnson and his government could have become so muddled as to make such a glaring, public error regarding one of their main targets.

Abramovich would not in fact become subject to UK sanctions until 10 March, sixteen days after Johnson's blunder in Parliament, eight days after Abramovich put Chelsea up for official sale.

The circuitous, turbulent story that led to the imposition of sanctions against Abramovich had grown early roots in the March 2018 Skripal poisoning affair, but almost four years later, an entirely new saga morphed out of the final build-up to Russia's invasion of Ukraine.

Brexit, the Covid-19 pandemic and Partygate had all conspired to leave Britain's beleaguered Tory government in a state of flux and frustration, unsure whether to offer a mutinous public one endless mea culpa or to launch a new charm offensive. Johnson's entire premiership was on the line, and behind the scenes his leadership group was scouring far and wide for potential voter-pleasing initiatives. Rivals, both inside the Conservative Party and out, had long since abandoned any cover when firing shots at his office.

Several insiders from the Tory Party and the Whitehall machine have explained how Johnson's government was determined to sanction Abramovich as much for his profile as for any alleged ability to influence Russian President Putin. None of this came as any surprise to the Chelsea owner or the rest of the club's leadership. While Abramovich and Chelsea had long anticipated sanctions could be in the offing, his move to put the club up for sale was designed to separate, even to a small degree, football and politics.

The British government had been battling to put its house in order on the sanctions front ever since the 2016 Brexit vote, and certainly after the January 2020 departure itself. The Office of Financial Sanctions Implementation (OFSI) was established in 2016 as a subsidiary of the Treasury. The new body quickly had to shoulder the burden of working out exactly how the UK would transpose EU sanctions law after Brexit, so that such measures could then be applied by Britain.

Staff who had spent entire careers drawing down on EU law and interpreting those regulations for UK implementation suddenly had to draft not just their own versions but also update the legislation to keep pace with international geopolitical developments.

Russia's annexation of Crimea in 2014 led to the largest suite of European financial sanctions against the country since the 1970s. Russia's status as the world's eleventh largest economy rendered the scope of the entire sanctions endeavour almost never-ending, especially given the frequent updating of regulations and their interpretation and implementation.

Diplomatic tensions created turmoil in global business, and in the six months in the build-up to Russia's invasion of Ukraine, UK and EU legal alterations were so common that top specialist lawyers, notably in private practice, were receiving hourly briefing updates via email. The picture was so vast and changeable that several sanctions law experts have termed the UK and EU response and its pace as breathtaking.

Foreign Secretary Liz Truss had announced to Parliament on 31 January 2022 that new amendments to 2019 legislation would allow an 'unprecedented package of coordinated sanctions' should Russia invade Ukraine. The UK's updated sanctions legislation would allow measures to be imposed against any company linked to the Russian state and also against individuals who owned or controlled those enterprises.

Staff at OFSI were inundated with enquiries from businesses and individuals but were considered extremely nervous to make substantive decisions, instead directing requests upwards towards those at ministerial level. While top politicians wanted to make broad, umbrella decisions, they expected to rely on lawyers and civil servants for policy detail, and external experts found themselves being sent from pillar to post, all too often struggling to obtain proper information.

This whirling wider context all whipped up towards Johnson's false claim on 22 February that Abramovich had already been sanctioned. While Abramovich had clearly not by that stage been placed under sanctions, a great deal of groundwork towards that aim was already in place.

The night of 22 February, after Johnson's House of Commons error, Chelsea defeated Lille 2–0 at Stamford Bridge in the first leg of their Champions League last-sixteen tie. The reigning European champions flexed their considerable muscle again thanks to goals from Germany forward Kai Havertz and USA star Christian Pulisic. As the Blues hit their stride at the Bridge, there were precious few clues of the chaos that would soon ensue, despite the day's intrigue at Westminster.

• • •

Even the day before Abramovich would actually be sanctioned, UK government chiefs were embroiled in private wranglings over whether to press ahead and enforce the highly punitive measures. Aims were split among the Cabinet between flexing every possible financial muscle against Russia and addressing concerns on the impact on Chelsea, English football and public opinion.

On 9 March, one day before sanctions were imposed on Abramovich, a delegation of influential Ukrainians linked to the country's government met with a group of MPs and peers for lunch at Parliament buildings in Westminster. The delegates from Ukraine made no secret of the fact that one of their main aims was to lobby against sanctions being imposed on Abramovich. Ukraine's position was that Abramovich had already risked much and made tangible progress in opening the lines of communication with the aim of brokering peace with Moscow. The case was made and the MPs and lords in attendance agreed to communicate the details to senior government figures.

The very same day, Ukraine's President Zelensky had a phone call with Johnson, during which he is understood to have requested that the UK refrain from imposing sanctions on Abramovich. The Ukrainian leader expressed personally his belief that Abramovich could continue to harbour a positive influence on efforts towards a possible peace.

Just as with the delegation in Westminster, Zelensky explained that the imposition of sanctions would hinder Abramovich's ability to travel to attend crucial meetings and back-channel talks. Zelensky would later make the same request of the USA.

Johnson adopted a sceptical stance to the request from Zelensky, which appeared at odds with the positive noises that the group of MPs and peers had made to the Ukrainian delegation at that lunch in Parliament. The overriding government attitude in the end was one of concern that Abramovich might try to exploit his peace-maker status to avoid sanctions, though Ukraine's President and its senior delegation continued to insist otherwise.

The UK government wanted to make an example of the high-est-profile Russians by imposing sanctions that could act as a major statement in the British efforts towards helping Ukraine. Johnson's administration considered Abramovich the prime target in this respect, believing that sanctioning the Chelsea owner would un-doubtedly generate the desired level of noise and the craved show of strength.

While several senior faces in the Tory government cautioned against a fallout for Chelsea that could jeopardise the club's future and also risk significant public anger, others focused only on the impact on the war effort. Debates verging on arguments raged on, all amid the preparation of a major announcement on a set of sanc-tions to be released the following day.

Abramovich's name is thought to have spent the majority of 9 March only pencilled into that announcement, as the varying factions at the top of the Tory Party continued to thrash out their differences. The amendments to the sanctions legislation that had come into force at the end of January had left government lawyers and Cabinet chiefs all in agreement that Abramovich would meet the lowered threshold for the measures, and so none of those de-bates was thought to have centred around procedure.

Several frustrated parties have suggested the government was overly focused on the optics of its sanctions suite, claiming this ul-timately tipped the balance in favour of sanctioning Abramovich.

Those who believed Abramovich did hold the power to influence President Putin dismissed those claims as spurious, continuing to insist that the Chelsea owner was a legitimate and important person to target with a British travel ban and UK asset freezes.

Such last-minute uncertainty at Westminster and Whitehall meant that even on the morning of 10 March neither Abramovich nor his staff, nor indeed anyone at Chelsea, had any idea of the events that were about to unfold.

•   •   •

When the UK government finally sanctioned Abramovich, the Tory administration delivered a full-court press, pushing the information as far and wide as possible. Just after nine o'clock in the morning on 10 March, an official press release started an extraordinary day's events.

Abramovich was among seven of Russia's wealthiest businessmen sanctioned in one swoop, all due to alleged links to President Putin. The government claimed Abramovich had held a close relationship with Putin 'for decades', alleging that he had benefited greatly from that claimed association. The Tory administration also alleged the manufacturing company Evraz, in which Abramovich was a major shareholder, had 'potentially' supplied steel to the Russian military that 'may have been used in the production of tanks'. Abramovich has always vehemently denied all of these claims.

The government press release announcing the sanctions was adorned with a photoshopped logo for what was unveiled as the 'Oligarch Task Force', a colloquial grouping of the varying offices of state that would combine to impose and enforce sanctions. A number of those who played key roles in the UK sanctions planning and enactment at the time were understood to have been left with a feeling of distaste at that 'Oligarch Task Force' moniker, for a perceived cheapening of both the process and the wider climate.

Prime Minister Johnson and Foreign Secretary Truss, however, both hailed a breakthrough moment in Britain's allyship towards Ukraine. After protracted deliberations behind the scenes before sanctioning Abramovich, once the announcement was made, there was no equivocation.

'There can be no safe havens for those who have supported Putin's vicious assault on Ukraine,' said Johnson. 'We will be ruthless in pursuing those who enable the killing of civilians, destruction of hospitals and illegal occupation of sovereign allies.'

Truss pulled no punches either, with a depth of criticism that surprised some of those close to Abramovich and many senior staff at Chelsea, even if in the end the sanctions had carried an air of inevitability. 'Today's sanctions show once again that oligarchs and kleptocrats have no place in our economy or society,' she said. 'With their close links to Putin they are complicit in his aggression. The blood of the Ukrainian people is on their hands. They should hang their heads in shame.'

While Johnson and Truss carried out a raft of media interviews, the wider game of football sought answers to just as many questions. In the first couple of hours after the sanctions were announced, the government had to move quickly to allay a host of fears, filling in a number of vital blanks.

All of Abramovich's UK assets were immediately frozen, including Chelsea, but the Treasury, via OFSI, issued a temporary operating licence to allow the football club to complete the season. That licence would expire on 31 May, and it quickly became clear that no one in either the Treasury or OFSI was of any mind to consider any extensions. This effectively imposed an immediate time limit for the completion of the club sale, but in order for a deal to be done, the government would have to grant a further, special sale licence. Under normal circumstances, a deal to sell an elite sports club could take nine to twelve months to compose and execute; the Chelsea sale would now have to be completed in less than twelve weeks.

The terms of the temporary operating licence were deliberately draconian, designed to stop Abramovich profiting in any way from the running of the club. No new tickets or merchandise could be sold and arbitrary spending limits were imposed, notably for travel costs for away matches and hosting home games.

Executives at Chelsea were immediately stunned by some of the terms imposed, fearing the restrictions would jeopardise the sale of the club by threatening the Blues' ability to function. The club's hierarchy launched straight into seeking meetings with OFSI and Treasury staff, to request alterations that would allow the club to carry out daily business in something approaching normality. The imposed limit of a £20,000 travel budget for a single away match proved glaringly problematic, at just half the industry standard cost, to give one example.

The suspension of all business other than paying wages for existing staff also meant that the club could not negotiate any new contracts for players. Top men's stars like captain César Azpilicueta, Toni Rüdiger and Andreas Christensen were out of contract at the end of that campaign and had been in talks on potential new deals. All such discussions had to be shelved, leaving Chelsea suddenly even more vulnerable to a number of elite stars simply walking away from the club for free that summer.

A glut of suitors had already revealed strong interest in buying the Blues, and Chelsea chiefs had been busy trying to arrange meetings with potential bidders, in an early attempt to steal a march on the sale process. The sanctions, the new operating licence and the sudden hard deadline of 31 May meant the sale mechanics would have to change radically.

Initially, the government released several briefings urging all interested parties to contact them directly, but eventually Raine would continue to manage the sale process. Culture Secretary Nadine Dorries issued a statement insisting the government wanted to avoid Chelsea being 'unnecessarily harmed' amid the 'important sanctions'. But even to Chelsea staff and supporters who could appreciate the rationale behind the sanctions, there appeared a distinct lack of planning, execution and detail on how the measures would affect the club.

· · ·

Just hours after the government's sanctions press release pinged around the world, hitting news websites, radio and TV station bulletins, Chelsea closed the doors on the Stamford Bridge club shop. The Chelsea Megastore had opened for business as usual on the morning of 10 March, but by early afternoon, all staff had left the building with no idea what to do next and when, or even if, they might be able to return to work.

A forlorn-looking employee taped an A4 sheet of paper to the inside of the glass entrance door, on which was printed a curt message explaining the extraordinary closure. The note read: 'Due to the latest government announcement this store will be closed for today until further notice. Kind regards, Megastore management.' Several onlookers to the closure of the store joked that the message on the shop door appeared as hastily drafted as the sanctions against Abramovich and Chelsea's temporary operating licence.

Guildford's Martyn Hardiman had the distinction of being the last supporter to buy a Chelsea shirt under Abramovich's ownership before the shop was closed indefinitely. Amid chaos and confusion about the immediate running of the club, namely quite how Chelsea could fulfil men's, women's and junior fixtures, Blues fan Hardiman had appreciated the historic element of his purchase.

'When we went round to the club shop it was still open, and as we went in, they closed the door behind us and put the signs up saying, "We're closed due to the ongoing sanctions"' Hardiman told the Press Association news agency. 'We went up, got the shirt and it turned out to be the last sale of the current era, apparently. It was a surreal moment but a cool bit of history.'

Once the club shop was closed, security staff at Stamford Bridge had to block off the Megastore entrance with barriers that would normally be used to direct queues of supporters on match days. While for some supporters the day carried a memorable feel, staff at all levels of the club feared for their jobs. Scores of casual and part-time staff, from match programme sellers to food vendors, were left in total limbo, with no idea whether they would be allowed to work their next scheduled shifts, let alone be paid. Club officials were desperately scrambling to gain answers from a government operation so bogged down by so many different sanctions issues that it could only layer on the detail regarding Chelsea as events developed.

Most third-party organisations linked to Chelsea continued to adopt a watching brief, determining that substantive action would still prove premature. The Premier League, for example, had only learned of Abramovich's sanctioning some fifteen minutes before the official government press release was issued. League bosses immediately launched a review of Abramovich's fitness to continue as a suitable club director but would not be drawn on the length or detail of that process.

The bulk of the club's sponsors were among those affiliated organisations refraining from making any quick decisions, opting instead to see how further events would unfold. Main shirt sponsor Three took a different tack, however. The mobile phone giants suspended a sponsorship deal that industry experts estimated as worth £40 million a year to Chelsea, citing a moral responsibility as central to the decision.

'In light of the government's recently announced sanctions, we have requested Chelsea Football Club temporarily suspend our sponsorship of the club, including the removal of our brand from shirts and around the stadium until further notice,' read Three's statement.

We recognise that this decision will impact the many Chelsea fans who follow their team passionately. However, we feel that given the circumstances, and the government sanction that is in place, it is the right thing to do.

As a mobile network, the best way we can support the people of Ukraine is to ensure refugees arriving in the UK from the conflict and customers currently in Ukraine can stay connected to the people who matter to them. Therefore, we are offering connectivity packages to all Ukrainians arriving in the UK, and those in Ukraine.

Chelsea chiefs had little choice but to accept this decision with good grace, but they also fully appreciated the extremes and difficulties of the situation. However, there were those at Stamford Bridge who felt uneasy about what was regarded in some internal circles as corporate opportunism by Three to include their offer of mobile connectivity to Ukraine and Ukrainians as part of their statement confirming the suspension of their sponsorship deal.

•   •   •

Anger and frustration swept through Chelsea's men's and women's squads, reaching new heights in the wake of Abramovich's sanctions. Both teams faced big matches on the night of 10 March, just hours after sanctions were enforced.

Chelsea's men were in Norwich, going through their usual daily routine in build-up to a Premier League night match, when the sanctions news broke. Staff, coaches and players have all branded this the most challenging day of the entire sale saga. Even though they had feared the worst in terms of sanctions for Abramovich and an enforced club sale, everyone involved had still hoped that some set of circumstances would materialise that could somehow yield a reprieve. Chelsea's full staff wondered, however privately and forlornly, whether by some quirk of fate the sale could be cancelled. The imposition of sanctions against Abramovich, coupled with the deepening war in Ukraine, ruled out any and all such slim possibility for good.

Chelsea's players could not comprehend the horrors of war, as impassioned boss Tuchel reiterated regularly, but the club's senior squads had still been left shocked and upset by the sanctions and the immediate imposition of that temporary operating licence. Even senior figures in the Chelsea executive had not fully appreciated the scale of the punishment that would be imposed, a first in English football.

Staff certainly felt that the punishments were being unjustly carried out against them and their ambitions and livelihoods, even though they could also appreciate the wider political importance of the sanctions regime. The anger was fierce and widespread internally, but tempered all the while by a determination to trust that the UK government had acted in the greater public interest.

Technical director Čech had to hold yet more talks with the teams, attempting to answer what questions he could about how the new licence and its restrictions would affect daily operations. Initially, players feared their seasons would be impossible to complete, though as the details of the licence filtered through, they started to see a tentative framework.

Čech felt a new level of intensity as he addressed Chelsea's men's delegation in Norwich that day, again insisting the club's hierarchy would find a way to minimise disruption. He explained to the men's first team group that in one way the reality of sanctions added some clarity to the situation. Čech urged everyone in Norwich to do everything in their power not to give Chelsea's detractors what they wanted, saying, 'We know people are waiting for us to fail. Well, don't give any of them any satisfaction whatsoever. Now let's show people that we are unbreakable.'

People in the meeting that day spoke of an immediate, almost visceral response, in which Chelsea's first team group grew tighter together. Čech had asked them again to draw on foundations and connections, and the response was palpable. By the time the game kicked off at Carrow Road that evening, Chelsea's players were fuming but focused, and had heeded all the words from coaches and directors to vent their frustrations in the most positive of ways – with a resounding victory. Just as in Luton eight days earlier, this was a match Chelsea were fully expected to win, with struggling Norwich languishing at the foot of the Premier League table.

Chelsea took to the field still wearing shirts adorned with the Three logo despite the company suspending its sponsorship. Kit staff had been unable to source fresh shirts without the logo in time for kick-off, and club chiefs opted against covering it up.

Norwich flew the flag of Ukraine at their stadium in a touching, if pointed, show of solidarity against Russia's war, but Chelsea's players were quickly able to dismiss any wider statement or judgement from the Canaries. When Trevoh Chalobah headed Chelsea into a 1–0 lead after just three minutes, all the fear, frustration and anger started to evaporate on that Norfolk night air. Born in Sierra Leone in 1999, Chalobah moved to London with his family aged two, before joining the Chelsea academy aged eight. He shrugged off two markers as though they were not there before nodding home to hand Chelsea the perfect start, as always exuding a calm and focus beyond his years that had roots in his religious upbringing but also his humble outlook.

Chalobah's fellow academy graduate Mason Mount then quickly doubled the Chelsea lead, drawing Ozan Kabak into stepping out too far with a smart feint, allowing the ball to roll across his body before lashing it into the roof of the net. As Mount raced away and slid onto his knees in celebration of Chelsea's 2–0 lead, he pulled his shirt and kissed the club's crest. The animated show of love for his boyhood club spoke volumes on the determination in the Chelsea ranks not to fold under the unique pressure of government sanctions.

Norwich pulled a goal back through Teemu Pukki's calm penalty, after a Chalobah handball. But neither Chalobah nor Chelsea were anywhere near unsettled enough to allow their hosts a comeback. Instead, Jorginho's inch-perfect progressive pass sent N'Golo Kanté racing through the lines on the inside right, and he in turn squared the ball across the area to the lurking Havertz. The Germany playmaker steadied with his first touch then fired home with his second, to put Chelsea 3–1 up and settle the contest.

Almost a mirror image of Mount's earlier goal, the build-up play and specifically the Chelsea players' positioning underscored manager Tuchel's uncanny ability to devise and implement bespoke attacking ruses designed to unpick specific opponents, which would be used in only one match then discarded. At the final whistle, Chelsea's victory brought relief and belief in equal measure to the travelling Blues, who strengthened their grip on third place in the Premier League table with a fourth league win in succession.

Chelsea's staff and players spoke with emotion and candour in the Carrow Road dressing room straight after the match. Here, they said, was a win that made good on all the pre-match promises; here was a win to show how unified the squad could be. And here was a win that pointed the way forward in terms of both attitude and performance for the remainder of the season.

Anger and frustration had been converted into psychological fuel when fear and uncertainty could easily have sapped Chelsea's resolve. Manager Tuchel told his players that even tougher times were bound to be waiting around the corner, given the continued lack of clarity in so many facets, but then he praised the Blues for setting the perfect tone for the challenge ahead.

• • •

Chelsea's women were also on their travels on the night that Abramovich had been sanctioned, making the short trip across London for a derby against West Ham in Dagenham. Manager Hayes's side found themselves in the relatively unusual position of needing to bounce back from defeat, and from a cup final loss to boot.

Chelsea had lost 3–1 to Manchester City in the Continental Cup final on Sunday 5 March, the Blues unable to retain their title in a frustrating showing at Wimbledon's Plough Lane stadium. Inspirational manager Hayes had insisted she had 'no anxieties' about Abramovich's wider situation and the ownership of Chelsea when speaking on the day before that Continental Cup final loss. If the decorated Chelsea women boss was worry-free at the weekend, by the time her side faced West Ham in east London in midweek, her outlook had shifted significantly.

Not only were Chelsea fixated on atoning for their shock cup final loss from five days earlier, they were also determined to deliver a show of strength, just as the men's side were aiming to produce at the same time in Norwich. Once Pernille Harder settled Chelsea nerves with the opening goal after twenty minutes, the Blues never looked back, powering to the kind of statement victory they had so craved.

Harder ended the night with a brace to take her season's goal tally to fifteen, while Niamh Charles and Sam Kerr also found the net. Dagný Brynjarsdóttir troubled the scorers early in the second half for West Ham, but Chelsea cruised to their 4–1 win, reasserting their supremacy as reigning league champions. Despite the comfortable evening's work on the pitch, manager Hayes was left with little choice but to accept the difficulties of the wider club situation.

'I think the club has to have time now with the government to dissect the implications of the sanctions and it has to be a two-way process to determine how to run, operate and how to exist in this period,' said Hayes, in the strongest public stance from anyone at Chelsea regarding interaction with Johnson's administration.

We all have a million questions, but I don't battle with things I can't control and I will probably learn more in the coming days and weeks. I believe in giving both sides the time to get it right going forward. It's important for the players, the staff and the fans to be patient and hopefully that process won't take too long.

Hayes had also revealed her team's collective relief at finally being able to think about football for the duration of a match in which her players certainly seemed to vent their own frustrations. Just as Chelsea's men had taken out their anger on Norwich, so too had the women swatted aside West Ham in some kind of elite sporting therapy. The reigning Women's Super League champions moved within five points of leaders Arsenal, but crucially with two games in hand, in a powerful return to form and an ominous warning about their desire to defend their title.

Two top teams both delivering statement victories at the peak of Chelsea's fears represented a stirring end to another turbulent, landmark day for the Stamford Bridge club. The political and legal wranglings would rumble on, but after weeks of heightened agitation both inside the club and for the fans, at least all connected to the Blues could hang their support on wins that would live long in the memory, as much for the right reasons as for the wrong.

• • •

Partisan Chelsea supporter fury was encapsulated in graffiti that appeared on building site walls close to Stamford Bridge, first spotted on the morning of 11 March. 'Europe is funding the war not CFC, leave our club alone,' read the spray-painted warning, in the kind of troubling conflation of politics and sport that everyone at Chelsea had been desperate to avoid but was now inevitable.

On 12 March, Abramovich was officially disqualified as a club director by the Premier League. Competition regulations technically stated Abramovich would then have twenty-eight days to sell his club shareholding, but Premier League chiefs were fully prepared to extend that deadline given that the Chelsea sale would be subject to government oversight. 'Following the imposition of sanctions by the UK government, the Premier League board has disqualified Roman Abramovich as a director of Chelsea Football Club,' read the league's statement. 'The board's decision does not impact on the club's ability to train and play its fixtures, as set out under the terms of a licence issued by the government which expires on 31 May 2022.'

The Premier League disqualification changed little in the overall picture, only further cementing the inevitability of the sale. Of more pressing concern to the Blues leadership was to try to negotiate concessions on the terms of the government's purposely draconian temporary operating licence. Chelsea chiefs were in constant contact with OFSI and Treasury staff in the days following the imposition of sanctions.

On 12 March, as Abramovich was disqualified by the Premier League, the government agreed to increase match-day cost spending limits from £500,000 to £900,000 and also to allow the club to have access to any earned competition prize money. The club was still blocked from selling any new match tickets, however, and the travel budget for away matches remained capped at £20,000. While the government remained determined not to make significant concessions for Chelsea, the club itself felt that the restrictions still threatened to harm the Blues in both the short and the long term.

Hyundai moved to suspend its Chelsea sponsorship on 12 March, after several days of deliberation, following Three's lead. Internet hotel search firm Trivago opted to stick by Chelsea, continuing its sponsorship and bucking a new trend of suspensions. Crucially, though, this move did not extend to showing any support for the outgoing Abramovich leadership group. 'The uncertainty over the current ownership situation of Chelsea FC has been challenging,' read a Trivago statement. 'Moving forward, it is important to us to continue supporting the club … We are looking forward to a transition of ownership as soon as possible and want to support the club in this process.'

Chelsea's ownership, staff and players, not to mention their supporters, were already in the grip of the five stages of grief, notwithstanding their horror at Russia's illegal invasion of Ukraine. Denial had already given way to the anger that was vented by players at Norwich and West Ham, and supporters chanting for Abramovich on the terraces, even before considering the graffiti artist who had ordered the government to leave Chelsea alone.

The third stage of grief, bargaining, was already in full swing too, especially in the form of Chelsea lobbying the government to ease up on the aggressively restrictive terms of the temporary operating licence. The more Chelsea argued that the terms were overly punitive, however, the more the government dug in its heels, determined to see tangible results from the sanctions against Abramovich. As ongoing discussions stretched out across a series of meetings, the polarised opinions became more entrenched, adding yet another new layer of jeopardy no one had anticipated.

CHAPTER SIX

SANCTION FC

Marina Granovskaia wanted to call the UK government's bluff and ignore the hard deadline to complete the Chelsea sale by 31 May. Chelsea's senior director had quickly come to the end of her tether, along with other members of the Blues' senior management team. Granovskaia did not believe the government was brave or foolish enough to let a London community institution fail just because of an arbitrary time limit for a sale that would be enforced however long was required. A global footballing giant and multi-billion-pound business, Chelsea would need nine to twelve months to be sold at full market value and amid standard due diligence under normal circumstances. In the days following Abramovich's sanctions and the imposing of that purposely punitive temporary operating licence for Chelsea, Granovskaia argued in internal club meetings that the government's sale deadline could be reasonably ignored.

Unless the government would permit amendments to the temporary operating licence, Chelsea were in real danger of failing to pay their bills and slipping into administration, even before the 31 May sale deadline. The temporary licence barred parent company

Fordstam, owned by Abramovich, from injecting funds into Chelsea as was otherwise standard. That block created the tangible possibility that Chelsea could fail, and quickly. Chelsea's senior leaders were equal parts vexed and perplexed at a government stance that jeopardised the club in the short as well as the long term, especially with the sale now entirely on the cards.

The Treasury held overall responsibility for Chelsea's long-term future, with OFSI as a subsidiary handling the details of the licence and keeping a watchful eye on the sale process. Several senior Cabinet members were said to be holding a hardline stance just as strong as that of Granovskaia – but at the other end of the spectrum. Fears were therefore genuinely heightened that the government would somehow be ready to see Chelsea go to the wall should Abramovich fail to complete the club's sale by that 31 May deadline.

While everyone in government was acutely aware of the seismic repercussions of a Premier League club and community institution being allowed to fail, there were those within the Johnson administration who were thought to be fully prepared to see the situation through all the way to the club's collapse. Chelsea's executive staff were being made aware of such entrenched positions held by some in government, and the back-channel messages only served to increase the tension still further.

As soon as the sanctions were imposed on Abramovich, Chelsea and government representatives were plunged into seemingly endless negotiations regarding the terms of the temporary operating licence. Buck took Chelsea's lead in meetings with the Treasury, OFSI and other government bodies and personnel, with Granovskaia battling to split her time between sale duties and general club responsibilities.

The more the meetings failed to bear fruit, either on concessions in the licence from the government or in a broader appreciation from Chelsea of the need for a punitive impact, the dicier the situation became. Granovskaia's anger towards the government only grew with that sequence of inconclusive or unhelpful talks.

All of Chelsea's senior staff were nonplussed and frustrated by the arbitrary but absolute 31 May deadline to sell the club. OFSI and the Treasury were petitioned on a number of occasions to relax that deadline, not to ease any intended punishment but to achieve the best possible outcome from the sale. Every request was summarily dismissed without any substantive discussion, and each outright rejection only served to widen the divide between the Chelsea executive and the government.

Running Chelsea while also trying to sell the club, and in double time, had left the Stamford Bridge executives exhausted and angry. The UK government sanctions meant Abramovich was barred from any involvement in either day-to-day club affairs or the sale process itself, but this suited his desire to throw himself fully into working for peace in Ukraine. Chairman Buck and senior director Granovskaia therefore had to balance their existing daily duties with overseeing large swathes of the sale process, in conjunction with US investment bank Raine, the deal brokers. Chelsea considered the entire situation to be creating undue and dangerous pressure, with everyone battling to beat the clock.

Granovskaia's response was to suggest quite seriously that Chelsea should work at a realistic pace towards the sale and inform the government that the 31 May deadline was simply untenable. Her reasoned and considered argument, delivered in private Chelsea meetings, was that the government would never bankrupt the club or let it disappear.

While sharing all her frustrations, Granovskaia's colleagues did not exactly warm to the idea of refusing to work to the government's timescale. Even though the other executives understood the rationale and were in broad agreement that the idea of the Tory administration allowing Chelsea to fold seemed absurd, generally this was regarded as too much of a risk.

As the deliberations continued, Granovskaia was still itching to push the point but gradually came to see that this was not the time for Chelsea to indulge in such a high-stakes game of chicken. For all her business and footballing world acumen built in a long and fruitful career, she had to admit internally that the one actor whose behaviour she could not model with enough confidence here would be that of the government.

After extended discussion, Chelsea's senior leadership opted to continue to work under the government yoke, rolling up their sleeves for some of the longest hours of their careers across a punishing three months. Several staff recall regularly returning home in the middle of the night for what felt like just long enough to shower, change and return to work, such were the relentless demands.

Once the sale process started to gather pace, everyone at Chelsea was motivated to ensure the club would be bought by the best possible owners. While Abramovich had to take a hands-off approach, he was driven by the desire to hand Chelsea on to the strongest possible custodians. And everyone below him at Stamford Bridge quickly turned their full focus to securing new owners with the power and fixation to keep the club in the manner to which it had long become accustomed.

The consensus at Chelsea was that the government was determined to make the entire sale process as difficult as possible, a stance which only served to add even more tension alongside the clear time pressure. Chelsea were also left frequently flummoxed in meetings where the government's representatives had neither the confidence nor the seniority to make decisions, leading to even more protracted discussions while requests were sent up and down various management chains. Despite the animosity, however, ultimately neither side was prepared to take a £4.25 billion gamble on the future of the club.

• • •

Abramovich adopted an air of realism when dealing with the implications of the sanctions, mainly because by the time the measures were imposed they had become inevitable. His London penthouse apartment numbered among a host of other UK assets to fall under the reach of sanctions, alongside Chelsea.

There were quirkier implications to the sanctions too, that somehow stuck out despite their entirely incidental nature. After the Blues defeated Brazilians Palmeiras 2–1 in the FIFA competition's final on 12 February, their UAE hosts threw a celebratory party for the victorious team.

Members of the Abu Dhabi royal family presented Abramovich firstly with a cake and then with an extremely thoughtful extra gift. The UAE Team Emirates professional cycling outfit's top rider Tadej Pogačar had claimed his first Tour de France triumph in 2020, and Abu Dhabi was still revelling in that landmark victory. Chelsea's hosts at that party to celebrate the Club World Cup win had done their homework. Wherever in the world Abramovich would travel during his Chelsea tenure, he would tend to address football first, other business matters second – and then look for places where he and his associates could ride bikes. Having discovered Abramovich's keen interest in cycling, the Abu Dhabi hosts presented him with a team bike that had been ridden during Pogačar's 2020 Tour de France win.

The evening event celebrating Chelsea's Club World Cup win went by in a flash, after which Abramovich and his cohort quickly returned to London on his private jet. On landing back in the UK, Abramovich left the special gift of that Tour de France bike on the plane, in what he considered at the time safe keeping. He needed to be quick in order to attend a meeting, so had planned to ask staff to transfer the bike to one of his London residences.

Somewhere along the line, the issue of moving the bike skipped collective minds, and so a prized present stayed put on the aircraft. And stay put that bike did, all the way up until the sanctions were imposed. It was only several days after the UK sanctions had come into effect that Abramovich and his team realised that such a generous gift was still on the jet, and therefore out of reach. While this was of course inconsequential amid the brutality of war and the threats to the livelihoods of Chelsea's staff, that bike came to represent the oddities of the sanctions that were at once fully understandable but also hard to fathom.

In the meantime, senior Chelsea figures were still locked in trying to improve the club's situation and ease the justifiable worries of club staff and supporters. Amid those tense talks with the government to try to relax the conditions of the temporary operating licence, Chelsea's fears continued to grip that they would be unable to pay their bills.

Amendments to the licence on 12 March at least allowed Chelsea to stage their Premier League match against Newcastle at Stamford Bridge the next day, with the game long since sold out. Those 12 March licence variations allowed for contractors and temporary workers to be paid, as match cost limits were raised to £900,000.

Casual staff were able to breathe a sigh of relief on being able both to turn up for work at Chelsea's match against Newcastle and to receive payment for that privilege.

Now gripped by the precarious situation, Chelsea's jittery supporters had to endure another tense afternoon, as much on the pitch as off it. Within hours of Abramovich falling under the UK asset freeze, rival fans had rebranded Chelsea as 'Sanction FC'. By the time Newcastle's vociferous support took to the Stamford Bridge stands, a new chant had already been devised, as simple as it was effective in the niggling repetition of its sole lyrics, 'Chelsea get sanctioned everywhere they go'.

The week's events looked to have taken their toll for a sluggish Chelsea side, whose malaise was matched by Newcastle's lack of impetus. Just when the Blues looked to be labouring to a goalless draw, up popped Havertz with a mood-lifting winner one minute from full time. The 1–0 victory kept Chelsea third in the league, marking the side's fourth win in a row in all competitions.

While players and staff could celebrate a last-gasp win, there were genuine concerns about the club's ability to keep paying its wage bill. Chelsea were confident of paying staff wages in full in the next monthly run, on 1 April, but continued to make it clear to OFSI and the Treasury that May's bill would be another matter entirely.

Wise to the turmoil, the majority of the Chelsea players' agents quickly sought legal advice, examining in what circumstances the club might end up in breach of contract. With the club barred from negotiating any new deals, any breach of contract claims en masse could have left Chelsea staring down an unprecedented summer exodus, even in the event of a successful club sale.

Granovskaia had already stepped back from her role in Abramovich's family office, which managed his personal life and travel arrangements. Although Granovskaia had started her career as Abramovich's chief assistant, her job had long since morphed into that central figure brokering transfer deals and negotiating contracts, acting as Abramovich's most senior representative in footballing matters.

In the course of Abramovich's nineteen-year tenure at Chelsea, Granovskaia's staff had grown, many employed in the family office set-up. Once the sanctions hit, those staff would have been all but out of work – except that Granovskaia continued to pay them out of her own pocket. She considered such largesse small beer in return for the dedication and loyalty of a close-knit, talented group of employees. Several other senior Abramovich aides followed Granovskaia's lead in paying staff out of their own pockets.

The personal staff of Abramovich and his executives, like the Chelsea employees at all levels of the club, were offering to continue working, where at all possible, even if payments would be delayed or might not materialise at all. Scores of employees who had worked for decades to earn their dream jobs were left suddenly fearing how they would find their next rent or mortgage payments.

External attitudes varied wildly, however: while Chelsea supporters and many general football followers showed sympathy to club staff, even the well-remunerated executives, other groups were quick to voice their hostility. Granovskaia received a glut of emails accusing her of having blood on her hands, claiming she had some kind of complicity in the war.

Suddenly, many senior Chelsea staff experienced the equivalent of a professional services cold shoulder. Only Abramovich was sanctioned, and yet a clutch of senior figures received correspondence from lawyers and accountants ending long-standing representation agreements. Despite all the bitterness and recrimination, Chelsea still had a football club not just to run but to sell, matches to play and win, and employees to try to protect through a duty of care that Stamford Bridge bosses took extremely seriously.

• • •

Straight after Chelsea's 1–0 Premier League win over Newcastle, Tuchel delivered a double boost to the Blues. Fresh from the Stamford Bridge dugout on 13 March, the German coach breezily insisted it was a no-brainer that he would stay on as Chelsea manager until first the end of the season and then well beyond. He quickly followed up that positive news by confirming that Chelsea were still expecting to travel by plane to the 16 March Champions League clash in Lille.

The temporary operating licence limited Chelsea's away-match logistics spending to a greatly reduced cap of £20,000, but travel to Lille had been booked and paid for in advance of government sanctions. In confirming Chelsea's ability to travel under previous auspices, though, Tuchel also reiterated his commitment to the club by declaring his readiness to take any means of transport necessary to do his job, one that he loved and refused to give up on without a fight.

'My last information is we have a plane,' said Tuchel on 13 March after the Newcastle win.

We can go by plane and go back by plane. If not, we go by train. And if not, we go by bus. And if not, I will drive a seven-seater! I will do, mark my words, I will arrive there. If you had asked me twenty, thirty years ago if I would join a Champions League match at the sideline and what I was willing to do for that, I would have said, 'Where do I have to be and when?' And why should this change? I will be there, and we will be there.

Tuchel's uncanny ability to lead by example through conviction and a semi-humorous quote had once again won the day for the Blues, raising morale and pointing the way forward into a pivotal week for the Stamford Bridge club. While Chelsea were clear on their travel plans for the Wednesday 16 March trip to Lille for their Champions League last-sixteen second leg, they were none the wiser on the FA Cup quarter-final away match at Middlesbrough just three days later.

Almost every match became a test case, the 1–0 win over Newcastle representing the first Stamford Bridge encounter after Abramovich had been hit with sanctions. The club might have been all but frozen, but the Blues had at least been able to find a way to keep staging home matches. But even as Tuchel was regaling the media with those promises to drive a minibus or even a people carrier to France, Chelsea were still no closer to knowing how they would make it to Teesside in six days' time, nor whether they could even stay overnight in a hotel.

Tuchel reaffirming his commitment to the Blues despite the sanctions went a long way to calming the fears of many of the players on their immediate and longer-term futures too. The Blues' relieved first team stars started to build confidence that if what lay ahead was good enough for Tuchel, then it would be good enough for them too. Not for the first or last time in the process, Tuchel offered the knowing wink, nod and grin of a savvy operator at his peak, then delivered a public intervention that kept Chelsea's show on the road. Metaphorically, Tuchel was behind the wheel, whether or not he would end up having to drive the bus.

• • •

If Chelsea had already resisted temptations to call the government's bluff on the 31 May sale deadline, relations with the Tory regime were still not improving. The start of a week involving two crucial away matches ought to have brought peace and quiet, and the chance for coaches and players to draw breath after beating Newcastle before summoning the strength and focus to push on again.

Instead, on Monday 14 March, Chelsea went public with their wrangles with the government over operating licence terms. What few concessions the government had given in terms of easing Chelsea's ability to function did not include any wiggle room on ticket sales. Chelsea were still blocked from selling any new tickets for any matches, sharpening club anger still further. Having sold fewer than 600 tickets of an allocation north of 3,000 for the coming Saturday's FA Cup quarter-final at Middlesbrough, Chelsea launched a very public and equally rare bid to shame the government into a change.

'We are pressing the government to allow our supporters to have access to tickets,' read the Chelsea statement.

Meetings are taking place daily in search of a resolution. In addition, the Premier League and FA are also discussing with the government the sporting integrity issues raised if they do not permit fans to attend. We are aware of the high level of frustration our supporters are facing over this issue, and we are doing everything we can to resolve it as soon as possible.

Supporters who have already purchased a ticket can attend the match. Tickets will be sent out in the post tomorrow (Tuesday). We have the remaining tickets for our allocation, but we are awaiting further updates from the government on whether we can sell these tickets or not before Saturday's game.

Chelsea were due to face Middlesbrough at the Riverside Stadium on Saturday 19 March, but their hectic week also included the small matter of another knockout match, against Lille. The Blues were of course scheduled to travel to France for that second leg of their Champions League last-sixteen tie on Wednesday 16 March, where they would take a 2–0 aggregate lead across the Channel.

Given Chelsea had seriously considered rejecting the government's deadlines outright, venting their displeasure publicly represented a relatively measured response. To the unsuspecting sporting world, however, Chelsea's stance appeared aggressive in the extreme, and while it was designed to provoke a response, the results caught everyone at Stamford Bridge on the hop.

Chelsea's attempt to put pressure on the government failed, with the club still blocked from selling any more tickets for the Middlesbrough match. On Tuesday 15 March, once Chelsea realised their requests had again been ignored, the Blues' hierarchy decided to double down. This time, their public position was that the match should be played behind closed doors to protect 'sporting integrity'.

'We are disappointed to announce we will not be able to sell tickets for Saturday's FA Cup tie at Middlesbrough,' read Chelsea's first statement on 15 March.

Despite engaging in extensive discussions with the Office of Financial Sanctions Implementation (OFSI), the deadline to purchase away tickets has passed without appropriate amendments being made to the government licence which would allow a full allocation of Chelsea supporters to attend. Executives at

Middlesbrough had been kind enough to extend their deadline for ticket sales and stadium allocation from 7.30pm last night until 9.30am this morning.

It is important for the competition that the match against Middlesbrough goes ahead, however it is with extreme reluctance that we are asking the FA board to direct that the game be played behind closed doors for matters of sporting integrity. Chelsea FC recognises that such an outcome would have a huge impact on Middlesbrough and its supporters, as well as our own fans who have already bought the limited number of tickets that were sold before the licence was imposed, but we believe this is the fairest way of proceeding in the current circumstances. We will continue to discuss the issue of ticket sales with OFSI as there are a number of fixtures still to be played this season and we hope to reach a resolution.

Championship club Middlesbrough's response was cutting and personal in its total rejection of Chelsea's FA request. Club chairman Steve Gibson called out his Chelsea counterpart Buck in several statements, adding an extra layer of enmity to sit above a caustic general club statement. 'I can't believe it, I can't believe this excuse of a man Bruce Buck,' lamented Gibson to *The Times*.

To try this is just unbelievable. Sporting integrity and Chelsea do not belong in the same sentence. For nineteen years Abramovich's money has fuelled Chelsea's success. If they were to beat us in the FA Cup, with no fans there, what would that do to the integrity of the competition? Are they going to play all their Premier League games behind closed doors too? This is pathetic by Chelsea.

Incensed and determined not to be dragged into Chelsea's fight,

Middlesbrough were immediately desperate to veto the idea to shut out supporters. Chelsea's chiefs had pounced on an opportunity to take their horse trading with the government into the public arena and were prepared to risk some flak if their hardline stance would ultimately force OFSI to back off and make further concessions to the temporary licence terms.

Experienced lawyer Buck was something of a Premier League sage after all his years as Chelsea chairman. He was broad shouldered enough to take the heat of Gibson's stinging rebuke, especially if the government would finally get the message and find a way to let Chelsea operate competitively for the remainder of the season.

Everyone at Chelsea remained stunned at the government's collective inability to grasp the necessities of elite sport. Stamford Bridge chiefs considered that not even the sport section of the Department for Culture, Media and Sport (DCMS) had a robust understanding of standard practices in either elite operations generally or Premier League clubs specifically. Imposing an away-match travel cost cap of £20,000, roughly half the standard Premier League outlay, left Chelsea feeling this entirely proved their point. The government position, however, remained one of battling to uphold the punitive elements of the temporary operating licence in order to maximise the impact of the sanctions.

If Middlesbrough's chairman refused to pull any punches in his personal commentary, neither did their more general club statement. 'We are aware of Chelsea's request to have Saturday's FA Cup sixth round tie played behind closed doors and find their suggestion both bizarre and without any merit whatsoever,' read the official club release.

All concerned are well aware of the reasons Chelsea have been sanctioned and that this has nothing to do with Middlesbrough Football Club. To suggest as a result that MFC and our fans should be penalised is not only grossly unfair but without any foundation. Given the reasons for these sanctions, for Chelsea to seek to invoke sporting 'integrity' as reason for the game being played behind closed doors is ironic in the extreme. We currently await formal notification from the FA of the next steps but rest assured MFC will resist Chelsea's actions in the strongest terms.

Eventually, the FA stepped in to halt an alarming escalation amid the bitter war of words. The governors of the English game convened emergency talks with Chelsea, talking the Blues bosses off the ledge of a request that never really had any chance of being accepted. For Buck and Chelsea, the government short-changing the club's fans by denying them access to tickets remained a major problem, but this entire episode was considered part of the bigger and continuing negotiation. Knowing in the end that their fight was not with the FA, Chelsea agreed to withdraw their request to have all supporters barred from the weekend's Middlesbrough match.

'After constructive talks between the FA and Chelsea, the club has agreed to remove their request,' the FA said in a statement. 'The FA remains in ongoing discussions with Chelsea, the Premier League and the government to find a solution that would enable both Chelsea fans to attend games and away fans to attend Stamford Bridge, while ensuring sanctions are respected.'

This time the Chelsea response was brief, and the acceptance tacit, as the Blues confirmed they were 'grateful for the FA's continuing efforts to help us find a solution'. The operative word of 'solution' referred not to the withdrawn request for the match to be played behind closed doors but to the continued problem of Chelsea not being able to sell any new tickets.

If government chiefs had not been wise to Chelsea's resolve before this spat, attitudes shifted in Westminster, with Cabinet ministers reacting privately with shock and anger to the fact that Stamford Bridge bosses simply refused to roll over and accept any and all restrictions. Boris Johnson and Chancellor Rishi Sunak particularly were described as frustrated to see the government's authority challenged, and so openly, while Chelsea were still trying to point out the problematic disparity in battling for sporting edges amid the wider context of Russia's illegal war.

• • •

Buried in the rubble of the ugly public spat with Middlesbrough, Abramovich was sanctioned by the EU on the very same day as Chelsea's aborted request to shut fans out of that FA Cup clash. Just one day out from Chelsea's Champions League knockout match against Lille, on 15 March Abramovich was hit with asset freezes and travel bans to cover the whole of Europe. Five days on from receiving UK sanctions, the scope of measures against the Chelsea owner broadened significantly.

By this point Abramovich had no desire to attend Chelsea's match at Lille, considering his presence inappropriate even aside from his more pressing matters trying to help facilitate talks between Russia and Ukraine. But once the EU sanctions took hold, his previous technical ability to attend the Champions League match was taken away.

While Ukraine petitioned both the UK and the USA against sanctioning Abramovich so that he could help with the peace process, President Zelensky did not seek similar talks with the EU. Ukraine's stance was that EU sanctions were inevitable by this point, and in any case, there was no one clear figurehead to whom he could make such a personal request.

Where Zelensky found no joy whatsoever with the UK and the EU, however, he was met with an entirely different response from the US. Zelensky spoke with US President Joe Biden directly, asking him in a phone call to refrain from sanctioning Abramovich. In the end, Biden agreed not to impose any sanctions, backing Zelensky's judgement that Abramovich could still play a crucial role and that imposing restrictions would hinder his ability to help. Following quickly on from the UK sanctions, the EU measures came as no surprise to Abramovich and his camp and, as before, his attitude was one of accepting the reality of the war and its wider repercussions.

The EU's fourth package of sanctions since the start of the conflict meant the bloc had imposed restrictions on 877 individuals and sixty-two entities since the measures had begun back in 2014. 'We are adding to our sanctions list even more oligarchs and regime-affiliated elites, their families and prominent businesspeople, which are involved in economic sectors providing a substantial source of revenue to the regime,' said Josep Borrell, the EU's high representative for foreign affairs and security policy.

Our message is clear: those who enable the invasion of Ukraine pay a price for their actions. As President Putin's war against Ukrainian people continues, so does our resolve to support Ukraine and cripple the financing of the Kremlin's war machinery. This fourth package of sanctions is another major blow to the economic and logistic base upon which Russia relies to carry out the invasion of Ukraine. The aim of the sanctions is that President Putin stops this inhuman and senseless war.

Chelsea were at least able to fly to Lille for the following day's Champions League match as originally planned. Amid seemingly endless political turmoil and plenty of public discourse on the wider situation, there was no need, this time, for manager Tuchel to make good on his pledge to drive the bus to France.

Chelsea made the trip across to northern France and set themselves up as usual the night before the match, with a 2–0 lead in the bag from the first leg and all eyes on the prize of a place in the quarter-finals. With every press conference and interview, the strain was starting to tell ever so slightly on Tuchel, a genial boss wearied by the endless sale and political talk despite his repeated demands that the focus shift back to the football. Despite the pressures, though, Tuchel had been able to generate new levels of motivation that continued to keep Chelsea's squad a remarkably close-knit group.

• • •

When Chelsea arrived at Stade Pierre-Mauroy for their 16 March Champions League clash with Lille, there was almost as much chaos in the directors' facilities as among Blues supporters who had made the trip across from London. As Chelsea's senior staff arrived and were welcomed by their Lille counterparts, the awkward exchanges and uneasy looks had the travelling Blues contingent wondering exactly what was up.

A few discreet enquiries later and the Chelsea cohort quickly arrived at the heart of the matter. Lille's leaders were panicking, unsure what they could and could not do in terms of hosting Chelsea. The French club almost did not serve the Chelsea executive delegation any food, fearing that to do so would be to breach the terms of the sanctions.

The EU sanctions had been laid down only the previous day, so no one at the French club felt that they had been able to scrutinise the rules properly. In their determination not to fall foul of sanctions law, Lille's executives ran the real risk of offending their visitors. By the time the catering and serving staff were given the green light to press on, however, both sets of executives were able to laugh off that initial panic.

If those early fears were quickly alleviated in the corporate boxes, the travelling supporters had been forced to deal with threats of an entirely more immediate level. Large groups of Chelsea fans had congregated in several of the main squares in the city, only for French police to deploy tear gas to disperse the travelling supporters.

There were no reports of major unrest or even signs of particular trouble, more the typical high spirits of excited football fans on an away trip. Chelsea fans who had been caught up in the overzealous tactics believed that the French police had overreacted, only to cause further problems that also affected people who had no link to the football.

When the Chelsea supporters eventually arrived at the stadium, the local police directed them into small sections outside the ground, penning them in seemingly without good reason and for an extended period of time. Supporters hemmed in later spoke about being unable to turn back and leave even if they had wanted to. Somehow both sets of fans made it into the ground without any major incident, but the Blues' travelling faithful felt this was rooted more in luck than judgement.

By the time the match kicked off, Chelsea's supporters, players, staff and executives all felt as though they had already been through the wringer, and there was still the jeopardy of a major knockout cup match to come. Chelsea carried a two-goal cushion into the tie and were odds-on favourites to progress to the quarter-finals, but the first half yielded only a patchy performance from the visitors.

When Jorginho handled the ball in the area, Burak Yilmaz stepped up and coolly converted a penalty to halve Lille's deficit, turning what could have been a procession into a serious battle. But just as Chelsea looked to be heading to the half-time interval trailing on the night, Pulisic delivered a crisp finish to level the scores at 1–1 for the second leg, putting the Blues 3–1 up on aggregate.

That breathing space allowed Chelsea to reassess at the break then return and set about shutting out the hosts to ease their way into the last eight, as originally planned. Captain Azpilicueta sealed progression to the quarter-finals by heading home Mount's cross, taking the aggregate score to 4–1 in the final exchanges. With so much upheaval and angst at every other turn, Chelsea's players and staff clung to the result with all their might.

Manager Tuchel met the 2–1 win on the evening and 4–1 aggregate triumph with the kind of animated celebration that matched even the passion he had shown when Chelsea won the previous season's Champions League final. The sparky German strode across the Stade Mauroy turf, making a beeline for the Chelsea supporters, and once he was as close as he could be while still on the field, he started punching the air, slapping his chest and joining in with their celebrations. The Chelsea fans responded by launching into a raucous rendition of their preferred chant for the former PSG boss. Somehow, the lyrics – 'We've got super Tommy Tuchel, he knows exactly what to do' – kept managing to carry more weight with each passing day in his savvy negotiation of mini-crisis after mini-crisis.

By the time Tuchel made his way to the post-match press conference, in the bowels of the stadium, he had finally regained his composure but was still all smiles as he took his seat. No sooner was he fielding the first question, however, than he was confronted with a fresh reality check that left him pleading for more than five minutes without having to consider the entire Chelsea picture in the round.

Chelsea were in the draw for the Champions League quarter-finals and Tuchel could not have been more delighted, but he had been brought back to Earth with a bump by the suggestion that Blues fans might be barred from attending any more games in the competition that season. Asked if he knew whether supporters would be able to attend the Champions League quarter-final legs, Tuchel replied:

Thanks for ruining my evening! I was in such a good mood, can we speak about it when it's confirmed? Let's wait for the confirmation of the confirmation. Let's see, today I'm happy that we are in the last eight. There were a lot of things to overcome, so I'm so happy and so proud. In three days we play Middlesbrough in the cup, then we have the national break, and then I'll think about a good answer. The fans are outside right now and it was brilliant to be with them.

Tuchel's exuberant celebrations took root in his personal view that reaching the Champions League quarter-finals represented a crucial benchmark for Chelsea's season – a minimum standard he set for himself, irrespective of any board or outside expectations. Tuchel was as excited as he was relieved to tick off such a big target, extending the Blues' defence of their title in the process.

Coming back down from his Lille high, though, Tuchel also had to turn his immediate attention to the weekend's fast-approaching Middlesbrough match, and all the controversy surrounding Chelsea still being barred from selling new tickets. Tuchel had studiously avoided the controversy in his press conferences before the Lille match but afterwards revealed the squad's frustration at how the build-up to the Middlesbrough trip had been enveloped in the Chelsea board's battles with the government.

'Let me put it like this, we love to play in front of spectators,' said Tuchel.

And I don't think that spectators for opponents should suffer from the consequences. So I think the proposal was withdrawn and it was absolutely the right thing to do, because that was from our side and hopefully it was not meant like this. It was not the very best idea to put it like this. We love to play in front of spectators. Me and the team were not involved in this decision and I'm happy that it was withdrawn, very happy.

Despite their buoyant mood, however, the Blues travelled back to London by plane with no idea how they would be making their way up to Middlesbrough just three days later. Tuchel's pledge to drive the bus to matches if necessary had been previously interpreted as a half-joke, but the team would certainly not be flying to Teesside without any last-minute changes to the away-match spending limits.

• • •

Chelsea's players were infuriated by the limits of the temporary operating licence, especially regarding travel and how it could affect elite performance. But rather than simply whinge about the situation, instead they clubbed together and requested to pay for air travel to the Middlesbrough FA Cup quarter-final out of their own money.

Captain Azpilicueta and several other players even collated a special fund and were fully prepared to make the payments themselves, such was the importance they placed on minimising travel time and the negative effect any disruptions could have on performance levels. The players approached Čech and Chelsea's other directors with the fund already established, volunteering to make the payment and remove any wranglings from the wider negotiations. The money was in place to pay outright for the special air travel required for the Middlesbrough match, and the players felt this ought to end the uncertainty.

Chelsea's directors quickly checked with club lawyers, only to discover that even such an outside payment was likely to breach not just the terms of the temporary licence but, perhaps more troublingly, Abramovich's sanctions. Their legal team explained to club directors that such a payment could easily be interpreted as acting as a benefit to Abramovich, in which case the sanctions legislation would most certainly have been breached.

So while the club's hierarchy respected and greatly appreciated the players' gesture and their obvious commitment, they had no choice but to reject the offer. Chelsea's players could not understand the rationale, which only deepened their latent resentment towards the government. For their part, the government had no specific proposal to reject, however, given Chelsea's legal team knew the idea could not be enacted.

As the organisers of the fund returned all the money to the first team, the players continued to question why private individuals could not just hire a plane and invite anyone they wanted to travel to Middlesbrough. But the terms of Abramovich's sanctions meant that he must not benefit materially in any way in the UK, and of course he still owned Chelsea.

As it turned out, by the time Chelsea were back in London and going through final preparations for that Middlesbrough trip, the government had finally agreed to raise the £20,000 expenses cap to allow the Blues to fly to Teesside for the 19 March FA Cup quarter-final. Despite that pledge, Chelsea were still waiting on official confirmation from any of the relevant government departments, just two days out from the match itself. So even though to the wider watching public another big hurdle appeared to have been crossed, the Blues were still watching the clock, waiting for the green light to travel by plane.

Even when manager Tuchel confirmed in his pre-match press conference that the team would fly north, the actual mode of transport for the trip was still to be determined. In fact, the lack of clarity on the issue led the club to make two sets of arrangements, with a coach on standby just in case of any last-minute hitches. And so the day before the match, with no official confirmation having been received that Chelsea could fly without breaking the terms of their temporary licence, the men's first team players and staff met up, fully expecting to have to travel by bus.

All were preparing to board the coach for the five-hour-plus journey to Middlesbrough on 18 March, then, when at the very last moment that key paperwork approving a flight came through. With the coach at hand and the players expecting to leave, a call came through to the group to tell them all to go home and reconvene later in the day to fly north instead.

Suddenly all the players were straight onto their phones to loved ones, some telling wives or girlfriends that they could take care of that nagging chore after all. Once Chelsea finally arrived on Teesside that evening, the players were still vexed but also relieved that another highly avoidable saga appeared to be at an end.

The war of words at the start of the week whipped up a niggly atmosphere for the match itself, once that contest finally became the main event. The fact that Chelsea had eventually withdrawn their request for the match to be staged behind closed doors meant little to a wound-up Middlesbrough fan base. The hosts had managed to fill the 34,000-seater Riverside Stadium, reclaiming the tickets that Chelsea had been blocked from selling to ensure a capacity crowd.

Middlesbrough chairman Gibson's personal public attack on Chelsea counterpart Buck only heaped further fuel on supporter fire, to the extent that the Blues' team bus was resoundingly booed on arrival at the stadium. Championship outfit Boro had already toppled Manchester United and Tottenham in a remarkable cup run and had undoubtedly done all in their power to try to exploit any perceived vulnerabilities from Chelsea's wider club situation in the build-up.

Once kick-off finally came, Chelsea moved quickly and decisively to snuff out any chance of a classic cup giant killing. Belgium hitman Lukaku side-footed home from Mount's inch-perfect low cross, handing the Blues the 1-0 lead on the quarter-hour. Just sixteen minutes later, Hakim Ziyech cut in off the right flank onto his favoured left foot and whipped a dipping strike into the corner of the net. The Morocco forward's twenty-yard finish owed everything to placement over power, underscoring the Blues' superiority in a game where they killed the contest from first to last, prevailing 2-0 at a relative stroll.

From the 2 March Luton match where Abramovich shocked the world by announcing the club's sale to the Middlesbrough encounter just seventeen days later, Chelsea's men had registered six wins in succession in all competitions. The Blues returned to London – by plane, no less – proud of generating a remarkable team spirit in the face of constant uncertainty and adversity.

All the demands that Čech and Tuchel had placed on the players, to keep a steely focus on the day job, had been met, and all the aims to disappoint those queuing up to revel in a potential Chelsea meltdown had been achieved. Dauntingly, however, after a two-week fixture break for international matches, Chelsea would have to start that entire process all over again.

· · ·

Tuchel had kept telling Chelsea's players to push hard until the domestic game's international break, then breathe and reassess. But Chelsea's board had to adopt the same approach, and with two weeks without any men's fixtures, the club pounced on the opportunity to up the ante and increase the intensity of talks with OFSI in lobbying for further concessions to the temporary licence.

Eventually, the government came to appreciate that without the flow of more funds through the existing systems, Chelsea were indeed at risk of insolvency. And so, on 23 March, the government confirmed another variation to the operating licence. Crucially, operating company Fordstam would be allowed to inject up to £30 million into Chelsea, to keep the club afloat while the sale process continued.

The limits around ticket sales were also relaxed, meaning fans could buy tickets for home matches in the Champions League and the Women's Super League, as well as for Chelsea's men's FA Cup semi-final clash with Crystal Palace. Bosses at OFSI and the Treasury had finally worked out methods of Chelsea selling new tickets while also upholding the sanctions against Abramovich.

Government representatives were said to have claimed that any perceived delays in such variations were down to the sheer volume of sanctions work stretching across all sectors of business and covering a vast swathe of individuals. Chelsea's board members were relieved in the extreme, however, that they now had the wherewithal to pay staff, avoiding any major financial problems and therefore allowing them to turn more of their focus to progressing the club's sale. While the government continued to claim publicly that the aim was never to risk Chelsea's future, the restrictions of the temporary licence and the sluggishness in carrying out variances undoubtedly plunged the club into a jeopardy that those at the Blues considered both unnecessary and avoidable.

If those first three weeks after Abramovich announced he was putting the club up for sale had proved turbulent both on the field and in political and legal terms, the developing saga among those battling to buy the club was just as dramatic. While Chelsea's players and staff had been able to shut out extraneous events beyond the many repercussions of the sanctions, the top Stamford Bridge executives were already entrenched in a frenetic contest to buy the club.

Scores of suitors were not just announcing bids in the public arena, they were also laying bare intimate details of their candidacy, as desperate to curry favour with the government as they were with Chelsea and Raine, the bank running the sale process. As bids were appraised and vetted in the court of public opinion, many interested parties revealed their hand in a flash, only to fall by the wayside just as quickly.

CHAPTER SEVEN

BEAUTY CONTEST

Beverly Hills' Maybourne Hotel sits in one of the most exclusive, upmarket pockets of not just Los Angeles or the US but the western world. Just as the official process of the Chelsea sale took off, in early March 2022, Todd Boehly joined his business colleagues Behdad Eghbali and José E. Feliciano for a breakfast meeting at the five-star Maybourne. Just a stone's throw from world-renowned shopping stretch Rodeo Drive, the group settled into the elegant surroundings, first running the rule over their recent conversations, in which Eghbali and Feliciano's private equity firm Clearlake Capital had explored a possible deal for Boehly's investment vehicle CBAM. Clearlake had been interested in learning about CBAM and had worked closely with Boehly in that explorative process. Even though CBAM was eventually sold to Carlyle, in a reported £787.2 million deal, Boehly, Eghbali and Feliciano struck a quick, firm working relationship across that fact-finding mission.

While they started off looking back at CBAM, the conversation quickly shifted to Chelsea, as by that time Boehly's name was already being linked to a bid for the Blues. Eghbali and Feliciano's proposal was straightforward and effective: Clearlake were prepared to put up a lot of the capital required for a competitive bid, but they and Boehly could be fifty–fifty partners in the deal.

Already comfortable with his relationship with Clearlake's co-founders, Boehly was quickly happy too with the terms of the mooted link-up, believing that the pair shared in his own vision for Chelsea's future. At that Maybourne Hotel breakfast, a mutual respect blossomed into a potent business relationship, as the group talked of the power of London and all the ways in which they could potentially harness that to Chelsea's advantage. They considered a heady mix of London's selling point for attracting players but also top stars from other fields who could collaborate with the club as just one route to building a young, exciting set-up that could flourish for the long term.

All three men appreciated the methodologies and successes of the Manchester City and Liverpool models, while also respecting the way in which Abramovich had created a paradigm shift at Chelsea. Immediately, they were excited and energised by the sizeable challenge of bidding to step into the culture he had built. Before breakfast was over, the three men were ready to shake hands and step forward together. Further meetings were held between Boehly and Clearlake, notably in Connecticut, where Boehly's Eldridge firm is headquartered, but it was at that Beverly Hills sit-down that the partnership initially came together.

Clearlake looked likely to be the single entity eyeing the Chelsea sale that would boast the most potent funding, with more than $90 billion of assets under management and $57 billion in global investments. Raine had therefore advised Eghbali and Feliciano to stay free from partners in the initial stages of the sale, to see how the process would unfold. Clearlake were intent on finding suitable long-term partners from the outset, however, and as with many of the Chelsea suitors, they took a host of meetings to assess their best options.

In the end, Eghbali and Feliciano considered Boehly, Mark Walter and Hansjörg Wyss tight-knit, focused and well-funded. Eghbali cited the three Cs of capable, confident and capital as he and Feliciano drilled down into the decision of partnering up with Boehly.

Boehly also felt comfortable with Clearlake and saw them as a good fit to round out the bidding partnership. The consortium came together quickly and efficiently, with Boehly, Walter and Wyss putting up roughly 38 per cent of the money between them, and Eghbali and Feliciano's firm Clearlake contributing the other 62 per cent. Boehly's investment was to be personal, and not from his firm Eldridge. Boehly and Eghbali agreed to have co-control, meaning the duo would be required to agree on all of the most important elements to their bid.

From the outset, anyone bidding to buy Chelsea knew the price would be steep. Boehly had considered not just the capital required to pull off a purchase but also the funds needed to both build and then grow the club for the future. It was clear too that Chelsea would need to solve the long-running issue of renovating or rebuilding Stamford Bridge, another project requiring major investment as well as expertise in real estate development and urban planning. The partners were aligned from the outset on their goals both for the bidding phase and for Chelsea's long-term future. Overall, the four partners entered the consortium aiming to build a team of investors with broad business expertise that could work together to promote the best interests of Chelsea and its supporters for a long time to come.

• • •

The official bidding for Chelsea started the moment Abramovich confirmed the club's sale on 2 March. The frenzy was so immediate that less than twenty-four hours later, several credible bids in the region of £3 billion had already been firmly tabled with sale brokers Raine. One of Raine's first jobs was to jockey for position to retain the exclusive rights to run the sale process itself. If Abramovich's status had been up in the air before the sanctioning, once he was a 'designated person', in the accepted terminology, UK government oversight and a level of control was mandatory. Raine's long-standing association with Abramovich and the Chelsea executive, allied to their previous work in exploring a possible sale, were the reasons why the Blues' hierarchy had commissioned the merchant bank to run the sale process in the first place.

As soon as Abramovich was sanctioned officially, however, Joe Ravitch got wind that some of Raine's biggest competitor firms were contacting the government directly and urging that a bank with no associations or affiliations at all ought to run the process. Raine's position was twofold: that the existing working relationship and the previously amassed intellectual property pertinent to the sale marked them out above all others who could run the sale, and that impartiality and neutrality would be required in order to complete the most effective sale, and therefore would be demanded by business interests as much as by corporate responsibility and ethics.

There were those observers who were attempting to claim that the government itself ought to run the entire process, in order to ensure operations followed all relevant legislation and procedures. Raine never gave much in the way of credence to such suggestions, and bosses at the bank need not have worried in any case. In a summit Zoom call in which Raine met with representatives of all the relevant government departments, with Ravitch logging on from his firm's London office in Berkeley Square, the heads of the US bank once again spelled out their first-class credentials not just to handle the sale but also to achieve the highest possible price – and most crucially of all, to conclude the entire transaction in the whistlestop timescale required.

The department heads on that call firstly summarily dismissed any talk of the government running the sale itself, then ordered Raine to sell the club and to turn the transaction around as quickly as possible. The government representatives insisted their main oversight of the process would be confirming that no money would find its way to Abramovich, while also ensuring that Chelsea would be transferred to fit and proper owners who could take the club forward into a new era, safeguarding a community asset and a major employer.

The call did not last long, predominantly because all parties on that Zoom were conscious of the huge workload in store. The scale of the task awaiting Raine was laid bare by the sheer volume of would-be bidders: the merchant bank running the Chelsea sale received 280 official expressions of interest and scores more enquiries beyond that.

Raine's ten staff seconded full-time to the Chelsea sale process, allied to Ravitch and partner Colin Neville, were working as close to twenty-four hours a day as they could manage. The bank's staff were fielding cold calls from all over the world, often from a family office associate who was unable to name their principal but could instead produce a line of credit, sometimes into a region as high as $10 billion. From Paris to Geneva, Montreal to Dubai, the approaches came from all over the world, many entirely out of the blue.

Raine's first duties then were to carry out due diligence on everyone from those making loose enquiries all the way up to the bidders with whom they had existing working relationships. Sifting out the serious bidders from the spurious opportunists proved a mammoth challenge in itself, but add in the intense public scrutiny and the glare of the media, and Raine were having to work at double the typical speed and twice the discretion.

The ultra-expedited process then required a new data room to be established, including all the fresh information on the Chelsea business that prospective bidders would expect to be able to access for their own due diligence. By the time Raine had managed to plough through all the approaches, which spanned a range from the fantasists and the fanciful to the robust, credible and heavily backed main contenders, there were perhaps as many as fifty genuine bidders. After a whittling-down process that was accompanied by a relentless rhythm of online commentary in both traditional and social media, some twenty-five bidders were deemed to boast the financial means to mount competitive submissions.

• • •

If the New York bank was inundated with a deluge of requests and approaches, for the first time ever in such a process, so were media outlets all over the world: almost everyone launching a bid behind the scenes also saw fit to make their intentions known in public.

Boehly's extended discussions on Chelsea in 2018 and 2019 and pre-existing relationship with Raine offered the Eldridge Industries co-founder one potential edge in the process, and with all the jigsaw pieces of his consortium quickly in place, a potent bid was being pulled together without delay. Boehly's partner Wyss was so enthused as to confirm his involvement publicly in early March, even though the other consortium members kept their counsel amid a low-key overall approach.

A number of the different bidders have described an atmosphere of chaos behind the scenes, as Raine fought to collate the information required to update their data from the 2019 interest in Chelsea and produce a pack for the actual sale, while all the interested parties clamoured to compile credible bids. While the likes of Boehly and company were aiming to stay under the public radar, scores of others took a polar opposite approach.

Turkish businessman Muhsin Bayrak was among the first to signpost a bid for Chelsea, generating as much fanfare as possible and launching a trend that a glut of other suitors would quickly follow. His declaration that 'we will fly the Turkish flag in London soon' instigated a type of beauty pageantry unique to football.

Britain's richest man, Sir Jim Ratcliffe, quickly ruled himself out, but only tentatively and indirectly. Ratcliffe had amassed his vast fortune of billions through his INEOS Group petrochemicals operation. Ratcliffe's brother Bob was running the group's football arm and therefore the French Ligue 1 outfit Nice, and he went on the record with the *Mail on Sunday* distancing INEOS from any kind of bid or interest in Chelsea. While no one connected to Ratcliffe or INEOS approached Raine in the developing stages of the sale process, no one running the Chelsea sale considered that position definitive. In discussing the prospect of Chelsea on the record, even by way of rejecting any interest, INEOS had still in effect floated the idea of a bid for the Blues – at least, this was how their position was interpreted behind the scenes among those piloting the sale.

Ghanian gold mine owner Bernard Antwi Boasiako was bullish in his public confirmation of a bid for Chelsea that his representatives

briefed would top £3 billion. London investment firm Aethel Partners also moved to flex their finance industry muscles in alerting
the public to their intention to join the fight, while the most prominent bid from the Middle East came from Saudi Media Group.
Chelsea fan Mohamed Al Khereiji fronted a consortium boasting
the deepest of pockets but also a candidacy that always faced an
uphill struggle for UK government approval.

Both Chelsea and Raine felt that in less politically charged circumstances, the field of main contenders could have been drawn
from a more diverse background. But against a deadline of less than
twelve weeks and with the UK government having ultimate sign-
off on the final buyers, the parameters for suitability were rendered
necessarily narrow. The Saudi Media Group insisted from the outset
that their bid was completely separate from the Saudi Arabian state,
but Raine harboured concerns of potentially terminal complications with the UK government from the outset.

Newcastle's £350 million sale to Saudi Arabia's Public Investment
Fund (PIF) in October 2021 had drawn sustained criticism in some
quarters. The Premier League had ruled the Saudi state had no
ultimate control of PIF, even though the country's crown prince,
Mohammed bin Salman, was listed as chairman of the investment
vehicle. With Raine requiring as much as craving a quick and seam-
less sale of Chelsea less than six months later, and the government
determined to avoid controversy, the less challenging the bid, the
greater the chance a consortium would stand of securing the Stamford Bridge club ownership.

In mere days, the serious bids for Chelsea had racked up and up,
an astonishing state of affairs given the asking price was expected
to set a world-record sports club sale. Perhaps more remarkable
still was one of the main reasons for such high demand: despite

the astronomical sums, the context of the enforced sale meant the buyers would be snaring themselves a relative bargain. Several of the senior figures involved considered that in different circumstances the final selling price for Chelsea could have risen comfortably by another billion pounds. Even aside from Abramovich writing off the club's debt, the circumstances of the war and the need for a rapid sale deepened the pool of billionaires with both the interest and the wherewithal to pull off a purchase.

New York Jets owner Woody Johnson and Sacramento Kings chief Vivek Ranadivé added further US flavour to a developing nucleus of suitors, before London tycoon Nick Candy announced his own candidacy. Property billionaire Candy, a boyhood Chelsea fan, went public with his bid for the club on 9 March, the day before Abramovich was sanctioned by the UK government.

Sir Martin Broughton, another Chelsea fan, confirmed his own bid for the Blues on 13 March, in the build-up to kick-off for the Premier League clash against Newcastle at Stamford Bridge. The former chairman of British Airways had also acted as chairman of Liverpool between April and October 2010, rescuing the Reds and facilitating the £300 million sale to New England Sports Ventures. Broughton's fine standing as a knight of the realm, his stewardship of a British institution in BA and his emergency caretaker role at Liverpool all conspired to elevate his Chelsea candidacy straight into the main reckoning.

As Chelsea edged past Newcastle 1–0 thanks to Havertz's late winner, Blues fans in the stadium were reading of Broughton's candidacy on their phones – and Broughton's rival bidders, wherever they were located in the world, shifted uneasily in their seats at the idea of such a heavyweight contender joining the fray.

The TV cameras picked out Candy in the crowd flanked by some family members during that Newcastle tussle, as the jockeying for position, coverage and acclaim suddenly ratcheted through the notches.

After the match itself, Tuchel of course delivered his twin boost to Chelsea supporters, in first confirming that he would stay in his managerial role for the long haul and then also pledging to drive the bus to away matches if required. In contrast, Newcastle boss Eddie Howe faced a relatively uncomfortable press conference of his own. While Tuchel had used all his savvy and charm to sprinkle some positive dust on the nervy Chelsea situation, Howe was in no such mood regarding Newcastle's ownership issues. The former Bournemouth boss flat-batted a series of questions from the assembled media regarding Newcastle's Saudi ownership.

When it was pointed out to Howe that a day earlier Saudi Arabia had executed eighty-one people, he kept his cool but refused to engage on his feelings about the north-east club's Saudi hierarchy. 'I'm just going to answer questions on the game and on football,' said Howe. 'I'm still bitterly disappointed from the defeat, so I think it's only right that I stick to football.'

Asked how he felt about having to field questions on global politics, just as Tuchel faced with Chelsea, Howe did, however, add:

I'm here to manage the football team and coach the football team, so I'm well aware of what's going on around the world but my focus is on trying to produce a team to win football matches and try to get enough points to stay in the league, and that's all I'll talk about.

Howe's blunt response generated an awkward air in the room and, coupled with a smattering of Newcastle fans waving Saudi Arabia flags in the Stamford Bridge stands, in one short swoop, many of the challenges facing Saudi Media Group's bid for Chelsea were laid bare.

•   •   •

If the Chelsea suitors' early public posturing was coated in a pristine polish, that veneer was quickly chipped away to reveal a murkier layer of skulduggery, which, however tentative, certainly shifted the mood and focus of all the serious bidders. Candy took the first public swing, reacting haughtily in scotching rumours that he may look to join Boehly's consortium.

On the morning of 16 March, Chelsea were in Lille, having flown to France for their Champions League match as normal. Players and first team staff were happily able to insulate themselves from the developing beauty contest playing out in the court of public opinion, especially given their more immediate concerns on the impact of sanctions for the remainder of the season. Anyone else of a Chelsea persuasion or with a vested interest, however, could only look on in a state of near bewilderment as ownership candidates lined up to build themselves up – and knock each other down.

From supporters to club staff and directors, from UK government officials to decision-makers at Raine, stunned onlookers could not quite believe what they were seeing and reading, starting with Candy's vehement rejection of the idea that he might join forces with Boehly. A simple assertion that his bid was his own would have sufficed, but Candy was characterised by many involved in the process as greatly frustrated by assumptions in some quarters that he lacked the clout to spearhead a consortium himself. Instead, Candy's spokesperson issued a statement that set the hares running on what became a far less palatable approach to the race to buy Chelsea.

'There are no talks under way with Nick Candy and the Todd Boehly and Jonathan Goldstein consortium, not least because Mr Candy does not want a lifelong Spurs fan as part of the future ownership of Chelsea Football Club,' said Candy's official spokesperson, deliberately sparking an entirely new debate in the Blues' ownership race.

British solicitor and entrepreneur Goldstein had by this time long since earned strong standing in London, and of course his partnership with Boehly dated back to their 2014 co-founding of real estate firm Cain International. Goldstein had chaired the Jewish Leadership Council too, lending another attribute to a business and community profile of the highest repute. Candy was doubtless aware of the myriad qualities to recommend Goldstein as a partner but chose instead to focus on a singular element of football tribalism.

Boehly's team, including Goldstein himself, were all thought to have swept aside the criticism without any reaction, confident that supporting Tottenham would have no bearing on the bidding for Chelsea. While Candy's candour generated immediate impact on social media and in the press, none of the decision-makers on the sale, from Chelsea's directors to Raine via the UK government, batted an eyelid at Goldstein's long-standing Tottenham fandom. The first blow that could be considered below the belt had been struck, however, and in circles where criticisms and critiques would rather be kept private if aired at all, Candy's intervention shifted the tone of both the campaigning and the lobbying.

While Candy's open criticism of Goldstein's suitability dominated the daytime news agenda, even before the night's Champions League clash with Lille could kick off, there was still time for yet another significant development in the battle for the Blues. Lille's directors were panicking over whether they would be breaking sanctions laws by serving food to their Chelsea counterparts when news broke that Sebastian Coe had joined the Broughton bid to buy the Blues. A Chelsea season ticket holder and major fan, Lord Coe's greatest achievement after his stellar athletics career had been to bring the Olympics to London in 2012. The intention was to add Coe to the Chelsea board should their bid succeed, and if their rivals had been twitchy days earlier during the Newcastle match, now there was genuine concern at the increased potency of the Broughton consortium.

Coe would add even further credibility in the eyes of the UK government, and his backing for Broughton left their rivals on message of the stature of British establishment figures potentially required to win the Chelsea race. As Tuchel's side eased past Lille 2–1 on the night at Stade Pierre Mauroy and into the Champions League quarter-finals, the reporting on the contest to buy the club had taken on something approaching equal footing to the football. The parallel narrative streams were driving stressed supporters to distraction, while players and staff struggled to keep pace with the developments, trying to sift through and pick out the pertinent issues.

• • •

The gloves were off in the early public relations battle, but any mild hostility or friction among the rival bidders suddenly paled into insignificance compared to a glut of threats, which were taken extremely seriously. Online abuse might sadly be par for the course for anyone in the public eye in the social media age, but the severity and seriousness of threats that were being directed at Raine's senior leadership team gave many at the company genuine pause.

A direct cyber attack on Raine's email system crashed the company's server, as Ravitch received some 36,000 emails all but simultaneously. As the number of unread emails in his inbox rocketed, he had to shut down his work account for several days while the cyber security experts solved the problem. The sophisticated email takedown was unsettling and problematic, but even that quickly took a back seat when the specific threats started filtering through.

Ravitch was subjected to a number of death threats, and not through social media alone. He and the rest of the company took the threats seriously enough to weigh up heavily whether he ought to employ private security, and his friends and family were urging him to do exactly that. While many of the abusive messages stemmed from a variety of troll farms, there were other threats that could not be so readily dismissed.

In the end, Ravitch decided against the private security, determined that he would not kowtow to trolls or online miscreants, especially amid the relentless pace of the work on the club's sale. Staying in London for the majority of the sale process, though, Ravitch did check in to his hotel under a fake name, just in case. Broad shoulders, long experience and cool heads were required to navigate the increasingly fractious climate now surrounding an already tense process, and Ravitch found himself having to shake off all thoughts of those personal threats in order to think clearly enough to be able to focus on the art of the deal.

The science and maths of the process were clear, in that bidders would have to reach a number of genuine significance in order to mount a competitive submission for Chelsea. The art element became a study in linking like-minded parties who had the capital to take significant stakes but would need partners to build suitably formidable consortiums. While the likes of Boehly and Clearlake had struck their partnership themselves, in that breakfast meeting in Beverly Hills, others were casting around for allies, and it was at this point that Ravitch started making connections.

Individuals with financial packages running to the hundreds of millions were approaching Raine looking for a good fit in terms of potential bid partners, and Ravitch would then scour the interested parties to see whether there would be any suitable matches. The due diligence on all those who had enquired about buying the club in the first instance came to carry an extra value and use to Raine, who could mine all that information and look for various groups who might just be aligned in terms of vision, culture and outlook.

So while the likes of Candy might have been all too ready to write off certain partners in public, behind the scenes, almost all the key individual investors were entertaining discussions with counterparts from other set-ups. Plenty of such talks never moved further than a feeling-out process, but just as many did bear fruit and lead to groups teaming up and forming credible consortiums. If the public relations element of the sale became a beauty contest aimed at winning government approval, then here was something of a speed-dating process. With precious little time for some partners to find their way to each other organically, Ravitch was happy to assume the role of bid team matchmaker.

• • •

The morning after Chelsea's 2–1 win at Lille, on 17 March, when the men's squad were back on home soil and immediately worrying about their means of transport to the weekend FA Cup clash in Middlesbrough, another blockbuster bid to buy the club was confirmed. The Chicago Cubs-owning Ricketts family had teamed up with Citadel hedge fund founder Ken Griffin to compose a consortium boasting a compelling mix of elite sporting acumen and major global financial muscle. Cubs chairman Tom Ricketts would lead the family's bid to buy Chelsea, boasting the crucial experience of successfully rebuilding Wrigley Field in situ and immediately raising the possibility of following suit with Stamford Bridge. When Griffin's financial backing and clout was factored in, the Ricketts' bid was immediately installed as another front-running candidate. Behind the scenes, the Ricketts would quickly add the further clout of another billionaire in the shape of Dan Gilbert, the head of Rock Entertainment Group, which owned the NBA outfit the Cleveland Cavaliers. The consortium partners were quickly well set, and bullish on their abilities not just to win the race to buy the Blues but also to lead the club into a fresh era of success.

The frenzy of bidders revealing their hands came down to Raine's first deadline for initial bid submissions, which candidates had been informed would cut off at close of business on Friday 18 March, little more than two weeks after the club had been officially put up for sale. Bidders would have the opportunity to revise and refine their bids in a second round before final submissions, but all parties involved were scrambling to put the finishing touches to their proposals in time to meet the deadline.

While Chelsea's players and staff were in limbo waiting to see if they could take a plane to Middlesbrough rather than a coach, then, serious bidders from all over the globe were poring over their submissions, checking and double-checking as the hours and minutes ticked down towards Raine's deadline. Raine had deliberately kept a low public profile, refusing to make any statements and not engaging on the record beyond confirming the company's status as brokering the sale. This afforded the bank's staff the breathing space to conduct their mountain of work relatively uninterrupted, but it also left several bidders chasing information and frustrated by the sluggishness with which it proved forthcoming.

Behind the scenes, beyond the polished, crafted and confident statements of intent and bold pledges to supporters, many of the bidders were still frantically shopping for consortium partners. Such negotiations continued right to the wire ahead of the first submission deadline, and there were even those consortiums still seeking extra investment further down the line in the process.

Broughton and Coe's bid might have boasted the heaviest establishment hitters that had been confirmed publicly, but the proposition was rumoured to have been slightly light on funding in the early phases. As the first submission deadline approached, however, it emerged that billionaire sports investors Josh Harris and David Blitzer were the powerhouse backers of the Broughton consortium. The position of the Philadelphia 76ers owners would be complicated by their shareholding in Crystal Palace, but Broughton was confident that any Premier League conflicts could be avoided.

Broughton was linked up with Harris and Blitzer by US investment specialist Michael Klein, a long-term business partner who also came on board for the bid. Klein had even played a key role in Broughton's short chairmanship of Liverpool, where he had steered the club into the hands of focused owners and to long-term stability. Broughton's bid for Chelsea had been sparked by his son Michael, who believed his father could pull off another white-knight rescue act to guide a troubled Premier League club to safety. Klein, Harris and Blitzer provided a major capital injection that would hand Broughton the wherewithal required to compete on an equal footing with any of the other bidders.

London property king Candy was also rumoured to have been

battling to source sufficient funding to match the potency of the main players, and his own search of the world's financial centres for suitable partners proved a dramatic affair. Just when time and opportunity looked like they might get the better of him, Candy managed to strike a key alliance with South Korean firms Hana Financial Group and C&P Sports Group. Sports agent Catalina Kim proved pivotal in brokering the agreement, confidently expressing her excitement at the prospect of ushering the first Korean owners into the Premier League.

As the first deadline of 18 March passed, all the early contenders let it be known by one means or another that they had submitted their bids. With Raine continuing to keep quiet, briefing notes were disseminated to journalists and media outlets from those bidders who wanted exposure on the status of their candidacy.

Boehly's bid was lodged well before the deadline without issue, while fellow high-profile contenders the Ricketts and Broughton made their submissions too. The likes of Saudi Media Group, Woody Johnson and Vivek Ranadivé all made the cut-off point, with plenty more bids going in further under the radar too. Still conspicuous by its absence, however, was any bid from Ratcliffe and INEOS: while all at Chelsea and Raine felt compelled to take the Ratcliffes at their word that the cost was prohibitive and no bid would be forthcoming, it was still considered incongruous that Britain's richest man, already a football investor and keen to expand his sporting enterprises, had not seemingly made any extended overtures towards buying the Blues.

• • •

The deadline for initial bids might have passed, but Raine were still keeping their eyes and ears open to other potential opportunities. The bank's top executives Joe Ravitch and Colin Neville had taken charge of the Chelsea project and were hyper-focused on brokering the best outcome for all parties – balancing the aim of realising the highest possible price with the need for the club to be transferred to responsible, committed and financially potent new owners.

While first-round bids had been lodged, no one vying to buy the Blues could ease off from perfecting their candidacy and consortiums. Just as Raine remained open to new opportunities, so too were the bidders continuing the hunt for both extra investment and further star or establishment power to bolster their offerings. On 19 March, as Chelsea were gearing up to face Middlesbrough in the FA Cup, having finally travelled up to Teesside by plane, one of the Stamford Bridge club's most famous sons stepped into the ownership argument.

Commanding centre-back John Terry had won the lot at Chelsea, every inch the 'captain, leader, legend' honoured in a semi-permanent Stamford Bridge banner. Terry had carried that popularity among Chelsea supporters far beyond a playing career comprising four Premier League titles, five FA Cup triumphs and of course that Champions League victory in 2012. Ranking among the most influential players of the Abramovich era, Terry had long been an outspoken supporter of Chelsea's transformative owner. By this stage in the sale proceedings, fans of the club were starting to wonder whether former players might start backing specific bids. The much-loved Gianluca Vialli had already thrown his weight behind Candy's bid, the former Italy and Chelsea striker's firm Tifosy Capital and Advisory joining forces with the London property tycoon. Where Chelsea fans were concerned, Vialli's affection for the club and London, having chosen to raise his family in the city after his playing career, carried considerable weight. Just as Candy's bid benefited significantly from Vialli's knowledgeable approval, then, so too could other candidates potentially gain favour from similar endorsements.

Terry's seal of approval was bound to prove impactful, and this influence was not lost on the ex-England defender. Refraining from backing a specific bid, though, Terry opted instead to take up a key cause of all football supporters. The 'golden share' concept had long been touted as a way for supporters to keep owners grounded via a percentage of club ownership, but it has rarely been employed in England. The UK government has long craved ways to implement regulations demanding clubs hand an ownership share to support-ers, allowing fans a say in the running of their club.

Chelsea's eventual new owners would have to provide a raft of commitments to the club's future in order to earn government ap-proval for a takeover, and the idea of offering Blues fans a share suddenly gained traction. So, rather than back one of the main runners and riders, Terry lent his support to a bid with a difference – the True Blues consortium. Led by financier Sandford Loudon, the True Blues were looking to levy funds to buy a stake in Chelsea through a community offering. Chelsea supporters would be offered the chance to buy in from as little as £100, with True Blues pledging to work with the eventual new owners on purchasing a club share.

Terry went public on his desire to protect Chelsea's history and future by putting his name to what in effect at that stage was simply a pressure group. The True Blues were not bidding to buy the club but attempting to convince the eventual new owners to take a sup-porter-led group under their wing. Along with Vialli's intervention, Terry trying to stand up for the average fan and hand them a voice in Chelsea's future tugged at heart strings across the sporting landscape.

As the public and private positioning continued apace, Raine's second big deadline in the sale process was fast approaching. Bosses at the New York bank had set the date of 25 March to draw up a shortlist of bidders who would progress to the final stages of the race for Chelsea. Even the consortiums with a degree of confidence in how their bids stacked up against the competition were suddenly in the dark about what would happen next, and quite when. But as it turned out, for several days in the run-up to that shortlist deadline, no news certainly represented good news.

Saudi Media Group had the unwanted distinction of becoming the first of the credible, competitive bids to be rejected from the process. Raine informed the bid leaders of their unsuccessful attempt, where the political climate around Newcastle's ownership had clearly taken its toll. Satisfying the Premier League that Chelsea's eventual new owners would prove fit and proper stewards might have been one thing, but meeting the government's expectations was deemed a long shot. In the prohibitively tight timeframe, Raine ultimately took the decision that there were too many unmanageable risk factors in a bid that could well have carried suitable financial backing and commitment.

New York Jets owner Woody Johnson was next to be disappointed by Raine, as the process of letting suitors down gently continued as discreetly as possible. Johnson might have started out with bold ambitions for his competitive, self-funded bid for Chelsea, but as the sheer scale of the figures involved unfolded in front of him, he felt his only move was to admit defeat gracefully. Johnson was thought to have possessed the ability to push his bid higher, but a handful of the other bidders seemed to boast more financial clout.

Raine kept to their word of not making any public pronouncements on the process, so the bidders themselves were left with the choice of whether and when to tell a wider audience. All interested parties were keen for the information to reach the public domain quickly, not only to stop any conjecture but also to avoid being considered to have tried to eke out their association to the sale when their involvement was already at an end. None of the consortiums whose initial bids had been lodged and then ratified were chasing exposure, and all were keen to ensure they were not perceived in such fashion.

The remaining players were still frantically compiling and refining the substance of their bids, while at the same time watching both clock and phone. With that shortlist deadline fast approaching, not even the consortium figureheads knew when the call from Raine might come, nor what the specific timing of that call might mean. While billionaires are not the type to sit and wait for opportunities to come to them, here was a rare scenario in which not even drilling down into their bid specifics could stop the main competitors from hanging on the telephone.

CHAPTER EIGHT

LA CONFIDENTIAL

The business acumen, financial muscle and laser-focus in the Todd Boehly–Clearlake Capital partnership were effectively put in place by the end of that Beverly Hills breakfast meeting, where Boehly had begun exploring the concept of joining forces with Behdad Eghbali and José Feliciano at the plush Maybourne hotel. Another significant element of the resources and experience that Boehly and Mark Walter brought to bear was situated across Los Angeles, nestled in the middle of Elysian Park. Dodger Stadium sits some ten miles across town from the Beverly Hills enclave where Boehly, Eghbali and Feliciano had thrashed out their initial agreement on what would become a formidable consortium proposition, the MLB arena surrounded on all sides by acres of hiking and biking trails, not to mention some of the best views of the city and a number of its main landmarks.

A trek to Angel's Point in Elysian Park affords a stunning city vista, with Dodger Stadium first rising to prominence, set in and around both the skyscraper clutch of downtown LA and the Hollywood hills, within sight of the famous white sign. By the time the Dodgers' ownership wrangle was resolved in May 2012, though, it was the famed old MLB franchise that had gone to seed, and not the picturesque park surrounding a beloved but fraying stadium. Mark Walter spearheaded the takeover that first secured the Dodgers' future then set about revolutionising both the entire baseball outfit and the fan experience. Boehly was part of that investor group too, which also included LA Lakers basketball icon Magic Johnson.

While Walter and Boehly would team up again when it came to Chelsea, a full decade down the line, in the interim there was the small matter of reversing the struggling Dodgers' fortunes. And turn the Dodgers upside down they did, outlaying $2 billion for the purchase itself, then another $1 billion in new players and upgrades to the stadium, training facilities and even the car parks. Long-term contracts for staff and players followed – lucrative, yes, but also designed to build stability and clarity of vision. As performances improved, the fans flocked back and by the time the Dodgers won the World Series in 2020, the stadium was among the best-attended in all of Major League Baseball.

Any time the Boehly–Clearlake consortium needed to point to tangible evidence of sports administration capability, the physical medals could easily be deposited on the relevant boardroom tables. Boehly had been able to appreciate first hand just how a big city team could work in tandem with its population, where the one could benefit the other, through a raft of community initiatives to boost local causes, as well as smart ideas that engaged supporters more closely with the team and its people.

Boehly had adopted a hands-on approach at the Dodgers, despite numbering among a nucleus of influential figures, and with Walter as chairman the lead operator. A regular at Dodger Stadium with his wife and three children, he made sure his young family were visible in the most inclusive and welcoming way at team offices too.

The openness and the family ethos chimed with Dodgers staff and players from day one and helped foster a positive atmosphere that fed into the ultra-focused pursuit of winning.

Boehly and his baseball partners built it, and the Dodgers won. The transferable skills were clear, and Boehly and his football colleagues were entirely confident that they could replicate their MLB success at Stamford Bridge, in both Europe and the Premier League.

• • •

The Ricketts family's bid was hardly even public knowledge when an anti-Islam storm whipped up that could have sunk the consortium's candidacy from the very outset. Initial reporting of the Ricketts family background covered everything from Tom Ricketts's successes and struggles as chairman of the Chicago Cubs to his sister Laura's work with the Michelle Obama Foundation and his brother Pete's governorship of Nebraska. Their father, Joe Ricketts, was the billionaire behind electronic trading platform TD Ameritrade, as much a business powerhouse as a family patriarch.

What was also woven into initial reporting, however, was the historical leak of a cache of emails from Joe Ricketts, revealing a glut of anti-Muslim sentiment and leading to widespread allegations of racism. Joe Ricketts described Muslims as 'my enemy' in those emails, leaked in 2019 but dating back far further, which led to a major controversy that affected the entire family.

The moment the incident was raised in relation to Chelsea, the Ricketts' bid was on the back foot. Neither Joe Ricketts nor his governor son Pete were set to play any part in the Chelsea consortium bid – Tom, Laura and Todd were the co-leaders of the proposal – but that did not prove a worthy distinction in the eyes of many Blues fans. In days, the hashtag 'No To Ricketts' was trending on Twitter, and despite the many compelling elements of the bid, in the court of public opinion at least, the Cubs owners were suddenly lagging behind the competition.

Siblings Tom, Laura and Todd Ricketts, the joint leaders of the Chelsea bid, were thought to have reacted with dismay. Those 'my enemy' emails had been pored over when they were first leaked three years earlier, and were written another decade prior to that. For Chelsea supporters, though, the Ricketts' bid team knew that this would represent fresh, shocking information.

Tom, Laura and Todd Ricketts had always been characterised as condemnatory of their father's choice of words, amid the trio's staunch anti-racism stance. Historically, the three Ricketts siblings had been described as feeling that the emails did not accurately reflect their father's views. No public explanation would have washed, but privately they had been said to feel that their father had meant that Muslim extremists, not all Muslims, were his enemy. The siblings had always been believed to be acutely aware, nonetheless, that what he had said in those emails was something entirely different. And details matter.

Just five days after the Ricketts' bid went public, Paul Canoville, Chelsea's first black player, stepped up and ventured his opinion that the family did not represent suitable owners of the Stamford Bridge club. 'So I've seen and heard enough, I'm saying a big fat anti-racism NO to the Ricketts bid!'

Canoville had suffered the pain and distress of being racially abused by his own fans on his Chelsea debut in April 1982. The skilful winger rose above the aggression and abuse to make seventy-nine appearances for the Blues in five years at the club, before injury stunted the remainder of his career. By the time of the Chelsea sale, Canoville had managed to reinvent himself as an anti-racism and anti-discrimination campaigner. Having fought off several bouts of aggressive cancer, Canoville had not only rejuvenated his health; he had built the anti-hate foundation named in his honour into a shining example of understanding and tolerance. Chelsea had even renamed Stamford Bridge's largest hospitality suite after their pioneering star.

So while Canoville might not have carried much clout when suffering the outrageous abuses of his early playing days, simply because of the unacceptable climate of that era, by 2022, people would listen. And on matters of race, integration and discrimination, he was not just a campaigner but a man bearing decades of lived experience who was regularly visiting schools, sharing his story and its repercussions.

If the Ricketts trio were concerned about the backlash from the renewed scrutiny of their father's historical racist emails, they most likely harboured palpable worry when Canoville entered the public discourse. Allied to critical commentary from the Chelsea Supporters' Trust (CST), Canoville's stance had left the Ricketts in no doubt that only a concerted effort to explain themselves in detail would allow any chance of reversing the overwhelming negativity. Tom Ricketts contacted Raine and Bruce Buck and asked if he could meet with both Canoville and the CST, and within days he would be jetting in to London to do just that.

In the meantime, Canoville was caught by surprise when he received a rare phone call from Buck himself. Despite his many and varied collaborations with Chelsea, it was unusual for the club's chairman to be on the phone in person. What was more unusual still was the request that went alongside that call. Buck asked Canoville if he would be prepared to meet Tom Ricketts and hear out the Chicago Cubs owner in person.

In the early '80s, Canoville had to handle his racist abusers with a mixture of tactics, which in those days did not all that often represent a direct, all-out challenge. The mood of the time meant that often those on the receiving end of the most disgusting abuse simply had to grin and bear it, or take it in their stride, or rise above it, or any number of similar euphemisms for letting it go unchallenged. His own Chelsea fans should have been doing everything they could to throw their support behind him, urging him on with the strength of their backing. Instead, in his playing days, he, had to endure monkey chants, being hit with bananas thrown from the stands, and even some rival club supporters wearing white pillowcases on their heads in a mixture of macabre taunt and threat.

When Canoville had read of Joe Ricketts's emails, many of the same feelings he had endured in his early playing days came rushing right back to the surface. A negative tweet was a mild response, even if he had not thought out his strategy in detail or at length. When Buck asked Canoville to meet Tom Ricketts, even though the ex-Chelsea winger knew it was his father who had made those statements rather than Tom himself, he was quickly transported back to the days of being given precious little choice other than to be forced into a reaction. But if as a young footballer in the '80s it had been safer and smarter to let things slide, here was an opportunity at a more established stage of his life, and in the context of an entirely different era, for him to confront an aggressor, in discrimination terms at least.

The day after Canoville's tweet, on 23 March, the Ricketts issued a statement as the first in a string of proactive steps to try to rectify the damage caused by those 2019 emails being brought back into the light. 'Our family rejects any form of hate in the strongest possible terms,' read the Ricketts family's statement.

Racism and Islamophobia have no place whatsoever in our society. We have developed deep and abiding partnerships with the
Muslim community in Chicago, as well as with all communities
of colour. Respect for diversity and inclusion are central to our
family's values. If we prevail in our bid for Chelsea, we commit to
the club and to the fans that we will actively promote these values.

Tom, Laura and Todd Ricketts then promptly hopped on a plane
bound for London, hoping to start building some bridges. But
whatever turbulence they experienced over the Atlantic would be
nothing in comparison to the Stamford Bridge storm that was still
brewing around their bid.

• • •

While the Ricketts were busy fighting reputational fires and battling
for Chelsea fan backing, Boehly, Clearlake and partners were still
working away in the background, slotting in more pieces of their
consortium jigsaw. All the equity partners, the funding and the percentage splits had quickly been resolved, which allowed attention
to turn to strategic support. The dauntingly tight timeframe meant
that Raine and the UK government would both be highly prizing
speed, efficiency and simplicity when it came to selecting a winner
and then ratifying that bid.

Boehly was of the firm mindset that speed and agility would be
everything in this race, not just in compiling a bid but also in the
ability to deliver pledges and expedite the sale transaction itself.
Any hitches, hold-ups or snags that would complicate a smooth
purchase, especially in terms of technicalities, would definitely dent
a proposition, Boehly believed. And so it was to that end that he

made sure one of his earliest moves was to seek out the services of top advisory staff who could command respect and influence in the halls of government. The government would not be selecting the new Chelsea owners, but they would have to ratify the candidacy of the eventual club buyers. While a veto appeared extremely remote and would doubtless have generated huge, unwanted controversy, it was also not entirely out of the realms of possibility, should the eventual bidder put forward to buy the club prove unsuitable in government reckoning.

Boehly therefore quickly engaged Robey Warshaw, which meant not only adding its head Sir Simon Robey but also bringing on Robey's colleague George Osborne. The former Chancellor had joined the Mayfair advisory firm the previous year, aiming to bring all his Westminster and Whitehall connections and expertise to bear for the boutique outfit. With plenty of former colleagues, friends and peers still in the Tory government, Osborne would be able to provide insight, understanding and also access to the Boehly–Clearlake proposition.

Boehly had already been confident his bid would be able to generate a straightforward deal for Chelsea, and after adding Robey and Osborne, he was left in total belief that his submission would end up being not just the most compelling but also the most agile when it would matter most, in terms of meeting all the requirements and terms of any eventual deal.

The chaotic grind of the sale had all those striving to compile bids for Chelsea fighting against the constant instinct to compare and contrast with rivals' prospects. Determined not to fall into any such traps, Boehly worked hard to stop his mind wandering into the realms of uncertainty. Purposely ignoring all the press and media coverage of the sale, leaving that to other staff and bid team representatives, Boehly instead mapped out the destination, put his head down and plotted a course for that end point. At every turn, he brought his outlook back to the aims of building the best possible team and compiling the best possible bid itself, which in turn meant a clean, simple and effective submission.

•   •   •

Providing all the credible Chelsea bidders with the vast information required for them to construct compelling, comprehensive submissions for the club turned into no mean feat in isolation. While Raine had set up a data room and similar facilities for interested parties to mine required information on the Chelsea business operation, when it came down to creating a shortlist of potential winners, those running the process needed to furnish the contenders with even more detail.

Conversations online or on the phone were simply not going to cut it and would certainly have taken too long. And so instead, Marina Granovskaia, Bruce Buck, Joe Ravitch and Colin Neville held lengthy, ultra-detailed presentations for as many as eight bid teams, in order to provide everything required to compile a suitable proposal for the Stamford Bridge club. Across a period of a week to ten days, then, west London played host to extended cohorts from those bid teams that were leading the running in the mid-section of the sale process.

The luxury hotels and residences of west and south-west London's most exclusive postcodes suddenly became crowded with delegates from the various consortiums all battling to buy the Blues. The staff who were organising logistics for bid teams running double-figures deep were not only required to secure accommodation of the requisite standard but also to ensure, somehow, that none of the rival bidders would be situated either in the same place or close by. Almost 100 key parties were filtering in and out of the city for crunch meetings with the group running the sale process, in what morphed into a mammoth undertaking.

Granovskaia, Buck and the Raine duo would present to each group as a whole, disclosing the detail on the Chelsea business in full. Where Granovskaia would lead a session on information like player acquisitions, other Chelsea staff were also drafted in to present on their own specialties. At the end of exhaustive presentations to each group, Buck and Granovskaia would then meet privately with the principal of each consortium.

As groups of lawyers for each side would also thrash out fine print, all the bidders were able to gain the strongest possible feel for the business that was Chelsea FC. Granovskaia and Buck apportioned a full day for each meeting, and each day was crammed full. The leaders of the bids were all determined to be as amenable and available as possible, which meant that a clutch of top business figures were circling the wider west London area for the best part of two weeks.

As the marathon talks were taking place in and around the Stamford Bridge area, the wider public was none the wiser, not least Chelsea fans. Thousands of supporters would have milled past the ground each day, unaware that one or other of the groups going all-out to buy the club would have been intently taking in every tiny morsel of information, hoping to turn even the smallest scrap of detail into a piece of actionable intelligence.

•   •   •

Paul Canoville met Tom Ricketts on 24 March, the day before Raine were due to finalise the shortlist of bidders for Chelsea. Bruce Buck met Canoville and his team in the grounds of Stamford Bridge, whereupon Ricketts arrived too. The group took a walk up through the Canoville Suite itself, renamed in his honour as part of Chelsea's bid to ease some of the hurt the club's first black player had endured back in the '80s. If anyone had been left in two minds about Canoville's influence, walking through the hospitality area bearing his name wiped out any remaining doubt.

Settling down for the crunch talks in one of the west London ground's other hospitality areas, Buck assumed a watching brief, as first Ricketts attempted to set out his stall to Canoville and then the ex-Chelsea star gave the Chicago Cubs owner an extended grilling. Ricketts spoke passionately about his abhorrence at his father's emails, refusing to make any excuses but instead offering simple, open apologies. Then he laid out his hopes and ambitions for his bid for Chelsea, explaining how he and his family saw opportunities to bring local communities even closer to the club.

Ricketts championed the Cubs' stadium renovation at Wrigley Field, insisting they could replicate the impressive feat at Stamford Bridge. He talked about his sister's work with the Michelle Obama Foundation and how the two bid leaders were determined that their vision for Chelsea would be based in multiculturalism. Keen to quiz Canoville on his experiences, Ricketts took the time to hear Chelsea's first black star explain some of his most challenging times from his Blues playing days.

Canoville spent time carefully but respectfully challenging Ricketts on everything from his apology to his ideas and aims for Chelsea's future, should his bid be a success. At the end of a lengthy, comprehensive process, Canoville found himself impressed. The anti-racism campaigner, who had been running his own foundation for years, was left with the distinct impression that Ricketts was neither saying merely what was expedient nor going through the motions. Instead, Canoville and his team were more than pleasantly surprised by not just the tone and the vehemence in Ricketts's condemnation of any and all forms of racism but also his explanation of their aims for the Blues.

Canoville can easily distinguish between those addressing anti-racism issues who are simply saying what they think people want to hear and those who actually mean what they are saying and are prepared to act on those stances. He certainly considered Tom Ricketts to be in the latter category, and at the end of a heartfelt, productive meeting, he came away believing that the Ricketts had all the credentials to be excellent Chelsea owners – barring, of course, supporter buy-in.

The former Blues and Reading winger was also left feeling frustrated, however, as he knew he would not be able to reveal the details of the meeting, nor mount any public support for either the Ricketts or any other bid. Even though he came away from meeting Ricketts having had his mind changed, confident that Tom, his sister Laura and brother Todd were not bigoted people, he also realised he would not be able to communicate that, especially not while the sale process was ongoing. Canoville felt the Chelsea fans would have both understood and been excited by the Ricketts' vision for the Blues, but however much he was itching to share what he had learned, firstly it was not his place to do so, and secondly it was paramount that he steered entirely clear of any actions that might be seen to influence the sale process.

Before the meeting, Canoville had been concerned that the

Ricketts would seek to excuse or even justify those historical emails, and that there would be some kind of attempt to rewrite the past. Afterwards, though, he felt reenergised by the refreshing candour of Tom Ricketts, who entirely shouldered the family's responsibility for those emails and accepted the full extent of the discrimination. As with the Ricketts' vision for Chelsea, Canoville could not share any of his emotional and instinctive responses to the meeting either. His hands were tied, and as he was unable to provide any balance to his tweet saying 'No to the Ricketts', he was left frustrated by his inability to level that particular playing field.

Tom Ricketts, meanwhile, was understood to have felt honoured not just to meet Canoville but to hear his remarkable story first-hand. Ricketts had become a Chelsea fan having spent time in London in the '90s and members of the bid team felt he was fully appreciative of the magnitude of Canoville's status, allied to the depth of emotion tied to his Stamford Bridge story. The wider bid team came to regard that meeting as a unique lesson on racism and discrimination, forgiveness and education, when Tom Ricketts relayed the events.

While the circumstances of that audience were more than deplorable, the Ricketts group came away relieved that Canoville had the grace and patience to keep an open mind and then to shift his point of view. All parties appeared to have left Stamford Bridge in buoyant mood, with absolutely no idea of the furore the meeting would cause in the future.

• • •

As the Ricketts rushed to defend the virtues of their bid and their family's very integrity, another fresh development rocked the entire sale process. The day before the deadline for forming the shortlist, an entirely new bidder – and a genuine contender – surfaced publicly. Boston Celtics co-owner Stephen Pagliuca stepped out of the shadows, at the very last minute confirming his bid for the Blues.

The public narrative was that of shock and surprise, and in some quarters a sense of vindication, because the notion of a mystery bidder had been gaining traction for several weeks. Among those who would speculate to such effect, names as spurious as Amazon founder Jeff Bezos, one of the world's richest men, had been bandied around, but never with any certainty or as a result of any definite sourcing. While the likes of Bezos had never taken any interest in the Chelsea situation, Pagliuca had, and from the outset of the process.

In the early phase of the sale, while Raine were busily introducing and matching possible partners, Joe Ravitch had teed up Pagliuca with Larry Tanenbaum, the chairman of the NBA and an investor in the Toronto Raptors as well as the ice hockey franchise the Toronto Maple Leafs. Further partners were John Burbank, founder of San Francisco hedge fund Passport Capital, and Eduardo Saverin, the Facebook co-founder.

Where other bidders had felt the need to publicise their intentions, Pagliuca had opted to stay entirely under the radar, sticking fast to long-held sporting administrative principles of aiming, wherever possible, to operate behind the scenes and only speak publicly when either necessary or with particularly substantive information to share. Pagliuca resisted any urge to meet the revelations of his bid with any kind of briefing or on-record statements, accepting that, at least in the short term, the Chelsea sale's by-now juggernaut narrative would motor on whether he or his partners added to it or not.

Pagliuca certainly had the financial muscle to compete with the top bidders, but an immediate concern was his acquisition as recently as February 2022 of a significant share in Italian club Atalanta. Along with a number of other investors, Pagliuca's group's 55 per cent share in the Serie A outfit meant that any purchase of Chelsea would likely have required him to divest that holding. So, as with Harris and Blitzer, who had backed the Broughton bid while holding a share in Crystal Palace, there were complications that could have put pressure on the kind of quick sale transaction that the UK government demanded, and that Raine and Chelsea therefore required.

Pagliuca's ability to keep his bid under wraps for such a long time unsettled some of his rivals and earned him some kudos in other areas too. Supporters were left with immediate mixed feelings, though, respecting the ability to control a narrative but questioning the intention behind entirely shutting down an important flow of information to the fans.

Chelsea's supporter groups wanted influence in the process too, given the government oversight and the extraordinary circumstances more generally of the club's perilous position. Pagliuca opting not to engage with any of the fan organisations in the early phases of the sale process left many supporters frustrated and seeking answers on the aims of his bid and his wider ambitions for the club.

As deadline day for Raine to name the shortlist of bidders inched along, the consortiums that had not yet been contacted were left to sweat still further. Close of business on 25 March was the final deadline for confirming the shortlist – and thanks to Raine's main location, that meant New York time. For the UK-based bidders, the wait felt even longer due to the five-hour time zone lag. The later in the day the phone call from Raine, the better, and the last groups to receive word were Boehly–Clearlake, Broughton, the Ricketts family – and Pagliuca.

For days, the shortlist had looked for all money as though it would be whittled down to just three bids, and all with a US influence, given Harris and Blitzer's backing for Broughton. But Pagliuca's emergence from the blindside had created not only fresh public intrigue but also a modicum of doubt in the other three finalist bidders.

As the four bidders were informed by Raine that they had made it to the shortlisting stage, there was no time to draw breath, let alone celebrate or even reflect. All four finalists had ultimate belief in their submissions, considering they could all offer a crucial point of difference that would tip the scales in their favour. They had all also met the minimum criteria required by Abramovich for future stewardship of Chelsea, which beyond winning the bidding process included pledging and planning to provide a long-term stadium solution and investing heavily in not just the men's and women's first teams but also the academy and the training ground.

●　●　●

The Ricketts certainly had no time to ease off the gas, because on the day the shortlist was finalised, the Chelsea Supporters' Trust issued a combative statement insisting they could not conscience supporting the family's bid to buy the Blues – and this was even after meeting the Ricketts personally in London. The Ricketts bid leaders had sat down with CST delegates in tandem with meeting Canoville on their flying visit to London.

The Ricketts bid group's general feeling was that the meetings had gone well, but any notions of winning the CST round evaporated in light of that 25 March statement, which put the Ricketts family on renewed notice that, as far as a large section of Chelsea fans were concerned, their candidacy was still not endorsed.

'It is essential that the new owners of the club have the confidence of the supporter base and demonstrate an understanding of the values that we stand for,' read the CST statement.

That is why the strength of feeling towards the Ricketts family bid from Chelsea supporters cannot and must not be ignored. The CST are grateful to the Ricketts family for meeting with us this week. We challenged them on all of the points supporters have raised concerns about. However, our concerns about their ability to run an inclusive, successful club on behalf of our diverse supporter base around the world have not yet been allayed. It is for the Ricketts family to demonstrate how they will address supporter concerns – especially with regard to inclusivity, given both past and recent statements by members of the family – and they have not yet done that. They must do so publicly and they must do so urgently. If they are unable to do this and gain the confidence of Chelsea supporters, the CST board does not believe it would be in the best interests of our members and Chelsea supporters for their bid to succeed.

Promising a member survey on the matter in a bid to gain a wider picture of Chelsea fan opinion on the Ricketts, the CST also accepted in the lengthy statement that the choice of future club owners would come entirely down to the existing club ownership, Raine and the UK government. At the same time, the CST's influence was clear: the Ricketts had taken the time to meet with them and talk them through their plans and ambitions towards the club.

If Canoville had already felt his hands had been tied by the inability to share the details of his own Ricketts meeting, after the CST statement he was left even more frustrated. While entirely respectful of the CST stance, especially in terms of protecting the club, Canoville felt the Ricketts had still not been able to achieve a fair public hearing.

At the same time, the depth of feeling and wide spectrum of views on such an emotive subject only served to vindicate his decision to keep his counsel and respect the deeper sale process. Beyond the public narrative, the varying PR strategies and the differing outlooks of the competing consortiums, the sale shortlist confirmed that, in the eyes of the decision-makers, any one of Boehly–Clearlake, Broughton–Harris–Blitzer, Ricketts–Griffin–Gilbert or Pagliuca–Tanenbaum would be deemed suitable and appropriate Chelsea owners.

While the men's team had dispersed for the international break, the women were pressing on through their standard schedule, and two days after Raine finalised the shortlist of Chelsea bidders, Emma Hayes's side ran riot on the road at Leicester. Guro Reiten, Sam Kerr and Bethany England all bagged goal braces, while Aniek Nouwen, Lauren James and Jessie Fleming also found the net as the Blues crushed the Foxes 9–0 at the King Power Stadium. In venting a whole heap of frustration wrapped up in the club's sanctions and the uncertainty around the future, Chelsea also leapfrogged Arsenal at the top of the WSL.

After the final whistle, boss Hayes admitted shedding a few tears on the morning of the match, but not for any of the reasons outlined above. Ever one to acknowledge the personal challenges of a career in football, Hayes revealed that the time away from her young son Harry, particularly on Mother's Day, was taking a sizeable toll. 'The girls asked me why I didn't bring him,' Hayes told Sky Sports. 'I said that's half the problem us parents have, the guilt of being the best at our jobs and being parents. I regret that one and I won't do it again.'

Amid all the talk of multi-billion-pound investment in Chelsea's future, hundreds of club staff were more commonly found fretting for their next paycheque than thinking overtly about which shortlisted consortium might make the best new owners. As ever, Hayes's ability to cut through the din and ground herself and her players in the most compelling manner paid the biggest possible dividend. After all, the horrors of the war loomed constantly over every single event at Chelsea, a spectre that remained unavoidable for club employees but that also had to be put to the back of collective minds in order for daily tasks to be carried out.

CHAPTER NINE

A FRAMEWORK FOR PEACE

Attempts to keep a lid on Abramovich's poisoning incident held relatively fast for almost a month, but at the end of March the story leaked out, instantly becoming global news. Eventually, Abramovich's senior aides decided to confirm several basic details of the incident, in order to calm the noise and help him continue his back-channelling efforts towards facilitating peace talks.

If the poisoning incident was making worldwide headlines on 28 March, however, Abramovich himself – and more precisely footage of the Russian-Israeli billionaire – dominated the news cycle the very next day. On 29 March, all parties involved in peace talks between Russia and Ukraine convened in Istanbul, for a summit where genuine hopes had been raised that a pathway towards peace could be drawn.

Turkey's President Recep Tayyip Erdoğan played host to the first set of direct, public-facing talks where both sides came to the table, in the presidential offices of the Dolmabahce Palace. Just as Abramovich had found himself shuttling between such historic and ornate buildings at the start of the month when moving from delegation to delegation, again he was on hand on the banks of the Bosphorus, still aiming to do what he could to bring all sides together for crunch talks.

The more formal and official nature of these talks meant a small collection of media personnel were on hand to cover at least an element of the event, and certainly to record the fact of the negotiations taking place at all. The moment Abramovich walked through the entrance vestibule and into the wide, open room in which the talks were to be housed, all the media in attendance latched onto the news value of his presence.

As video footage of Abramovich's arrival beamed around the world, this, like the poisoning incident's confirmation a day earlier, would lead countless bulletins. The footage allowed TV outlets to press the story harder and further than before, building their reports around the new content. The video also acted as categorical proof that Abramovich was indeed taking on the role that he and his people had previously described, albeit in purposely scant detail.

Where on 28 February vocal detractors like MPs Chris Bryant and Margaret Hodge had poured public scorn on reports that Abramovich was attempting to foster peace talks, on 29 March when the footage of his presence was broadcast around the world there was only silence. Abramovich himself had never been greatly concerned with what was written about him and did not deviate from his natural approach on this occasion. Members of his staff, however, had felt far more keenly the heat of criticism from sections of the UK political elite specifically, and the dissemination of incontrovertible proof of Abramovich's involvement yielded a feeling of relief.

After the buzz of arrivals from both delegations, the Russian and Ukrainian parties took their seats at the long expanse of table, the two sides facing each other. At the head of the room stood a lectern, from which President Erdoğan addressed the convened negotiating teams. 'The world is waiting for good news, and good news from you,' said Turkey's commander in chief. After the kind of pithy opening address that left no one in any doubt of the day's agenda, the media receded and let both parties thrash out their points.

Abramovich did not have a seat at the main table, commensurate with not being part of the formal negotiating groups, as he and his staff had maintained from the outset. The Chelsea owner sat at a nearby table, next to the Turkish presidential spokesman Ibrahim Kalin.

The wide-ranging talks ran on in private for the entirety of the morning. By lunchtime, both sides emerged with an optimism as high as it was cautious. Turkish foreign minister Mevlüt Çavuşoğlu told a press conference that 'we see with satisfaction that both sides are getting closer at every stage' before adding that he hoped Russia's and Ukraine's most senior politicians would meet at future peace talks.

Some UK politicians were sceptical not just about Abramovich's involvement but more broadly about the sincerity of Russia's wider motivations. Smaller European countries were thought to have warned Ukraine not to take Russia's negotiating position at face value, while the likes of Germany and France were characterised in some quarters as quietly hoping this would be an opportunity to end the war. The two delegations, however, considered that great progress had been achieved in the course of many painstaking, delicate and at times perilous meetings.

The press conferences at the palace gave way to less formal meetings at the nearby Shangri-La Hotel, an opulent five-star complex less than ten minutes away on foot. On the terrace overlooking the Bosphorus Strait, pockets of delegates huddled over papers, talked animatedly or just soaked up the scene. When the day's events were at an end, a compulsorily opaque process cleared ever so slightly: the two sides agreed and then set out in writing the terms by which a potential peace could be explored.

Here was a framework that might just have paved the way for a resolution to a conflict unwanted by so many. What came to be known as the Istanbul Communiqué was never made public, but both sides were clear on a host of the terms and requirements that were written into the document.

In 2024, Samuel Charap, a senior political scientist at the RAND Corporation, an American non-profit global policy think tank, and Sergey Radchenko, a professor at Johns Hopkins University School of Advanced International Studies in Europe, analysed the agreements that had been drawn up in Istanbul. Their findings were presented in US magazine *Foreign Affairs* in an article titled 'The talks that could have ended the war in Ukraine'. Charap and Radchenko asserted that 'in the midst of Moscow's unprecedented aggression, the Russians and Ukrainians almost finalised an agreement that would have ended the war and provided Ukraine with multilateral security guarantees, paving the way to its permanent neutrality and, down the road, its membership of the EU'.

Charap and Radchenko had not only obtained a copy of the treaty but also interviewed a number of participants in the negotiations, who suggested that the Ukrainians had largely drafted the communiqué and the Russians provisionally accepted the idea of using it as the framework for a treaty.

As for the conditions, the proposed treaty would set up Ukraine as a permanently neutral, non-nuclear state. Ukraine would end any plans to join military alliances and would veto foreign military bases or troops on its territory. Guarantors for the treaty were listed as the permanent members of the UN Security Council, including Russia, along with Canada, Germany, Israel, Italy, Poland and Turkey. Terms were written in that would oblige guarantor states to provide assistance to Ukraine to restore its security should the country come under attack.

Despite the proposed neutrality for Ukraine, the framework also set out that the country would still have the opportunity to join the EU in future. The guarantor states would be required to confirm their support for Ukraine's future EU membership. This particular term was widely regarded as extraordinary, due to Russia's historical and recent robust opposition to Ukraine joining the EU. The communiqué had also included another provision, calling for the two sides to seek a peaceful resolution to their dispute over Crimea during the following ten to fifteen years.

These negotiations took place months before Russia announced it had annexed areas in and around four Ukrainian oblasts – Donetsk, Kherson, Luhansk and Zaporizhzhia. The issue of newly drawn borders was not addressed in the treaty but was instead left for Presidents Putin and Zelensky to agree in future summits, should a treaty be accepted.

The day after the Istanbul summit, Russia's chief negotiator, Vladimir Medinsky, told reporters that 'the Ukrainian side for the first time fixed in a written form its readiness to carry out a series of most important conditions for the building of future normal and good neighbourly relations with Russia. They handed to us the principles of a potential future settlement, fixed in writing.'

Those sceptical of Russia's intentions only interpreted these details as more evidence that President Putin and his peace envoys were acting in a manner less than straightforward. Those involved in the talks, however, were determined that the Istanbul agreements were a major step forward and a potential precursor to a genuine peace.

•   •   •

Even into mid-April, both Russia and Ukraine continued to work hard on the details of that craved peace treaty, whatever the circumstances on the various fields of battle. Russia characterised its withdrawal from Kyiv as part of efforts to build trust in the peace talks, but Ukraine felt varied gains in the fighting meant they could claim enough of an upper hand to turn the wider tide of conflict in their favour.

As details of the Istanbul Communiqué began to circulate around the international diplomatic community, several of the commitments were seen as problematic for a number of the partners who would be required to act as guarantors towards Ukraine. Misgivings were thought to have been expressed in Washington among the US administration, while the UK's concerns were already well voiced.

The UK warnings revolved around concerns that Russia might agree to and sign one set of terms, then promptly act in an entirely different manner. Other European leaders were of similar mind and were said to have expressed those concerns to President Zelensky. Boris Jonhson took things several steps further than that, arriving in Kyiv on 9 April in a surprise visit, not only boosting Ukrainian morale but also making a raft of new promises to Zelensky and to the country.

Just as it seemed the US would require much more convincing in order to sign any peace treaty and shoulder responsibility to keep that in place, so too were UK chiefs prepared to express their misgivings with the terms on the table. Johnson was reported to have told Zelensky not only that the UK would not agree to the specifics of the proposed treaty but that Ukraine should not be signing any documents in any case.

Johnson's administration was hardly keeping its staunch support for Ukraine's war effort behind closed doors either. On the day of Johnson's snap trip to Kyiv, the government vowed to send 120 armoured vehicles and new Harpoon anti-ship missile systems to Ukraine, and that after pledging an additional £100 million of military assistance just a week earlier.

The arms, the financing and the moral support were all designed to embolden Zelensky and Ukraine in the campaign against Russia's invasion, and all three appeared to hit the mark. After meeting with Zelensky, Johnson spoke publicly about his visit and his assessment of the conflict's status.

> Ukraine has defied the odds and pushed back Russian forces from the gates of Kyiv, achieving the greatest feat of arms of the twenty-first century. It is because of President Zelensky's resolute leadership and the invincible heroism and courage of the Ukrainian people that Putin's monstrous aims are being thwarted.
>
> I made clear today that the United Kingdom stands unwaveringly with them in this ongoing fight, and we are in it for the long run. We are stepping up our own military and economic support and convening a global alliance to bring this tragedy to an end and ensure Ukraine survives and thrives as a free and sovereign nation.

The UK's allyship was seen as more proactive than that of other NATO partners, leaving Zelensky and his Ukrainian leadership team continuing to weigh the potential peace treaty in an increasingly complicated round. Johnson's overwhelming support for Ukraine received almost universal praise, and the war effort raged on bloodily, although peace efforts never stopped.

By the tail-end of 2023, however, Johnson's visit to Kyiv had in some quarters come to be seen as a pivotal act in hindering the floundering peace process. Davyd Arakhamia, who had led the Ukrainian peace delegation, said in an interview on Ukrainian television that Johnson's Kyiv visit had played a role in the Istanbul Communiqué failing to achieve peace.

'The war could have ended in the spring of 2022 if Ukraine had agreed to neutrality,' Arakhamia told Ukrainian TV station 1+1 on 30 November 2023.

Russia's goal was to put pressure on us so that we would be neutral. This was the main thing for them: they were ready to end the war if we accepted neutrality, like Finland once did. And for us to make a commitment that we will not join NATO. This is the main thing.

Asked directly why the proposals were never agreed, Arakhamia replied, 'Firstly, it was necessary to change the constitution, and secondly, there was no trust in the Russians that they will do this. Further, after we returned from Istanbul, Boris Johnson visited Kyiv and said that we should not sign anything with the Russians and "let's just fight".'

President Putin has since used Arakhamia's comments to blame western Europe and the UK for the collapse of peace talks, claiming that Ukraine is in some kind of thrall to its allies. Johnson himself and the UK government would always argue that the country placed itself on the right side of not just the conflict but also the approach to aiding Ukraine. In February 2025, with the war still grinding on, President Zelensky publicly rubbished all claims that Johnson had held any sway over the chances of a peace accord in spring 2022. 'There were several approaches with ultimatums and I never gave my approval for it,' Zelensky told *The Guardian*. On whether Johnson had any impact on his decision not to enter into any agreements with Russia, Zelensky insisted, 'It doesn't fit with logic; what was he supposed to be talking us out of?'

Another potential blocker to any peace treaty came in the shape of alleged war crimes and atrocities claimed to have been carried out by Russia in the Ukrainian town of Bucha. Zelensky visited the town on 4 April 2022, accusing Russia of perpetrating the alleged crimes in a video call to the UN Security Council the next day. A range of journalists from across Europe were able to visit the town and report on a litany of horrors, but despite the bleakest of events, the Russian and Ukrainian delegations maintained their efforts towards a treaty. Resolving to continue talks with Russia, on 4 April Zelensky told the BBC, 'Ukraine must have peace. We are in Europe in the twenty-first century. We will continue efforts diplomatically and militarily.'

However influential or otherwise Johnson's snap Kyiv visit had been in terms of swaying Zelensky's approach, the Istanbul Communiqué would always have required buy-in from many western partners, not least the US and UK. Though the Istanbul Communiqué represented a remarkable body of work, tireless effort and no little risk on the part of those on both sides of the conflict, and many neutrals too, the cold realities of western powers brokering a diplomatic security guarantee with Russia were perhaps always at the crux of the ultimate challenge of brokering a lasting, effective peace.

CHAPTER TEN

BRIEF ENCOUNTER

Tom Ricketts's meeting with Paul Canoville passed initially with-out incident, with all parties coming away from the 24 March sit-down with only positive feelings. Canoville felt he had had many of his concerns eased, even finding himself impressed with the Ricketts' bid and their suitability as potential Chelsea owners. Tom Ricketts was thought to have enjoyed the meeting, relishing the face-to-face contact with Canoville and the privilege of hearing his story first-hand. Bruce Buck had attended as a courtesy, having been asked to facilitate the meeting by Raine, and while he was there, he had not taken any part in proceedings.

No one present had given the meeting much thought in any wider context, then – that is, until the Ricketts' rivals got wind of it. The other bidders were left with more than a few suspicions about the nature of the arrangement and duly took those concerns to the public domain. Several of the consortiums insisted that the rules of the sale process had been breached by the Ricketts family contact-ing Buck directly.

Claims of an unfair advantage started to fly, with the Ricketts' rivals maintaining that all contact should have been conducted through Raine, rather than the Chelsea executive, as per their reading of the sale process rules. 'If they want the Ricketts family to buy the club from Roman Abramovich, just tell the rest of us now and spare us what is an awful lot of hard work,' an unnamed bid adviser told *The Times*. The fallout from the complaints suddenly blew up, in person, in traditional media and on social media platforms too.

At Raine, Ravitch and Neville were nonplussed, confident that no processes had been flouted; they had asked Buck to set up the Ricketts meeting, after all. Buck was left at once surprised and not surprised, being experienced enough to have expected that the hysteria around the entire sale would naturally lead to flashpoints. Issues that would develop into spats in football would often never even surface in other business settings, and in his nineteen years at the Chelsea helm Buck had often seen such storms brew, rage and then disperse.

He also knew that all the bidding groups had the facility and opportunity, within reason, to arrange meetings with any fan organisations, former players or other bodies associated with Chelsea that they wished. Raine had always made it clear to the bidders that such meetings could be organised, and so from Buck's standpoint, he had only followed up on a request from Raine that appeared to conform entirely to expectation. Buck was fully anticipating the other bidders would organise exactly the same meetings, with the floor open to all comers.

The Ricketts' rivals felt the Chicago Cubs owners had jumped the gun, however, and that any such discussions with Buck, Granovskaia or anyone else from the Chelsea hierarchy were meant to wait until Raine had selected their shortlist of potential Blues owners. Tom Ricketts's meeting with Canoville, attended by Buck, had taken place on Thursday 24 March, the day before the four-strong short-list of bidders was confirmed.

As the brickbats were lobbed back and forth, Canoville was left shocked and dismayed, especially at accusations that he had sought out the meeting and, moreover, that he had somehow tried to insert himself into the sale process. The club he had graced with distinction under no little duress, that he still supported and worked closely with, had asked for his help, and he had agreed, as he always would. Social media's lack of appreciation for nuance and distinction left Canoville exposed to criticism, enmity and in some cases outright abuse.

Canoville's original tweet, and its staunch nature, had engendered a response from the Ricketts that led their proactive bid team to try to step onto the front foot, take ownership of the issues and explain their situation and wider context in person. Once the furore broke, Canoville was able to reflect immediately on his tweet and wish he had perhaps kept his counsel, only grasping in hindsight the full reach of an influence that his natural humility had not allowed him to appreciate.

Members of the Ricketts bid team were thought to have already felt for some time that several of their rivals were trying to brief the media negatively against the family's candidacy, and they considered that those suspicions were effectively confirmed by the uproar over their meeting with Canoville. The entire Chelsea sale process had of course been coloured from the outset by Nick Candy publicly criticising Jonathan Goldstein's status on the Boehly–Clearlake bid because the prominent London businessman just so happened to be a Tottenham fan.

From that point on, many of those in the varying bid teams felt as though the gloves had come off, with the net result that consortiums were not just accentuating the positives of their own submissions but also highlighting perceived weaknesses among their rivals. The atmosphere became poisonous as a nucleus of those around Canoville, not least colleagues in his foundation, felt compelled to come out fighting in defence of his actions.

A number of people involved in the bid felt the complaints from rivals betrayed the fact that they were concerned about the strength of the Ricketts' candidacy. The Ricketts' rivals, of course, considered that the Chicago Cubs owners had stolen an unfair march by organising such meetings prematurely.

• • •

The public storm raging around the Ricketts showed no signs of abating whatsoever, to the extent that what had started as a Twitter hashtag of 'Ricketts Out' slowly morphed into a physical protest against the prospective Chelsea owners. The fortnight's international break, which had given Chelsea's men's team a total break from club duties, had come at a welcome time from the point of view of the coaching staff and playing squad, so shattered mentally had they become by the increasingly fraught circus that was following the sale, let alone all the restrictions imposed by the sanctions. As public anger around perceived shortcuts from the Ricketts were heaped upon supporter frustrations regarding Joe Ricketts' historical racist emails, Chelsea's home Premier League clash with Brentford on 2 April was targeted as the ideal staging post for a demonstration against the Chicago-based consortium.

Protests against the proposed European Super League had raged at Stamford Bridge on 20 April 2021, when fan power helped convince Abramovich to abandon support for the ever-controversial project of a pan-continental league competition. Scores of angry supporters had besieged all the Premier League clubs that were attached to the prospective Super League launch at the time, but the Chelsea demonstration proved the most attended and the most boisterous, ahead of the Blues' goalless Premier League draw with Brighton.

Technical director Petr Čech had even taken the remarkable step of leaving the stadium and returning to the street to beseech the supporters to calm their protests, amid club concerns that the demonstration could slip out of hand, especially considering England was still in the grip of the tail-end of Covid-19 lockdowns that had put much of the public in a generally mutinous mood. As that Super League protest raged, with supporters marching to Stamford Bridge brandishing banners and letting off blue smoke canisters, the Chelsea executives were hurriedly reassessing their entire connection to the Super League project.

Chelsea's default approach had been to retain cautious involvement in an enterprise that had offered automatic qualification to founder members. As opposition to the project intensified, however, Rola Brentlin was among a nucleus of senior Chelsea staff who told Abramovich that the club should consider cutting ties with the Super League altogether. A long-time adviser to Abramovich, Brentlin acted as spokesperson for the Chelsea owner and had spearheaded the club's Say No To Antisemitism campaign. Brentlin had also helped coordinate Chelsea's community-focused initiatives during the UK lockdowns, including opening up Stamford Bridge as a Covid-19 vaccination centre and allowing NHS staff to stay in the hotel at the Chelsea ground for free.

Amid fierce opposition from supporters, allied to public criticism from Prince William, who warned that such an enterprise could irreversibly damage the English game, Brentlin pressed home her point with Abramovich that the mooted competition would never proceed under the circumstances and that Chelsea should be the first to step back. By the time the match with Brighton kicked off that 20 April 2021 night, Chelsea had been the first team to withdraw support for the competition, with Brentlin informing the media that the Blues were pulling out. By the end of the night's Premier League fixtures, none of the English clubs who had been invited were involved either.

For the Chelsea supporters, that frenzied Super League demonstration would for ever represent the gold standard of fan power in action. And it was with the reverberations of that seismic stand-off still in mind that fans had even considered the notion of another protest when it came to the Ricketts and early April 2022. The days leading up to Chelsea's home clash with Brentford were laced with the natural excitement that follows the end of the international break, with supporters delighted that the league's hiatus would be over. That build-up was also punctuated, however, by conspicuous social media planning aimed at generating as large a pre-match protest as possible against the Ricketts family's prospective club ownership.

By the time the protest swung into action, though, it was immediately clear that this would be no repeat of the widespread, visceral demonstration that had helped topple the Super League almost twelve months earlier. Instead, perhaps fifty to a hundred people gathered outside Stamford Bridge, chanting and waving signs demanding that Chelsea not be sold to the Ricketts. As it became apparent that no massive numbers of protesters were on their way, the demonstration quickly petered out. Several observers noted that a clutch of fans who had left the Butcher's Hook pub opposite

Stamford Bridge to join the demonstration were back inside the drinking establishment less than an hour later.

While several of those taking part agreed to conduct media interviews with various TV stations in attendance, the entire protest dispersed quickly, with ultimately precious little in the way of lasting impact having been achieved. Several members of the Ricketts bid team attended the Chelsea–Brentford match that day and had been in and around the stadium at the time of the protest. If they had arrived in the Chelsea area that day fearful for what would unfold, by the end of the protest they were thought to be both relieved and encouraged. Relieved at the modest numbers in attendance and encouraged by the possibility that Blues fans might be starting to understand the Ricketts' distinction between family patriarch Joe's historical views and the diametrically opposed ideas of Tom, Laura and Todd, the heads of the Chelsea bid.

The damp squib of the protest was difficult to square away with the social media hype. Members of the Ricketts bid team had no proof but were thought to wonder if elements of the protest had been at least encouraged by factions either supporting or attached to rival bidders. An overriding sense started to build within some bid team members that they were facing a targeted campaign, but the family had neither the time nor the inclination to investigate, given the pace and complexity of the bidding process.

As the fever pitch of the sale left many involved desperately fighting to avoid paranoia, each time the Ricketts family members let their minds wander to such nefarious thoughts, they pulled them back, preferring instead to focus on the detail and the strength of their bid for the club. Another accounting for the discrepancy between the social media vitriol and the tameness of the in-person protest was simply that it was easy to join an online bandwagon and far more laborious to get out on the street and march for or against a specific cause.

If the real-world demonstration had failed to land, a snap poll conducted by the Chelsea Supporters' Trust certainly represented a blow to the Ricketts. As the Blues were gearing up to face Brentford and that protest was petering out, a CST statement laid bare their members' mistrust of the Chicago Cubs owners. The body claimed that 72 per cent of their members canvassed did not believe the Ricketts could run an inclusive and successful Chelsea, while 77 per cent said they did not support the family's candidacy.

Having already held several meetings with the CST that were designed to explain in full the family's position and its bid, the Ricketts were left frustrated but relatively unsurprised by either the poll or its results. They issued a statement pointing out that more meetings were already scheduled with the CST to continue working towards composing the kind of bid that the club's supporters could throw their weight behind.

After all that, Chelsea took on Brentford, mentally refreshed after the international break but seeking to resume in the same rhythm that had punctuated their fine run of results before the domestic hiatus. The Blues had won six games in a row in all competitions in an intense run before the international break and hoped to pick up right where they left off against their west London near neighbours. The hosts missed several chances in a galling, goalless first half, only for Toni Rüdiger to lash in a fine thirty-yard strike shortly after the interval to hand the Blues the lead. The Germany defender had tried and failed with a string of similar pot-shots across the course of the campaign, but this time he connected sweetly, and the resulting goal brought down the house, as much for the effort as for the reward for one of the side's most popular figures.

No sooner had Rüdiger fired Chelsea into that lead, though, than Brentford wrestled total control of the contest away from their hosts. In an alarming capitulation that appeared to highlight a level of weariness in the Chelsea ranks, Brentford delivered four unanswered goals, giving them their first victory over the Blues since 1939. Vitaly Janelt netted twice, either side of a first goal for the club from Christian Eriksen, a finish that once and for all cemented his comeback to football after he had suffered a cardiac arrest on Denmark duty at Euro 2020.

Three minutes from time, Yoane Wissa's effort wrapped up Brentford's 4–1 win, a thumping and then some that left Blues boss Tuchel concerned about the mental state of his players, especially in the continued battles against sanctions and the club's sale saga. 'Nobody saw it coming, and for sure not after we were one-zero ahead, it was very untypical for us,' Tuchel later told reporters. 'But we stopped defending, we were not aware enough of the danger, we were sloppy in defending and we got punished.'

After such a compelling and morale-boosting run before the international break, here was a particularly ill-timed drop-off by the Blues: Real Madrid were due at Stamford Bridge just four days later for the first leg of the Champions League quarter-final. Suddenly Chelsea were about to put the defence of their European title on the line against the then thirteen-time tournament winners, off the back of arguably their worst performance of the campaign. Having battled so hard to stave off the impact of the sanctions and build a powerful siege mentality across three relentless weeks, in a flash all that progress was once again at risk, and with the toughest possible challenge imminently in store.

●　　●　　●

The very next day, Tom and Laura Ricketts attended the Chelsea women's match against Reading at Kingsmeadow, with the Blues looking to extend their four-game winning run in the WSL. The Ricketts bid team leaders were treated to a serious display of power by the hosts, who swept Reading aside 5–0 to end the weekend once again top of the table. Sam Kerr and Beth England both netted twice after Jessie Fleming had opened the scoring, as Emma Hayes's side followed up the 9–0 thrashing of Leicester with another entirely dominant performance. Kerr's brace took her tally of WSL goals and assists to fifty since January 2020, topping the league's stats chart, with teammates England and Fran Kirby alongside her for company in the top five.

The Ricketts siblings kept a low profile at the match, aiming to soak up the full atmosphere of the club's overwhelmingly success-ful women's set-up. While Tom Ricketts had been a long-standing Chelsea fan owing to his time working in London in his twenties, Laura's fascination with football was only just beginning. At that Chelsea match she was thought to have caught the bug, especially for the women's game, and also enjoyed some impactful meetings with club fan groups. One lengthy conversation with Tracy Brown, co-founder of the club's official LGBTQ+ supporter group Chelsea Pride, was said to have left a lasting impression on Laura Ricketts, the two striking up a connection that would run well beyond the club's sale process.

The Ricketts' latest trip to London had not just been about enjoy-ing matchday experiences, however, and on that same day, Sunday 3 April, the bid team released an eight-point pledge to Chelsea supporters representing the main commitments they would vow to uphold should their candidacy for the club prove successful. Among the pledges, the most eye-catching was the vow never to participate in a European Super League, the Ricketts determined to lay out in public exactly how they had listened and then acted upon their meetings with supporters. Also pledging to do everything possible to rebuild the stadium so Chelsea could remain at Stamford Bridge rather than find a new site, the Ricketts further vowed to protect the club's colours and crest and to create an advisory committee of diverse representation, including fan groups.

'Over the past fortnight, the Ricketts family has met with several Chelsea supporter groups and carefully listened to all their feedback,' read the family's statement.

As we enter the next phase of the process, we are sharing a list of specific commitments that give fans a pivotal role in protecting Chelsea's heritage and building for future success. We will continue to discuss our ambitions for the club with fans and the wider football community in the coming days.

The first of the bidders to offer such a set of iron-clad promises that would have to be upheld given their public expression, the Ricketts were understood to have felt they were turning the tide and shifting the mood, one careful move at a time. After every face-to-face meeting with Chelsea supporters or fan groups, the Ricketts bid team were thought to feel they were winning people over – not necessarily to consider them a first choice but certainly as acceptable potential owners, on the same footing as the other bidders.

• • •

As the four bidders were all jetting in and out of London for meetings with the Chelsea executives and Raine, and also to try to win round supporter associations, Tuchel's side were gearing up to host the decorated, dangerous and perhaps resurgent Real Madrid at Stamford Bridge. The Blues' west London stadium would play host to talks with various members of the four bid teams during weekdays, then continue to stage the biggest matches by weeknight or weekend.

On 5 April, the day before Chelsea would host Real, the team that had won the European Cup more than any other in history, Tuchel delivered an impassioned rallying cry to both players and supporters. Chelsea had toppled Madrid in the semi-finals of the previous season's Champions League, before edging out Manchester City in the final in Lisbon to claim their second European crown. The semi-finals against Madrid from the previous season had been played without the presence of supporters, due to the Covid-19 pandemic lockdowns, but this time, in a keenly anticipated two-legged rematch, fans would very much be a part of the narrative of two blockbuster nights.

After Chelsea's shock 4–1 home reverse to Brentford, where the Blues' faithful were stunned into silence, amid an attendance limited by the sanctions-imposed restriction on selling new tickets, the ever-savvy Tuchel made a rare intervention to call on the fans to raise their own game in exactly the same way he was about to demand from his players. 'We need to be better on the pitch, but we also need the crowd to be better,' said Tuchel.

Everyone has to be on the front foot for a big opponent on the big occasions. We normally have these atmospheres in evening games and big matches. In the Champions League matches they gave us a huge push in energy and atmosphere. It is crucial in these games. It's much harder to play against the spectators as

well. We felt it in Malmö and St Petersburg earlier in the competition, we will face it again in Madrid next week, and everyone
needs to arrive tomorrow to support us.

Gauntlet duly laid down to fans in Tuchel's inimitable style, then.
The Chelsea boss was perhaps not thinking of Todd Boehly when
picturing the archetypal Blues supporter he wanted to incite towards
new levels of passion in the stands. Boehly caught most people by
surprise, however, by numbering among the Chelsea faithful for
that compelling Madrid clash the next day, Wednesday 6 April, for
the hotly anticipated Champions League quarter-final first leg.

The atmosphere around Stamford Bridge was already crackling
with the kind of excitement that a crucial night match in European
competition can provide, supporters milling around outside stadium entrances, filing in and out of pubs and bars or simply waiting on street corners for friends and family. As a group of police
horses clopped by, Boehly walked breezily through the Stamford
Bridge gates, dressed casually in jeans, trainers, shirt, jacket, scarf
and baseball cap. Precious few people noticed his low-key arrival,
but the TV cameras were eagle-eyed enough to pick him out in the
crowd.

Chuckling audibly to himself as he realised the cameras were loi-
tering with intent for him, Boehly made no statement but was laughing lightly and smiling as the TV outlets shot footage that would be
quickly beamed around the world, only serving to push the already
huge intrigue in the Chelsea sale even further. Boehly was unfazed
but still surprised by the attention, especially as people were by now
starting to recognise him in and around the stadium area. While
he had long been a part of the LA Dodgers ownership group, the
American sports culture proved a very different experience for the

prospective Chelsea owner: where he could move freely around Dodger Stadium and hardly draw any attention to himself, immediately he realised the climate in and around Chelsea would be something else entirely.

A big night for Chelsea in the midst of a momentous three months for the club, but Boehly's presence could not inspire the Blues to another European match to remember under the Stamford Bridge floodlights. Instead it was the golden oldies of Madrid who took control of the two-leg affair, even by the tie's halfway stage. At the ripe old football age of thirty-six, Croatia maestro Luka Modrić had no right to be conducting midfield proceedings, let alone have the legs to last the course, while dead-eye striker Karim Benzema looked a full decade shy of his thirty-four years as he stalked the final third of the Stamford Bridge pitch with menace and intent.

Vinicius Junior outfoxed Chelsea time and again on Madrid's left flank, with Benzema dropping into the inside-left channel to combine with the Brazil tyro. It was from one such link-up that Madrid plundered the lead. As Vinicius whipped in a cross from the left flank, France hitman Benzema shaped to dart deep into the box, only to drop off his defender instead, before thumping a header into the back of the Chelsea net.

Just three minutes later, Benzema steered another header home to send Madrid into a 2–0 lead inside the opening half-hour. This time, Modrić picked up possession on the inside right, checked to hold the defence and then lofted the ball into the penalty area, allowing Benzema to guide a deft header over Edouard Mendy and home for his and his side's second goal of the night.

The one-two punch combination had Chelsea against the ropes, but just before half time the Blues were able to clear the stars in their eyes and lay at least a glove on the dominant visitors. Jorginho received possession in centre-field in the vicinity of the box, rolled his studs over the ball and then dinked a teasing cross into the area, which dropped invitingly for Kai Havertz. The Germany forward timed his run perfectly and nodded past Thibaut Courtois, the ex-Chelsea goalkeeper frustrated not to have tipped the ball around his post.

The game was finely poised at the break, with Chelsea relieved to be back in the bout and Madrid determined not to cede control after the interval. Neither side had settled by the time the outcome of the first leg was decided, however, as Blues keeper Mendy desperately undersold a pass to Toni Rüdiger, on which Benzema immediately pounced. Mendy had been forced to race out of his area to sweep up from an overhit Madrid pass but promptly found himself stuck in no man's land. His underhit pass left Rüdiger with no chance to remedy the situation, and Benzema not only latched onto the ball; he also stepped forward and slotted home into the empty net.

As Mendy closed his eyes and trilled his lips, Chelsea's French goalkeeper knew full well that his mistake might ultimately prove the end of his side's Champions League defence. This was the toughest of blows for an eminently likeable character who had grown to be relied upon by the Blues in almost all circumstances. For a player who had once found himself without a club and signing on for unemployment benefit in France, his career had come full circle with winning the Champions League the season prior. Here, though, was an error that compounded the odd trouble he had with the ball at his feet, and left the Blues floundering just when they needed their very best.

After ten wins in fourteen matches in all competitions, suddenly Chelsea had leaked seven goals in consecutive defeats, the Madrid loss coming straight after that 4–1 reverse to Brentford. In the post-match media debriefs, Tuchel pulled no punches on Chelsea's chances of overturning their 3–1 deficit in the second leg at Madrid's imposing Bernabéu Stadium a week later. 'We have to find our level back, I don't know where it went since the international break,' lamented a frustrated Tuchel.

Our first half here is a repetition of the second half against Brentford, in a quarter-final of the Champions League against Real Madrid; we were so far off our level in absolutely everything the game demands. After the international break we don't look the same and I don't really have an explanation; we didn't change anything, it's alarming. If we don't get our heads and legs straight then we will not beat Southampton on Saturday and this tie is not alive either. If things change, maybe, but we need three goals and how often does this happen? We need to find our competitive spirit and then we can talk. If we keep on playing like this, then we don't need to talk about the Bernabéu, we will get hammered in the Bernabéu.

•   •   •

The bidders' charm offensive continued in earnest the next day, as Laura Ricketts released a lengthy statement detailing her personal hopes for her family's tilt at buying the Blues. A rarity as an openly gay sports team owner in the US, Ricketts revealed a life of striving for equality, in the latest attempt to separate the Chicago Cubs owners' candidacy from their father Joe's Islamophobic emails.

'I can assure all Chelsea fans that it has been my life's work to fight against discrimination and bigotry of any kind,' said Laura Ricketts.

Coming out as an LGBTQ+ woman has influenced my perspective and sensitivity about diversity and inclusion. I can't know what it's like to walk in another person's shoes, but I can begin to understand and have an awareness of their different experience. And that's a gift. In the position that I'm in, I feel a sense of responsibility to be an advocate. To me, being an advocate means speaking up, and also listening.

While the Cubs owners were heading home to the US after their latest trip to Chelsea to meet the team running the sale process as well as various fan groups, the heads of the rival consortiums were busy taking up their own opportunities to meet Paul Canoville. Chelsea's first black player was still reeling from the criticism that was flung his way after the meeting with Tom Ricketts, which had led to accusations of favouritism in the sale process.

After all the bad blood, Canoville had jumped at the chance to level the playing field, in the perceptions of some, when attending meetings with both the Boehly–Clearlake and the Broughton consortiums on 8 April. Again organised through the official channels, this time Buck did not attend either meeting, given the controversy of his presence when Canoville met Tom Ricketts. The fact that Buck took no part in that Canoville–Ricketts meeting, merely observing, had long since fallen on deaf ears, and the Chelsea chairman thought the only prudent course was to step away.

First up for Canoville was Michael Broughton, Martin's son, a key part of the bid and a successful specialist in digital sports investments. Michael Broughton took Canoville through their bid's key plans for a club board pulled together from diverse backgrounds, in order to boost inclusivity at a strategic level. He also explained growth projections from plans to harness online supporter engagement that they believed could see the club's value soar, thereby future-proofing the Blues' ability to stay at the elite game's sharp end. Canoville was impressed with Broughton's approach and personality but was left hoping the diversity angles were not just rooted in the celebrity power of several high-profile stars from other sports who were attached to the bid.

Next, Canoville met the Boehly–Clearlake team, at the central London offices of Cain International, the company founded by Boehly and bid partner Jonathan Goldstein, who hosted the meeting himself. Chelsea fans Daniel Finkelstein and Barbara Charone had already been coopted to the bid and were on hand for the meeting too. Tory peer Lord Finkelstein and music PR guru Charone were already well acquainted with Canoville, which put his mind at ease, and the conversation quickly started flowing. Boehly had managed to delay a flight back to the US and so was able to join the meeting some ten minutes in.

Canoville was surprised by Boehly's informal, calm and natural approach, and also that he focused on how to foster stronger links with the club's former players, taking a leaf out of the Dodgers' book. Several people at that meeting remarked that Boehly talked to Canoville simply as a former Chelsea player, and not specifically as a black former Chelsea player. The distinction carried weight with Canoville, as did the fact that Boehly appeared already well-versed in his background and story.

Boehly and his bid team members exuded an infectious excitement that left Canoville with a positive outlook on the meeting, and their only request was that no one talk in any detail about the meeting itself. Canoville was able to say the meeting had taken place but otherwise respected the privacy of the Boehly bid. Though he felt he could have helped the process and handed fans more information by explaining his meetings further, he understood why those details had to remain under wraps. Canoville would later be pleasantly surprised and impressed by the fact that no one in the Boehly bid team briefed any of the details of the meeting either. Not only had he found Boehly and his partners open and genuine; he had also found them true to their word.

Back at Chelsea, Tuchel spent the Friday press conference previewing the next day's Premier League trip to Southampton, admitting he had held a meeting and read the modern-day, gentle equivalent of the riot act to his players after the heavy defeats by Brentford and Real Madrid. 'It was not a discussion type of meeting, it was more I gave my point of view and that's sometimes necessary,' said Tuchel.

> We always take the players' view into account, but over the last two games we felt it was maybe necessary to give our point of view. It was behind closed doors, where everybody can take criticism. We don't point fingers, we don't look for people who are guilty, we are in this together.

By the time Chelsea kicked off at Southampton the next day, Saturday 9 April, Tuchel's tough love had clearly had the desired effect. The Blues ripped through the stunned hosts, with Timo Werner and Mason Mount both claiming a brace, to add to goals from Marcos Alonso and Kai Havertz. The 6–0 thumping even had Tuchel suggesting he had spoken too soon when all but writing off the return-leg Champions League clash at Madrid that coming Tuesday night. In a season typified by dogged resilience, Chelsea had once again found a way to hit back, and beyond, after their two dispiriting defeats.

• • •

Chelsea arrived in Madrid with Tuchel's words ringing in their ears that they would need 'a fantastic script' to overturn their 3–1 first-leg deficit and reach the Champions League semi-finals. The relentless sale narrative continued to prove every inch as extraordinary as the turnaround Chelsea were seeking in Madrid, meanwhile, as the Ricketts added Karan Bilimoria, the founder of Cobra beer, to their bid for the Blues. Lord Bilimoria had pledged to act as a club ambassador should the Ricketts win the race for Chelsea, but before any of that he could help liaise with and lobby the government.

As the hours towards kick-off at the Bernabéu ticked down on 12 April, Stephen Pagliuca finally broke his silence on his bid for the Blues. Having opted to go about his business under the radar until this point, Pagliuca revealed he had been in attendance at the weekend's 6–0 win at Southampton. In confirming a list of pledges that met all the same standards as the other bidders had agreed, Pagliuca also explained that he preferred to work away in the background rather than signpost his every move. The deadline for final, fully updated bids was fast approaching, on 15 April, which just so happened to be Good Friday. The bidders were running out of time to court public opinion, and Pagliuca had certainly left it late to state his case to the Chelsea supporters.

The running sale commentary nearly clouded the main event, until everyone in Madrid arrived at the almost fully rebuilt Bernabéu to marvel at a fine reconstruction job. The Real fans unfurled a Tifo banner that read 'Don't mess with the kings' amid an intimidating and boisterous build-up to kick-off, only for Chelsea to shake off all their surroundings and haul themselves right back into the contest.

Mateo Kovačić, Ruben Loftus-Cheek and Timo Werner all combined neatly to send Mount racing in on goal, and the England forward lashed into the net to hand Chelsea a 1–0 lead on the night. The Blues took that slender advantage into the break but were still trailing 3–2 on aggregate and in need of further inspiration. Shortly after the interval, though, Rüdiger delivered that spark, heading home from a corner to level the aggregate at 3–3.

Marcos Alonso thought he had snatched the overall lead for Chelsea when cutting inside and lashing into the net from N'Golo Kanté's fine pass, only for the goal to be chalked off for a handball in the build-up. Benzema then thumped a header against the bar, in a warning to the Blues that the hosts could always catch them on the break. With a quarter-hour to play, however, Kovačić sent Werner racing through on the inside left and the Germany forward cut inside twice before squeezing a finish just beyond Courtois and into the net.

Leading 3–0 on the night, Chelsea had wrestled a 4–3 aggregate lead, in the kind of 'fantastic script' that Tuchel had been praying for in the build-up. Madrid refused to be beaten, though, especially Luka Modrić, who delivered a sumptuous lofted ball into the box that begged to be swept home – and Rodrygo duly delivered. Madrid's solitary goal put the aggregate at 4–4, and so extra time was forced. As the game broke up amid tired bodies and taxed minds, Real set Vinicius Junior free down the left flank, and he delivered the perfect cross for Benzema to power home another header, which this time would kill off both Chelsea's resistance and the tie.

Just as Benzema had done for one of his goals in the first leg, so too here had the France striker shaped to push deep into the box only to drop off and wrong-foot the Chelsea defence before thumping in the header. Chelsea pressed and pressed as the minutes ticked away but to no avail. The Blues won 3–2 on the night but were still eliminated on the 5–4 aggregate.

A vainglorious Champions League exit despite beating the mighty Madrid in their own backyard somehow came to encapsulate the challenges of one of the most turbulent seasons in Chelsea's history. Proud amid defeat, Chelsea's coaches and players were still left with the nagging what-if feeling when they ran the rule over several mistakes that had led to Madrid goals in both legs. As it was, Tuchel and company had to shake off the fatigue and frustration without delay, as just five days later Crystal Palace would lie in wait at Wembley for the FA Cup semi-final.

•   •   •

Eugene Tenenbaum was in Israel for Passover, observing the Jewish festival with friends and relatives, his mind regularly wandering to the latest events in the Chelsea sale, when news broke that would change his and his family's life for ever. The Pagliuca consortium had just confirmed that their bid would be fully financed by equity and no debt, which meant that all four final Chelsea bidders were primed to submit potent, compelling and well-funded propositions for the Stamford Bridge club. That information, and all other thoughts of the sale, quickly disappeared from Tenenbaum's mind, however: the life-changing news was that the UK government had imposed sanctions against him. The government's reasoning was brief: Tenenbaum had been sanctioned as a person 'associated with Roman Abramovich', so in effect the move was off the back of the sanctions imposed against the Chelsea owner.

Tenenbaum and fellow Abramovich associate David Davidovich

were both sanctioned at the same time – but what set Tenenbaum apart from others who had been sanctioned was his UK citizenship, having lived in England for some thirty years. Only a small handful of UK citizens were sanctioned due to Russia's invasion of Ukraine, and the global impact of the penalty ran far wider and harsher than for those from overseas.

'We are tightening the ratchet on Putin's war machine and targeting the circle of people closest to the Kremlin,' said Foreign Secretary Liz Truss. 'We will keep going with sanctions until Putin fails in Ukraine. Nothing and no one is off the table.'

Just as Abramovich has always vehemently denied the links to Putin alleged by the UK government, so too has Tenenbaum entirely rejected the association. The UK government also claimed Abramovich had transferred the company Ervington Investments Limited to Tenenbaum and the firm Norma Investments to Davidovich on 24 February.

Tenenbaum rejected the allegation against him relating to Ervington, insisting in a statement at the time:

I am not the owner of these companies nor the beneficiary of the assets these companies possess, nor have I ever been. I do not hold assets for Mr Abramovich or his family and Mr Abramovich or his family have not transferred any assets to me. Contrary to what has been reported, I have no ownership or control over these assets, and I was not an active director when the sanctions against me were introduced.

Notwithstanding this statement, the UK government still heralded sanctions that would freeze up to £10 billion in assets that they were linking to Abramovich, and in their eyes Putin, and trumpeting again their claimed crackdown on the economic machine surrounding Russia's invasion of Ukraine.

The sanctions against Tenenbaum and Davidovich came hot on the heels of the Royal Courts of Jersey freezing more than $7 billion worth of assets they claimed were linked to Abramovich, on 13 April. The 'formal freezing order' was issued on 'assets which are suspected to be connected to Mr Abramovich and which are either located in Jersey or owned by Jersey incorporated entities'. Offices that the Jersey authorities believed were linked to Abramovich were also raided under the terms of search warrants on 12 April, just hours before Chelsea would play out that Champions League classic encounter at Real Madrid. Jersey officials would be forced to apologise and pay damages for the searches, which a Jersey court ruled were illegal, in November 2022.

Tenenbaum meanwhile found his life dramatically changed, as he had to confront a situation neither he nor anyone connected to Abramovich had seen coming. He had never thought for a second that he could fall into the category of people at risk of sanctions, so the announcement took him by complete surprise. His wife and children were on holiday in Florida, so as he battled to come to terms with the shock and the scale of the punitive measures, he had to do so without his immediate family for in-person support.

Born in Kyiv but raised in Canada from a young age, Tenenbaum moved from Toronto to London in 1994 to work for US investment bank Salomon Brothers. Abramovich's company Sibneft was a Salomon Brothers client, and it was while Tenenbaum was working on the account that the two met for the first time. Their relationship grew quickly, to the point where Tenenbaum joined Sibneft in 1998 before going to work for further companies owned by Abramovich.

Already on board by the time Abramovich bought Chelsea, Tenenbaum spent roughly the first decade of the Blues' new era as both adviser to and translator for Abramovich. If the translating duties waned over the years, Tenenbaum remained a constant in Abramovich's wider Chelsea set-up, advising the owner on many things Stamford Bridge-related but also working on a number of other assets and projects for the Russian-Israeli billionaire.

As brief as the UK government's public reasons for sanctioning Tenenbaum were, he received next to no further information behind the scenes. Ultimately, he was sanctioned in order that he might influence Abramovich to influence Putin to stop the war, in what lawyers told him would be technically referred to as the process of signalling. Given Abramovich's position that he had no ability to influence the Russian government, Tenenbaum found himself flummoxed as to quite how he could exert any kind of pressure that in turn might reverse his own situation.

While sanctions are not designed as outright punishment, more as a political instrument, Tenenbaum was left floored by the repercussions on his life. For British citizens, the UK regulations apply worldwide: Tenenbaum had to leave the UK, his assets were frozen across the globe and he was not able to get a job or even open a bank account wherever he might go. Unable to receive even gifts from others, Tenenbaum felt trapped, and while living with friends in Israel, he was left with precious few options.

The UK government position was staunch in that anyone they deemed to be associated with Putin or Russia would be liable for sanctions, and that the concern to be put above all others was finding a way to stop the war in Ukraine. Tenenbaum had lived in England for thirty years, he had married an English woman and all four of his children were born and raised in England. Perhaps it was the emotional impact of the sanctions at the time, but he found himself feeling British, but not British enough.

Tenenbaum remained reluctant to relate his personal experiences in detail, acutely aware that the trials and tribulations of a wealthy businessman would not, and perhaps should not, engender a sympathy that he absolutely did not seek. At the same time, however, his experience was one of substantive loss and great change – personal, emotional and situational.

A man finding himself without recourse or agency, left simply to hope for and wait until a sufficiently substantive political change that would lead sanctions to be lifted – which ultimately could only mean the end of the Ukraine war, and even then a resolution palatable to the UK. Far more concerned for the fallout as regards his family than for himself, Tenenbaum found himself repeatedly drawn to Thomas Hobbes's famed refrain from *Leviathan*: 'No arts; no letters; no society; and which is worst of all, continual fear and danger of violent death; and the life of man, solitary, poor, nasty, brutish and short.'

CHAPTER ELEVEN

FOUR BECOME THREE

Easter weekend 2022 started with the promise of a renewal for Chelsea befitting of the Christian festival, given the Raine chiefs were all geared up to receive the four shortlisted bidders' full and final offers for the Stamford Bridge club by close of business on Good Friday, 15 April. Searing sunshine swept across the Blues' pristine Cobham training pitches as Tuchel's men prepared in earnest for their Easter Sunday FA Cup semi-final clash with capital rivals Crystal Palace. As the players completed their morning training session preparations, boss Tuchel wheeled round into the bespoke press conference room, for once confident he could face the media and talk football and only football.

With Chelsea's sale moving impressively swiftly towards a resolution that would safeguard the club's future, Tuchel's days of acting as a de facto club spokesman on everything from the war in Ukraine to the UK government's sanctions suite appeared to be approaching an end. Even the assembled media, story-getters and inquisitors by nature, exuded a collective relief that for the first time in some time, perhaps Chelsea would stage a press conference where football would take top billing.

Tuchel reeled off a fitness update that would prove noteworthy, with Belgium hitman Romelu Lukaku available for selection after injury, although neither Ben Chilwell nor Callum Hudson-Odoi would be fit in time to feature at Wembley that Sunday. Chelsea would be facing one old boy in the shape of Marc Guéhi, the Cobham academy graduate defender who had been sold to Palace the previous summer. The Blues would not have to go up against one of their squad mates, however, with Conor Gallagher blocked from facing his parent club as per the terms of his loan to the Eagles.

Tuchel admitted he felt for Gallagher, who had performed impressively in his season-long loan at Palace that term. The Blues' German boss had even apologised to Gallagher some weeks earlier, when bumping into the midfielder in a restaurant. A loanee being barred from facing their parent club was par for the course in elite football, but that did not stop Gallagher raging against the machine, or Tuchel accepting his developing midfielder's frustrations. Yet no amount of sentiment would lead Chelsea to relent and allow one of their own players the potential to knock them out of the cup.

For the first time in months, Chelsea had negotiated a full press conference where the cut and thrust, the questions and answers, represented something approaching routine. The journalists' attentions were quickly returned to the specifics and mechanics of the sale after the press conference in any case, and the quest to discover if, when and how the four remaining bidders would submit their final offers for Chelsea that very day. The overwhelming expectation was that all four consortiums were raring to go and fully ready to submit their final bids. The calm of all four bidders on 14 April had contributed greatly to that routine, almost run-of-the-mill air to that morning's Chelsea press conference, with the media for once not anticipating any major controversies.

As the various journalists and camera operators departed the state-of-the-art Cobham training ground, with thoughts on confirming the final four submitted bids as quickly as possible in order to free up time for Easter weekend family activities, precious few people involved with the Chelsea sale in any capacity had any idea of the size, scale and speed of the shock that was about to be delivered.

At noon UK time, the Ricketts family issued a statement that would rock the sale process to its core: they were pulling out of the fight for the club completely. The Chicago Cubs owners and their partners would not be submitting a bid for Chelsea. After weeks of twenty-hour days, millions of pounds of fees paid to a bid team including investment specialists, lawyers, accountants and publicists... nothing. No final bid, no battle to the last to try to take custody of Chelsea, and no more turning of the tide of that anti-Ricketts sentiment, which had appeared to be on the wane.

'The Ricketts–Griffin–Gilbert group has decided, after careful consideration, not to submit a final bid for Chelsea FC,' the Ricketts family revealed, in a statement released to the Press Association. 'In the process of finalising the proposal, it became increasingly clear that certain issues could not be addressed given the unusual dynamics around the sales process. We have great admiration for Chelsea and its fans and we wish the new owners well.'

Suddenly a quiet day in the life of Chelsea FC became anything but, with the confusion sown from the withdrawal of what had appeared a rock-solid bid from a leading contender giving everyone involved pause on all the other remaining consortiums. If four could become three without any requirement for an elimination, and on the day that the final bids were meant to be lodged, then all bets for the remainder of the process seemed once again off. Just when even the unprecedented Chelsea sale process itself was preparing to fall into a reassuring rhythm, here was yet another jolt to kick the entire undertaking out of kilter.

Bid chiefs insisted in off-record briefings that the withdrawal had nothing to do with the almost endless fallout from patriarch Joe Ricketts's historical anti-Muslim emails. Immediate partisan commentary refused to accept this assertion, and questions were rapidly and relentlessly launched concerning the 'unusual dynamics around the sale process' that had been cited as the reason behind the Ricketts' withdrawal. Several theorists posited the notion that there had been friction between consortium partners Ken Griffin and Dan Gilbert, centring on the equity split in the proposed shareholding set-up. The shareholding divisions had long since been settled by the bid chiefs, however, with all three major parties happy with the arrangement and their levels of individual investment.

Despite the running speculation and rumour, the Ricketts and their representatives never added any further explanation to what was quickly being branded a mystery decision of equally puzzling timing. Even at the close of business on 13 April, all three partners in the Ricketts set-up were excited, confident and ready to submit their final bid. The bid leaders had overriding confidence that their submission would at least run the decision close, and they all felt their proposition was the most compelling.

At the very last, however, just as the bid leaders were preparing to submit the final package to Raine, Gilbert withdrew. He contacted the other partners and explained that he had woken up that day with something approaching cold feet. The Ricketts and Griffin camps were both stunned. Both groups suspected that the reality and complexity of satisfying the UK government's purchase requirements had ultimately proved too much for Gilbert to countenance.

In a flash, from a complete proposal that was fully funded with cash and no debt, suddenly the Ricketts' bid was missing a sizeable chunk of capital – with less than twenty-four hours to replace Gilbert's multi-million-pound investment. The time limit effectively left even the notion of seeking a replacement partner a complete non-starter. The other final bids were all cash too, so Raine were likely to look unfavourably on a late addition of debt, which it is understood the Ricketts bid team never considered.

Try as they might, through strategy and theorising, no one in the two remaining camps could find an answer or way forward. And so, faced with only one course of action, the bid leaders informed Raine of their decision to withdraw, and then quickly made their public announcement.

All three rival bidders were just as stunned as the Ricketts family and Ken Griffin. The withdrawal gave them all pause, and each in turn was left to conduct one extra final check of their submissions before making the requisite lodging with Raine. The entire process had been spooked, leaving many of those involved looking over their shoulders and wondering what could possibly happen next.

• • •

Once the final bids were in place, attentions switched to the crucial task of liaising with the government, which would await whichever consortium won out in the race to buy the Blues. The Boehly–Clearlake bid already had Goldman Sachs advising, but on 16 April, the involvement of Robey Warshaw was also confirmed. The addition of the boutique advisory firm would not have proved significant in isolation, save for the fact that a certain George Osborne had joined the London-based investment outfit the previous year.

The former Chancellor had quit frontline politics in 2016, racking up a clutch of private sector jobs, including editing the *Evening Standard* from 2017 to 2020. A lifelong Chelsea fan, Osborne was on hand in Munich when the Blues claimed Champions League glory in 2012 and was even pictured with the trophy that night. His firm friend and fellow Chelsea fan Lord Finkelstein had also helped advise Boehly to bring Robey Warshaw on board.

Osborne's continued association with the Tory Party leadership and Cabinet immediately put the Boehly–Clearlake bid in pole position when it came to back-channelling influence with the government. All the bidders would need to foster the strongest possible links with not just the Johnson administration but also the staff at the Treasury and OFSI, especially as the government's purposeful default position had been to communicate as little as possible with the Abramovich camp or indeed with Raine. The Johnson administration's decision to allow Raine to run the Chelsea sale themselves meant that the government vetting process would not be carried out officially until the preferred bidder was chosen. The race against time left the Treasury and OFSI carrying out preparatory work and extensive background checks on all the final shortlisted bidders, but the finer details of the vetting process would still have to wait until a winner in the race to buy Chelsea eventually emerged.

The Broughton bid offered plenty of establishment clout too, through the principal's own knight of the realm status and his work as British Airways chairman and then in rescuing Liverpool. The addition of Lord Coe only added further influence and ability to interact seamlessly with the government; as with so many other facets of the sale process, the enlisting of the ennobled and entitled became something of an arms race in itself. Boehly and Eghbali certainly felt they possessed the trump card in the shape of Osborne and the further backing of reputable and successful firm Robey Warshaw.

As the weekend edged into Sunday, Chelsea's men found themselves back at Wembley, this time competing for a place in the FA Cup final. City rivals Palace were painted as the plucky longshots aiming to topple the decorated and moneyed west Londoners, while Chelsea themselves had bucketloads of underdog energy given the constant siege mentality that had been fostered throughout the restrictions of the sanctions and the sale process.

The drama of Chelsea's compelling, galling and last-gasp Champions League loss in Real Madrid in midweek sucked some of the usual vigour out of the Blues' approach. The first half proved a tense affair, with Chelsea battling to shake off the understandable fatigue of those extra-time exploits in Madrid, not to mention the emotional toll of having had their Champions League trophy prised from an almost vice-like grip. The challenge of managing the required mental and physical peaks and troughs of playing multiple knockout matches in the space of just a few days cannot be overestimated. And for once, Chelsea's rhythm fell out of sync with their fixture schedule.

The teams turned around goalless at half time, after which point, the longer Palace kept the game scoreless, the more the pressure ramped up on a Chelsea side comfortably installed as favourites. Eventually, though, the resolve that had allowed the stubborn Chelsea players to drive through the many and varied setbacks and limitations of the sanctions kicked in.

First, Ruben Loftus-Cheek kept his technique in check to deliver a rasping volley that was still rising as it ripped into the back of the net. Then, Mason Mount combined with Timo Werner to thread his way through the Palace defence, before rolling a deft effort into the far corner of the goal.

Chelsea's reward for a dogged victory was to secure a repeat of the Carabao Cup final – another Wembley final showdown with Liverpool. A third FA Cup final in a row underscored Chelsea's continued influence on England's elite game, and boss Tuchel was immediately, though quietly, nudging his players to prepare to make up for the previous two years' showpiece losses to Arsenal and then Leicester.

'We controlled the match and were very, very disciplined, and we took care of the counter-attacks before they could launch them,' a delighted Tuchel told the BBC.

It was not the moment to take risks today, they did not allow a lot of chances, so we had to stay patient and keep the focus, and we did, and I'm very happy. I'm very proud that we will be here at Wembley again for a second final, after the Carabao Cup final. There's room for improvement result-wise, but it means a lot because it's the oldest and most traditional cup competition that you can play. It's a dream come true, so we will be ready.

That Tuchel could still focus on living his footballing dream amid numerous nightmarish elements of the sanctions and the enforced club sale underscored again his uncanny natural ability to motivate the Chelsea collective. His energy, focus, tactical nous and emotional intelligence had proved vital to the Blues' progress once again. The club's directors were again left in thrall to his remarkable managerial powers, relieved at the team's strong form and ability to recover quickly from varied setbacks.

The likes of Buck and Granovskaia certainly felt eternally grateful to Tuchel for a stewardship of the men's team that undoubtedly added an impetus and buoyancy to the entire sale process. A winning team is a popular team, and a popular team is a saleable asset, and the Raine executives too were left to feel that the form of both Chelsea's men and women only served to aid their job in realising the highest price for the Stamford Bridge outfit.

•   •   •

Once the three finalist consortiums were confirmed, a fresh round of meetings took place between Raine, Buck and Granovskaia and all the bidders in turn. If previous meetings at the exploratory stage had been designed to inform the bidders of the detail of the business, to add to their own due diligence, this time the suitors were doing the legwork.

The Boehly–Clearlake, Broughton–Harris–Blitzer and Pagliuca–Tanenbaum bid teams all descended once again on London, pulling out all the stops for the final pitches in gruelling, ultra-detailed meetings and presentations at Stamford Bridge. The strength of all three bids meant the race remained relatively even, despite each consortium head naturally believing their own submission to be by far the strongest.

All the while the football ground on, with Chelsea capitulating 4–2 at home to rivals Arsenal in the Premier League on 20 April, in what Tuchel branded an 'unacceptable' third Stamford Bridge loss in succession across all competitions. The home defeats by Brentford and Real Madrid had started that three-match Stamford Bridge losing streak, even though the Blues had since won their last three matches, held on the road. While the picture was perhaps rosier than Tuchel made out, Chelsea were starting to make heavy weather of securing a top-four league finish and the important Champions League qualification. Tuchel told his players not to get 'superstitious' and start looking for problems that did not exist – or, in other words, he urged them to hold their nerve and not overcorrect themselves.

The next day, Lewis Hamilton and Serena Williams's ambassadorial roles in Broughton's consortium made their way into the public domain, as the fervour around the sale from all angles simply refused to abate. The global sporting icons added star power, glamour and an elite winning mentality to the Broughton set-up, not to mention both were prepared to act as key figureheads in the team's bid to build an impactful approach to diversity in its ranks.

As the week unfolded, Chelsea were preparing to host another London derby, with West Ham pitching up at Stamford Bridge on Sunday 24 April, when Tuchel finally confirmed that talismanic defender Toni Rüdiger would leave the club on a free transfer that summer. One of the worst-kept secrets in football by this point, Rüdiger was on the cusp of agreeing a stunning move to Real Madrid. Tuchel could not hide his disappointment but felt that the sanctions had left Chelsea with no chance of retaining one of their top talents.

Chelsea made it known that week that Rüdiger had been offered a new contract – before the sanctions hit – that would have made him the highest-paid defender in the club's history. Rüdiger thought he had plenty of time to negotiate, and he would have done had the sanctions not blocked Chelsea from conducting any transfer business. The lure of Real Madrid might have proved too strong even against an open, full attempt at a new deal from the Blues, but Stamford Bridge bosses like Granovskaia still believe they could, and would, have convinced him to stay in west London given the unhindered opportunity.

Chelsea stepped into that West Ham clash at home dispirited by the impending loss of Rüdiger and with that run of three Stamford Bridge defeats to try to arrest. Nonetheless, Tuchel had insisted that Rüdiger would throw everything in his power at trying to cap his hugely impressive Chelsea tenure with another trophy before the end of the season, and the Blues were still focused overall on a positive end to the campaign.

The sanctions bit again as Chelsea could only host their home fans' season ticket holders at Stamford Bridge, leading to a reduced crowd of 32,231 for the Hammers' visit. Another nervy, tetchy encounter ensued, in which despite struggling to find fluency in attack Chelsea did defend manfully and retain focus and shape. Just as Chelsea appeared to be grinding to a galling, goalless draw, however, Craig Dawson hauled back Romelu Lukaku in the box, gifting the hosts a penalty in the tie's dying minutes. Jorginho stepped up with his trademark hop, skip and jump run-up, only to undersell the dummy and leave Łukasz Fabiański with a relatively straightforward save.

There was still time for further drama and a reprieve for Jorginho, though, as Christian Pulisic swept home Marcos Alonso's low cross in the final minute, sealing the win and ending the Blues' three-match losing streak at home. A palpably relieved Tuchel admitted afterwards that his players had desperately needed the confidence boost of a return to winning ways at home, in a victory he hoped would smooth the path back to top fluency and form.

•   •   •

As the final round of meetings between Raine, Buck and Granovskaia and the three shortlisted bidders started to draw to a close, a new demand was tabled that caught the consortiums by surprise. On

27 April, Raine requested that all three bidders raise their offers for the club by an extra £500 million. The size of the demand stunned all three parties, but the relentlessness of the race for ownership of the Blues, and the depth of feeling associated with the sale process, left all parties quickly minded to agree.

By this stage of the process, all the negotiating was taking place behind closed doors, so only off-record briefings would allow journalists to piece together events in order to keep relatively up to speed with proceedings. The request for the bidders to raise their offers significantly and at the last minute was characterised as a demand that came directly from Abramovich, and which was rooted in his desire to be able to donate as high a figure as possible to the intended humanitarian aid foundation.

Raine, for their part, were battling to assimilate information from all sources at a breakneck pace for a transaction of such size and magnitude, which led to an unusually high level of fluidity in terms of detail. While the late bid to drive higher value out of the sale could have caused friction, the Raine bosses were always confident the bidders would take the request in the spirit in which it was intended.

Senior staff at Raine had been receiving calls regularly throughout the process from a variety of people attached to all the key consortiums, with the bidders desperate to know what exactly they could do to drive their own candidacy over the line. In such a context, and with time running out, Raine were always confident the bidders would react to something approaching a take-it-or-leave-it situation by taking, not leaving.

And in the event, less than a day after Raine had put the request in front of the final bidders, all three consortiums had come back and confirmed they would raise their offers accordingly. The agreement across the board set the scene for the Chelsea sale to total a world-record sports outfit sale of £4.25 billion, which would be broken down into a £2.5 billion payment for the club itself, with £1.75 billion required in spending commitments split between renovating Stamford Bridge and investing in the academy, training ground and men's and women's playing squads.

While the bidders were coming to terms with such a significant uplift in the potential purchase price of the club, Chelsea's men were gearing up to take on Manchester United at Old Trafford in Premier League action on 28 April. All the talk of top-flight ownership issues had led the United fans to stage the latest in a long line of pre-match protests against the Glazer family, the widely unpopular owners of the Old Trafford club. Chelsea fans on hand in Manchester looked at the protests with a new level of vested interest, namely keeping everything crossed that the eventual new Blues owners would carry the club forward and deliver another fruitful era.

Once the action finally hit full swing, Chelsea dominated, only to find David de Gea in scintillating form in the United goal. The Spain stopper thwarted both Kai Havertz and N'Golo Kanté as the match crept towards the hour mark still in stalemate. Exactly on the dot of the hour, however, up popped full-back Marcos Alonso with a neat volley, to wrestle a hard-fought but deserved lead for the travelling Blues.

Deadlock broken, Chelsea set about trying to hold out for what could have proven their ninth consecutive win on the road in all competitions. Instead, that lead lasted just two minutes, as Cristiano Ronaldo lashed home an equaliser with his seventeenth goal of the season for United. Reece James struck the post for Chelsea as the visitors went in hunt of that craved win, before Edouard Mendy denied Ronaldo a second with a smart save.

Chelsea held on to third place in the league table but were left frustrated not to have claimed victory in a match they dominated almost from first to last. Despite continuing to perform admirably, especially in the circumstances of the sanctions and resulting constraints, Chelsea's staff and players were still mindful of having let several opportunities slide to nail down that top-four finish. The Blues came away from Old Trafford buoyed by knowing that seven points from their five remaining matches would be sufficient to secure Champions League qualification but also frustrated not to have already wrapped up that aim.

•   •   •

The morning after Chelsea had been held to that frustrating 1–1 draw with Manchester United at Old Trafford, Sir Jim Ratcliffe called Bruce Buck and asked for an urgent meeting. In next to no time, Ratcliffe swept into the board room at Stamford Bridge, a man with a purpose and in a hurry too. Britain's richest man was at Chelsea to make a last-minute bid to buy the club, in a bold attempt to circumvent the entire sale process, gazump the final three shortlisted consortiums and swipe the Blues away, in what would have proved a remarkable smash-and-grab raid.

Sat in the grand surroundings of the Stamford Bridge boardroom, where Abramovich and Buck had held court for almost twenty years, Ratcliffe made his big play. Tapping his chest repeatedly, Ratcliffe told Buck he had a piece of paper in the breast pocket of his shirt – on which was written an offer to buy Chelsea. Without delay, Buck asked Ratcliffe simply to reveal the value of that bid. Almost ignoring the question, Ratcliffe turned matters back to the detail of his pitch, how his proposed offer would represent the only bid with entirely British money and backing.

Again, Buck asked how much Ratcliffe was willing to bid, but again that piece of paper stayed in his shirt pocket, as the petrochemicals magnate preferred instead to keep laying out the minutiae of his pitch. The more Ratcliffe became energised about the specifics of his candidacy, the less chance Buck appeared to have of stopping the billionaire in his tracks.

When Buck could eventually break Ratcliffe's flow, he explained that even if anyone running the process would be minded to consider the INEOS bid, he was effectively too late. A preferred bidder had all but been chosen, and Raine were about to start informing all the parties of the result of the arduous, turbulent and relentless battle to buy the Blues. Buck went on to explain that in all probability, only an offer of significantly higher value than the three that had made the final reckoning was likely to be seriously considered.

Ratcliffe had still not removed that piece of paper from his pocket, and with Buck none the wiser at this stage of the value of his hypothetical bid, the last-minute interloper could easily have kept his paper where it was, turned on his heel and left, never for the incident to be discussed again. That, however, was not how events unfolded; as with so many other extraordinary incidents across the three-month sale process, what had been started was going to be finished, right through to the bitter end.

Warning Ratcliffe that there could be no guarantee his bid would even be considered given that the process was almost over, Buck agreed to arrange for him to meet Raine chiefs Joe Ravitch and Colin Neville that same morning. Buck was also at pains to point out that Ratcliffe's bypassing of the sale process proper would be viewed in an extremely dim light by all the other contenders, and that the INEOS chief's lack of due diligence or a bid proposal would most likely greatly hinder his last-ditch effort to hijack the Chelsea sale.

Ratcliffe had numbered among the original 280 expressions of interest in buying Chelsea, all the way back at the start of March after Abramovich had confirmed the club was for sale. Quickly, though, he and his team politely withdrew from the process, considering that the fast-rising price point was beyond their determination, though certainly not beyond their means. Walking away in the embryonic stages only to saunter back in at the last minute with an offer on a sole piece of paper – when others had produced ultra-polished 140-page bid documents – not only raised eyebrows internally among those running the sale; it also left the decision-makers feeling the strategy could not pass muster.

Buck also explained to Ratcliffe that the nature of the government's unmoveable 31 May deadline meant that neither Chelsea nor Raine could risk angering everyone else in the process by progressing this extraordinary bid. Had Ratcliffe's bid been chosen only to fail, if the other bidders were left alienated, Chelsea could again have been at risk of ruin. Just when the process looked to be inching towards a conclusion inside the unforgiving timeframe, neither Buck nor Granovskaia, nor indeed Raine, was in search of any further drama or jeopardy.

After hearing all Buck's cautions, Ratcliffe still requested to meet with Raine, whereupon that very same morning he submitted a formal bid of £4.25 billion to buy Chelsea, the same value as the three offers to make the final shortlist. Buck, Granovskaia and Raine were left with the distinct impression that Ratcliffe was convinced that his status as the sole bid composed entirely of British money and personnel set him apart from all competition, by virtue of the government's oversight of the sale and required sign-off to trigger the transaction.

By mid-afternoon, despite being told by both Buck and Raine that the Boehly–Clearlake consortium was in all probability about to be named the preferred bidder, Ratcliffe had not only lodged his own offer but INEOS had released a lengthy statement in confirmation. 'This is a British bid for a British club,' read the INEOS statement, which confirmed that Ratcliffe had offered to meet all the same commitments as the other bidders.

Ratcliffe had grown up as a Manchester United supporter but had held Chelsea season tickets for a decade before the Covid pandemic, becoming a Stamford Bridge regular on frequent work trips to London. INEOS's varied sports portfolio by that stage included taking over the former Team Sky cycling outfit, bankrolling Sir Ben Ainslie's bid for the America's Cup and even taking a stake in Mercedes' Formula One team. INEOS's ownership of French top-flight club Nice would have left Ratcliffe having to sell or divest his shareholding were he to buy Chelsea, to conform to elite club competition regulations.

Of course, Ratcliffe's brother Bob had distanced the INEOS operation from a bid for Chelsea in early March, in an interview with the *Mail on Sunday* in which he insisted the petrochemicals firm had not shelled out 'silly money' building their set-up at Nice. If the Ratcliffes were happy to imply publicly that Chelsea was overpriced in early March, which tallied with the pair privately baulking at the asking price and quitting the official sale process, by the end of April, the tune was in an entirely different key. 'If you look at the big football clubs and American teams, Chelsea sits about right in the hierarchy in value,' Jim Ratcliffe told *The Times* in a wide-ranging interview on 30 April. 'It's expensive but not foolish.'

The other bidders were distinctly unimpressed with Ratcliffe's actions, as predicted by Buck in that shock, snap meeting with Ratcliffe at Stamford Bridge on 29 April. The bad news did not stop there for Pagliuca and Broughton, who would discover on the very same day that their own candidacies had proved unsuccessful. Both consortiums took falling short with good grace and, crucially, both asked to remain in the sale organisers' thoughts just in case any last-ditch problems might emerge with the Boehly–Clearlake proposition.

By the time Ratcliffe's major public play for the Chelsea hotseat hit the print edition of *The Times* on 30 April, Boehly and Clearlake had already been informed that they had won the race to buy the club, nominally at least, in the first instance. The terms would still have to be thrashed out, and days of non-stop negotiating lay in store, but Boehly and Eghbali were effectively victorious, at least in principle. Ratcliffe knew all of this, and yet he continued to press his claims both in public and in private, emboldened by separate, low-key discussions with the government, which had been interpreted positively.

• • •

After Ratcliffe's last-minute disruption act on 29 April, Buck and Raine were still recovering their bearings when convening to finalise the formal choice of preferred bidder. Buck and Granovskaia sat with Ravitch and Neville from Raine in a room next to Abramovich's office at Stamford Bridge. The discussion started off with a light-hearted joke that if ever there was a time to pick a winner, it would be at the end of a day of such magnitude, but quickly the semi-humour subsided and Buck and Granovskaia told Ravitch their first choices.

The Chelsea executives both selected the Boehly–Clearlake consortium, and seemed to have come to that conclusion for the same general reasons. Having considered all the final bidders in the round, meeting all the main partners and assessing their suitability in detail, in the end the decision on the preferred bidders came down to fine margins. All three final bidders had submitted bids to the same value and largely offering the same pledges and securities for the club's future. All three bids impressed both Raine and the Chelsea executive with their professional, comprehensive and committed composition.

Granovskaia felt Boehly, Eghbali and partners would prove to be the bidders who could most closely match Abramovich's aptitude for decisive and quick but also considered action. Under Abramovich's leadership, senior staff were given responsibility and trusted to carry out his wishes, much as Granovskaia and Buck had been across the sale process itself. Boehly and Clearlake proved themselves prepared to build an off-field structure that would allow for the kind of agility that had so characterised Abramovich's Stamford Bridge ownership.

After all had been said and done across the nineteen-year Abramovich tenure, Chelsea fan Buck could not shake the thoughts of his fellow Blues supporters when judging who should take the club forward into a new era. Buck had bought two Chelsea season tickets for the 1989–90 campaign and had never relinquished the seats, not even during his chairmanship. In a kind of semi-superstitious magical thinking, he had considered that retaining his season tickets would somehow help extend the remarkable ride of Abramovich's ownership. Plus, Buck always knew that Abramovich's tenure would come to an end some day, at which point he would be extremely glad of the opportunity to return to attending matches purely as a fan.

Across the course of Abramovich's ownership, Buck's family and friends would use his season tickets, but he had always known the day would come when he would want to be back in his original Stamford Bridge seats, which he had taken up when he had settled in London due to his career in law. As he thought about who he, or any other supporter, would want at the Chelsea helm out of the final bidders, when he pictured himself back in his original Stamford Bridge seats, the overriding image was of Boehly and Eghbali directing operations from the owners' and directors' boxes.

Allied to the raft of expected commitments, Boehly and Eghbali had made it clear in their pitches to buy Chelsea that they were prepared to invest the most heavily of the bidders when it came to adding talent to the club's playing squads. While the scale of the eventual investment was not divulged, Buck was left with the overriding impression that the Boehly–Clearlake consortium was prepared to invest well above the market average in order to take Chelsea forward on all fronts. For Buck, this was the most prominent distinguishing factor and the attitude that he felt would prove the strongest Stamford Bridge fit.

With Buck and Granovskaia in total agreement, a call was made to Eugene Tenenbaum to pass the news up the chain of command. Tenenbaum called Abramovich to break the news and check for a green light to proceed, and in next to no time, the quartet at Stamford Bridge had the go-ahead to inform Boehly and Eghbali of the best possible news.

Fielding the call that would set in motion his consortium's ownership of Chelsea, Boehly kept his cool and thanked the sales process
leaders, revealing his delight but in an ultra-professional manner.
Acutely aware that being named the preferred bidder would come
to mean nothing unless both sides could strike the specific terms of
the deal, and fast, Boehly told Buck and Company over the phone
that he was looking forward to exploring the finer details in a bid to
close the transaction without delay – so that Chelsea as a club could
get on with its life.

• • •

Though Boehly and Eghbali were already installed as the preferred
bidders, the LA consortium still had to pass official checks from the
Premier League and the government. Any official confirmation of
the Boehly bid's status was kept under wraps to allow those checks
to be completed. To the wider public, then, Ratcliffe still appeared
to be in the running to disrupt the entire sale process and force
a say in the eventual outcome. Ratcliffe too refused to give up on
his last-ditch Chelsea pitch, suddenly ramping up the noise on his
candidacy.

If Ratcliffe had attempted to swoop in on the Chelsea sale process
with something of a bang, the fireworks affecting the Blues were
worryingly real on the night of 30 April. With Ratcliffe's interview
in that morning's *Times* still doing the rounds, Chelsea's men were
on Merseyside that night, preparing to face relegation-threatened
Everton at Goodison Park the next day. Everton's survival fight
had become so desperate that some of their fans opted to set off
fireworks outside Chelsea's hotel, disturbing the Blues' sleep in the
middle of the night.

By the time the Premier League clash came around on Sunday afternoon, Chelsea struggled for fluency and incision and slumped to a 1–0 defeat courtesy of Richarlison's goal. Manager Tuchel was later forced to insist the fireworks at the hotel had not had an overt impact on the result at Goodison, but whatever the reason, Chelsea had missed the chance to reaffirm their spot in third place in the top-flight table.

Ratcliffe continued to match the noise of those rowdy Everton fans with their midnight fireworks as the first week of May unfolded. Raine, Buck and Granovskaia by this point were all convinced Ratcliffe knew his charm offensive would fall on deaf ears, and yet he continued unabashed. On the morning of Wednesday 4 May, the BBC started trailing an exclusive video interview with Ratcliffe, the teasers for which flagged that he would be spilling the beans on his Chelsea bid.

As the hours ticked by towards the evening news and the broadcasting of that interview with Britain's richest man, INEOS then took a step that appeared to undercut that BBC story. A company spokesman confirmed in the middle of the day that the INEOS bid for Chelsea had been rejected out of hand, to respect the other bidders and the integrity of the process.

Ratcliffe himself told the BBC that he refused to give up on his fight for Chelsea, insisting, 'Consideration should be given to a British bid.' While both Raine and Buck had already told Ratcliffe that his bid was not successful, he still refused to accept defeat.

'We had a communication with Raine and met with them at the end of last week,' said Ratcliffe. 'We presented a bid but have heard very little back from them. My message to Raine is: don't discount our offer. We are British and have great intentions for Chelsea. If I were Raine, I wouldn't close any door.'

Many neutral observers questioned Ratcliffe's ultimate motivations, and he was even asked in the BBC interview why a Manchester United fan would not try to buy the Red Devils instead. Ratcliffe explained that United were simply not for sale. While some Chelsea fans reacted with scepticism to a multi-billionaire who felt prepared to split his loyalties between two Premier League giants, others theorised that this Chelsea bid was merely a public forum for Ratcliffe to make it patently clear to United owners the Glazer family that INEOS might very well have designs on owning the Old Trafford club.

Ratcliffe had conducted himself well in his TV interview and was doubtless still determined to swipe Chelsea from under Boehly's and Eghbali's noses. The immediate contrast of Ratcliffe's BBC interview with his spokespeople confirming that Raine had dismissed his bid proved significant and impactful enough, however, to stop the INEOS chief's work in its tracks.

For a second time, the Boehly–Clearlake bid appeared in the clear and all set to claim total control of first the sale process and then the club itself. This time, the Boehly bid was indeed the only one left in the frame, but just because no rival bids were now in competition did not mean that all the hurdles had been negotiated. With only one bid left on the table for the club, the power dynamic shifted: Raine and Abramovich's representatives could ill afford to let Boehly and Eghbali walk away during negotiations over the purchase agreement. As the turbulent sale finally entered its endgame, all of a sudden the buyers held the upper hand, with the clock ticking down ever closer to that immovable 31 May deadline.

CHAPTER TWELVE

FOUNDATIONS AND FRUSTRATIONS

At the start of 2021, Mike Penrose fielded a call from Abramovich's spokesperson and adviser Rola Brentlin, who had spearheaded Chelsea's Say No To Antisemitism campaign. Brentlin asked Penrose to advise Abramovich on the best way for the Chelsea owner to make a significant humanitarian donation, to outline the mechanics and how to maximise the impact of any such aid.

Already one of the world's leading philanthropists by that point, Abramovich had given more than $2.7 billion in global charitable contributions over twenty years. With a significant charitable footprint towards UK causes too, Chelsea Foundation became the Premier League's largest charitable vehicle. Despite such widespread charitable work, by 2021 he was still seeking further, impactful philanthropic investment. Abramovich was interested in a multi-million-pound donation to a cause-based initiative that would combat major global problems.

With almost thirty years' experience delivering aid in conflict zones, including his prior role as executive director of Unicef UK, Penrose was Brentlin's first and only call for this specific task. Penrose was chairman of Soccer Aid during his Unicef tenure, and

Stamford Bridge had played host to the annual football charity initiative raising funds for the humanitarian organisation. Chelsea had been impressed by Penrose's attitude and dynamism, before even considering his CV.

If Penrose was the obvious choice to explore the options open to Abramovich for such a donation, something that would prove at least bespoke and possibly unique, the initial motivations behind the task were not laid out beyond the Chelsea owner's desire to launch another new philanthropic initiative. After several conversations and meetings with Brentlin, Penrose set to work quietly behind the scenes writing a detailed paper for Abramovich, balancing that task with his other roles, having helped found the Sustainability Group and Future Plus.

Putting his head down and pressing on, Penrose did not consider the issue beyond the scope of the tasks set by Brentlin, on which he delivered a comprehensive treatise, drawing on a career comprising crisis work in more than sixty countries, including senior roles with Action contre la Faim and Save the Children.

The paper for Abramovich had long been put to bed by the time Russian troops were again lining the border with Ukraine in early 2022. As tensions rose and war inched closer, Penrose received fresh contact from Brentlin. This time, the question was just as clear but far more stunning. Penrose was asked, 'What if the size of donation were not in the region of several hundred million pounds, but more like two billion?'

Precious little might shock a man who had been kidnapped during the Chechen War, but Penrose caught himself in a double take at the question and its deeper significance. If the wider impact of the figures discussed did not fall into place straight away, the speed of events eventually slotted the jigsaw together.

By the time Abramovich announced that Chelsea was for sale, on 2 March, Penrose had already agreed to lead a new independent foundation, designed to use all proceeds from the club sale as humanitarian aid in global crises. Abramovich's initial statement on the Chelsea sale, pledging that all proceeds would be 'for the benefit of all victims of the war in Ukraine', formed the basis of Penrose's brief.

Even as Penrose got to grips with the initial planning, it was clear that this amount of capital would represent the biggest single humanitarian donation in history. In preparing a foundation to control the biggest independent charitable fund of all time, Penrose recruited a clutch of peers to act as directors, all with similarly strong humanitarian backgrounds.

Penrose was recruited not for any familiarity with Chelsea or the Abramovich leadership but instead for a neutrality and impartiality respected as much in political circles as in the world of humanitarianism. A reservist soldier who had also worked for the UK government's Department for International Development, Penrose's credentials were impeccable – but his was also a career that hinged on upholding that hard-earned reputation. Abramovich needed an individual to run this foundation who could stand beyond reproach in every measure, and Brentlin and other senior figures close to the Russian-Israeli billionaire considered Penrose the ideal figure.

When war officially broke out, Penrose immediately travelled to Ukraine to carry out assessments for UK-Med, the humanitarian medical aid charity born of the NHS. On the ground in active war zones from Kharkiv to Zaporizhzhia, Penrose played a central role in initial British support to the region, helping the only UK-based non-governmental organisation verified by the World Health Organization as an emergency medical team.

In this conflict as in so many others across his almost thirty years of humanitarian war zone work, Penrose saw first-hand just how futile it could be attempting to limit the scope of aid funding. Aid is extremely difficult to deliver during a conflict, and rebuilding and restructuring a country can clearly only happen on cessation of action.

Those preparing to set up the new foundation were all of the same mind: that if invested and managed prudently, the vast funds would never run out, allowing the organisation to offer aid globally in effect in perpetuity. To that end, Penrose lined up a number of top financial minds and bodies in the US who were prepared to guarantee investment returns for a set number of years given the foundation's charitable mission and compelling potential for good.

In penning the initial deed of undertaking, Penrose crucially stated that the foundation should exist to be of benefit firstly 'for Ukraine and the consequences of the Ukraine war' but with the intention for the scope to be extended eventually worldwide. In Penrose's expert view, war does not respect borders: the consequences of Russia's illegal invasion could never be contained within Ukraine itself. From the spread of refugees right across Europe to the wider geopolitical repercussions, there would be no chance of limiting the impact of war, and therefore the locations where aid was needed. As the foundation planning began to take shape, Penrose's clear position was that the body must exist to tackle all broader consequences – and that this was an enterprise requiring ambition beyond any comparison.

In the midst of the horrors of war, witnessed first-hand by Penrose and colleagues, hopes were quickly raised that the proceeds of the enforced Chelsea sale could provide the catalyst for an organisation that could transform the face of humanitarian aid for ever.

• • •

As the sale progressed and once sanctions were imposed on Abramovich, Penrose stepped up meetings with the UK government aimed at thrashing out the particulars of the foundation. Ministers and civil servants from OFSI and the Foreign Office were collectively concerned that the entire idea of the foundation was to act as a complex ruse by which Abramovich would bid to funnel the sale proceeds back to himself. Such insinuations were commonplace across the sale period, in private meetings, off-the-record media briefings – and even expressed to Penrose and those in Abramovich's camp too.

A nonplussed Penrose continually leaned on the many and varied legal frameworks and regulations through which it would ultimately prove nigh-on impossible for the money to be moved without complete government oversight. He had even provided the government with a scoping document that detailed how the foundation would be set up, who would manage the funds and how the money could be protected. As the days and weeks progressed, however, even though the sale itself was moving along at pace, the foundation planning remained in limbo.

Penrose had found himself hoping that the 7 May landmark of Boehly–Clearlake being named as the winning bid would break the deadlock, but to no avail. Some nine days later, with Chelsea's sellers and the club's buyers racing to beat the 31 May deadline to complete a whirlwind deal, Penrose went public with his plans for the foundation. He was determined to outline publicly the stunning scope to transform the humanitarian sector – but also to shine a light on the bureaucracy he already by that point feared might scupper the entire enterprise.

At a time when the details of the foundation should have been taking shape, Penrose instead found himself driven beyond distraction and into drastic action. 'The only thing between this becoming a reality and now is politics,' Penrose told the Press Association on 16 May.

> I have absolutely no interest in the politics of the sale. I have no interest in the politics of the government. If politics gets in the way, then that is to me almost criminal, it really is. I've written into the document that's gone to the government that no one who has ever been associated with the club, associated with the owner, can or will ever receive financial benefit. And that would go into the articles of association of the foundation. That's written into the document that's now in the hands of the government.

In other words, a vastly experienced professional whose best work was usually conducted behind the scenes and in low-key fashion had opted to stake his reputation on going public with his deepening concerns. Such was the scale of the opportunity that might go to waste, Penrose was more than prepared to put the greater good ahead of any reputational risk.

Not only had Penrose put all the planning and methodology on a plate for the government, he had also reasserted the already existing legal framework by which the proceeds of the Chelsea sale would be protected. The continued fears in the corridors of power that funds could be misappropriated appeared unfounded from his standpoint.

'I'd like to say I was confident, but I'm nervous about the politics of it all,' said a frazzled Penrose at the time.

I've spent my entire life in humanitarian aid, and I'm very worried that what might come out of this is politics over decent humanitarian action. But on the other hand I also hope that this government sees the opportunity that it has here. The UK government could create the world's leading humanitarian foundation.

What Penrose left purposely unsaid was the growing suspicion in some circles that top Cabinet figures were attempting to explore ways in which they could boost their personal legacies through their involvement with the Chelsea sale. The enormous sum of money involved had effectively been apportioned immediately by Abramovich himself, in his stated intention that the proceeds from the sale should go to aid all victims of the Ukraine war. While there was no suggestion that the money would be used to any other benefit, there were rumours circulating that top Cabinet figures wanted to find ways of claiming extra credit for ensuring those funds would aid Ukraine, boosting their own profiles in the process.

Behind the scenes, such suggestions were scotched from the outset both by direct government sources and by those close to senior figures in the Tory administration. But such rumours persisted, and some of those linked to both Chelsea and Abramovich have always felt that some of the hitches in setting up the foundation had their basis in senior Conservative figures aiming to claim extra credit for ensuring the money would be spent on aid for Ukraine.

Penrose's public statement on 16 May that he refused to play politics ultimately urged all involved to rise above any other concerns and find a way to ensure that the potentially transformative foundation could become a reality. Stationed close to the front line of the war in Ukraine at the time, Penrose saw his frustrations and fears over potential political interference collide with the realities of the conflict. Part of his duties on the ground in Ukraine had been to help train local emergency services in how to respond to chemical attacks.

Where it could take up to six months for humanitarian aid to reach a conflict zone from standard organisations, Penrose was confident that the unrivalled agility of such an independent foundation could see funds helping on the ground within days of the organisation's launch. But as the compelling reasons for action stacked up, not least the hellish toll of war in Ukraine itself, so too were the impediments continuing to block any tangible progress with the foundation.

• • •

High-level meetings aimed at groundbreaking humanitarian giving remained a world away from Chelsea's daily grind, but somehow the Blues kept the show on the road. Boehly and Eghbali might have won the fight for Chelsea, dispatching all other suitors, but the takeover was far from complete. While Penrose was hitting brick walls in terms of the foundation, Chelsea's top executives, Abramovich's personal staff and the Blues' prospective new owners were all working night and day to meet the government's 31 May sale completion deadline.

Chelsea's players and staff could look on the future no more than tentatively, as any delays or hitches in negotiations on the details of the deal could still have plunged the club into jeopardy. A cloud of concern still darkened both the men's and the women's teams, and not even two FA Cup finals in as many days could lift it. Chelsea were fixated on two revenge missions at a bumper Wembley weekend, with the men facing Liverpool on 14 May and the women Manchester City a day later. Tuchel's side were gunning to turn the tables on Liverpool after losing that 22-penalty shoot-out to the Reds in the Carabao Cup final in February, while Hayes's women were out to avenge their 3–1 Continental Cup final defeat by City from March.

Tuchel's men pushed Liverpool to the very limit once again, in another turbulent contest that somehow remained goalless after extra time. Just as in the League Cup final, neither team could break the deadlock, and so another penalty contest ensued. This time there would be no seemingly endless battle, but though the shoot-out was shorter, there was no lack of drama

Captain Azpilicueta fired against the post in an agonising early blow to the Blues, while every other initial penalty taker continued to bury their spot-kicks in the back of the net. Jorginho converted the last of Chelsea's allocation, leaving Sadio Mané needing only to slot home to hand Liverpool the cup. Practically everyone in Wembley expected the Senegal forward to deliver, and his confident walk to the spot suggested he himself thought along the same lines.

Step forward Edouard Mendy, then, Mané's Senegal teammate, who read his international colleague's run-up, pulling off a remarkable save. As on 27 February, the only way to settle a cup final between Chelsea and Liverpool would be through not just penalties but sudden-death spot-kicks. Unlike 27 February, however, there would be no near-flawless roll call, because Blues academy graduate Mount stepped up for the first sudden-death penalty and duly saw it well saved by Liverpool stopper Alisson. Liverpool were in no mood to spurn a second opportunity to end the penalty battle, and Kostas Tsimikas quickly dispatched his effort to end the argument and wrestle another cup out of Chelsea's hands.

As Mount dropped to his haunches on the Wembley turf, inconsolable amid the penalty agony, Liverpool lapped up their second domestic cup success over the Blues of the season. Chelsea's third successive FA Cup final defeat proved an unwanted record, while boss Tuchel was left to reflect with equal parts pride and sadness.

Denmark defender Andreas Christensen wound up conspicuous by his absence, having stood himself down for selection citing illness, despite having no injury. In a match in which veteran Thiago Silva had been forced to play through the pain of an existing problem, Blues boss Tuchel was frustrated and not particularly interested in hiding his feelings.

Christensen's summer free transfer to Barcelona had effectively been ratified by this time, but no one at Chelsea could fathom quite why the talented centre-back would want to relinquish the chance to end his Blues tenure with another trophy high. Germany defender Rüdiger might have been heading to Real Madrid that summer, but he had no qualms at all about committing fully to the Chelsea cause in the final weeks and months of the campaign.

In the bowels of the cavernous Wembley edifice, once post-match press duties were complete, Tuchel cut a nonplussed figure when attempting to run the rule over Christensen's absence. For once the Blues' German boss could not find an answer, and his air of resignation only served to heighten the continued worries of Chelsea's limbo.

Despite the deadline for the completion of the sale looming in just two weeks, Chelsea were still subject to all the transfer embargoes related to the sanctions. While Tuchel understood the reality of that continued ban, he knew Chelsea were losing ground on rivals who were free to strengthen their squads with new recruits for the following season without restriction.

The next day, it was the women's team's turn to take an FA Cup final to extra time. Hayes's side rose to the occasion of a record 49,094 crowd at the national stadium, but they had to do so the hard way. Sam Kerr's opener was cancelled out by City's Lauren Hemp, only for Erin Cuthbert to swipe a 2–1 lead for the Blues just past the hour.

As Hayes's side looked set to close out the victory in the dying stages, though, Hayley Raso levelled for City just a minute from time. Both sides had spurned fine openings throughout an engaging encounter, and extra time unfolded in a nervy jumble – until Kerr kept her cool to slide home the winner. In retaining their FA Cup title, Chelsea added a league and cup double to the previous year's domestic treble. Ultra-focused and composed boss Hayes had insisted throughout that her players and staff were capable of shaking off the outside fears and delivering on the pitch. When the time for reflection came afterwards, however, the main feeling flooding through the women's ranks was that of relief rather than sheer elation.

While the women's season was at an end, Tuchel and company still had two more crucial Premier League matches with which to seal Champions League qualification. Just five days after their gruelling FA Cup final loss on penalties, the Blues hosted Leicester at Stamford Bridge. Marcos Alonso's crisp strike secured a 1–1 draw that would all but wrap up the all-important qualification. Afterwards, Tuchel branded Chelsea's potential third-place finish in the league a 'miracle' given talisman midfielder N'Golo Kanté had missed almost half the season through injuries. Even as he cited Kanté's injury troubles as the biggest hindrance, that trademark wry smile crept across the wily coach's face. Everyone in the press conference room knew full well that Chelsea's real miracle had been to keep a stressed squad focused and motivated amid all the fears for the future.

Chelsea rolled into the last match of the season on 22 May technically needing at least a point against Watford to seal a third-place finish, highly creditable in the circumstances. Amid all the continued uncertainty on whether the Boehly–Eghbali takeover would beat the fast-approaching 31 May deadline, what was largely overshadowed was the final match of the Abramovich era. Boehly and consortium partner Hansjörg Wyss were on hand at Stamford Bridge to watch Chelsea edge to a 2–1 win that sealed that third-place finish and Champions League qualification. Ross Barkley's last-minute header swiped all three points, the former England midfielder claiming his first goal of the campaign on the season's final day.

Boehly and Wyss cut relatively circumspect figures walking the Stamford Bridge turf after the match, unable to indulge in any premature celebrations on their impending ownership. While not quite an interregnum, the clear limbo left supporters just as unsure how to approach the presence of the prospective owners as the men themselves. If the Watford match was a strange afternoon for the new consortium waiting not quite in the wings, the whole day proved bizarre and wistfully poignant for many key figures from the Abramovich era.

The political situation and general sensibilities meant Chelsea were in no position to mark the end of the Abramovich era even if they had so desired. The likes of senior director Granovskaia were in the Stamford Bridge stands that day knowing full well that this would represent the last official match of Abramovich's ownership – and with it the kind of ending that could not provide anything even remotely resembling closure. While anyone pining for a way to mark the end of the Abramovich era knew full well that was both impossible and inappropriate, a nucleus of his senior staff could not help but reminisce on some snapshot memories of happier times.

When Abramovich first took the Chelsea helm, the Russian folk song 'Kalinka' would be blasted out in the build-up to kick-off at Stamford Bridge. When the players had taken to the field to face Watford in what technically was the final match of Abramovich's stewardship, there were those on hand who quietly wished to hear those familiar Russian folk tune strains one last time. Old time's sake had no place in proceedings, however, and despite a robust Premier League finish amid the rocky wider situation, the entire day carried a decidedly circumspect air.

Tuchel had the last word, lamenting Chelsea's hands still being tied in the transfer market despite the presence of the incoming owners at the match. With just nine days until the deadline for the sale to be completed, and no public signals whatsoever of a finish line from any of the key parties, if the day itself had felt humdrum, the mood going forward was positively ominous.

• • •

While Penrose was desperately trying to avoid being buried in bureaucracy, Chelsea and Abramovich's top executives were negotiating with the government, trying to thrash out the terms of the special licence that would allow the club's sale to go ahead. The Treasury and OFSI would have to create another licence that would give the green light for Boehly and Clearlake to negotiate with Chelsea and eventually draw up and sign sale contracts.

In order to draft the sale licence, which would cover the full terms and mechanism of the pending £4.25 billion transaction, the

Treasury would also have to agree a separate deed of undertaking with Abramovich concerning the foundation that Penrose had been tasked to launch. Abramovich had made his position clear from the outset with his statement that Chelsea was for sale all the way back on 2 March, where he promised the loan to the club would be written off and called for the sale proceeds to be used to benefit all victims of the war in Ukraine.

The government's powers through sanctions extended only to freezing, rather than seizing, assets, so no one in Westminster could spend the proceeds of the Chelsea sale. The government adopted a cynical view of Abramovich's intentions from the outset, fearing that the Russian-Israeli billionaire would somehow attempt to funnel the funds back to himself after Chelsea's sale. The government were also sceptical of the pledge that the £1.5billion loan to Chelsea would be cancelled, even though Abramovich and his advisers had long since confirmed the intention publicly.

The government feared Abramovich would renege on his pledge to write off the loan and try to find a way to call it in once the sale funds were being processed, despite the fact that legal experts considered this in effect impossible. Such Cabinet worries led to extended hiatuses in negotiations around the drafting of the sale licence, but Abramovich for his part had no qualms about having safeguards blocking any loan repayment being written into the document.

Staff at the Treasury and OFSI were breaking new ground as regards implementing sanctions legislation, and deciphering the legal complexities of even where to house the Chelsea sale proceeds had proven a painstaking challenge. Eventually, it was decided that the proceeds of the Chelsea sale would be deposited in the bank account of Abramovich's holding company Fordstam, the parent company of the Stamford Bridge club. The account was already frozen under the terms of Abramovich's sanctions, leaving any funds that would be deposited ultra-secure.

Once the basic logistical and legal elements of the sale licence had been thrashed out, the government turned its attention to the details of the foundation and the mechanics of how the funds from the Chelsea sale would be distributed for aid. Despite Abramovich's pledges towards the independent foundation and Penrose's separate work, the government's opening stance was to try to impose total control and distribute the money itself.

The limits of the sanctions legislation meant the government could not simply seize the money but instead required Abramovich's approval for anything amounting to a sequestering of the funds. Abramovich and his advisers flatly refused. The first of many mini-stalemates came to pass, but in the end the government had to relent, instead attempting to add a time limit for the distribution of the funds, beyond which point the Treasury would seek to seize the money.

The levels of suspicion on both sides had boiled up by this stage, to the point where Abramovich and his advisers did not harbour great confidence in the government's ability to work to its own self-imposed timescale. And so, as with the government's first suggestion of simply controlling the money from the outset, again Abramovich and his team refused the updated Treasury suggestion.

As the two sides became increasingly entrenched, confusion and frustration grew, along with a sense of fear that the entire sale process was only ever one mix-up away from collapse. Several of Abramovich's senior staff felt the dialogue with the government was going round in ever-decreasing circles and at the most critical and time-sensitive stage of the entire process. Chelsea's top aides were driven to distraction as much by the fluctuating positions of several OFSI and government staff as by the pressures of working twenty-hour days through the process.

Heading into the second half of May, however, just when the impasse appeared to be stretching into panic stations, the government appeared prepared to accept the securities of the sanctions in allowing the Chelsea sale funds to be deposited in the frozen Fordstam bank account. And when the Treasury and OFSI agreed to accept that the deed of undertaking on the foundation could be referenced in the official sale licence, suddenly there appeared a breakthrough.

Two days after the end of the men's Premier League season and the underwhelming atmosphere around the Watford win, on 24 May, the Treasury issued the licence document that would allow the sale to go through. Almost simultaneously, the Premier League certified Boehly and his consortium partners as having passed the owners' and directors' tests. After so much pressure, angst and graft against the clock, suddenly the endgame for the entire process was genuinely in sight.

Abramovich signed the deed of undertaking that detailed the commitments of the proposed foundation to use the Chelsea sale money as humanitarian aid, and the Blues owner and his team all breathed a relative – and tentative – sigh of relief. No sooner had those of a Stamford Bridge leadership persuasion finished that weary exhalation, however, than an entirely new obstacle was strewn into the path of the ever turbulent sale process.

• • •

The ink was hardly dry on that OFSI sale licence when an entirely new problem threatened the sale again, this time in the shape of the Portuguese government. Some UK government sources say that representatives of the Iberian nation contacted their UK counterparts, insisting that the Chelsea sale could not be signed off without EU approval. Other sources have claimed that it was the UK government that reached out to Portugal, to check whether EU ratification was required. Portugal suddenly considered it held a key role in the Chelsea sale process due to Abramovich gaining citizenship of the country in 2021.

Abramovich had qualified for a Portuguese passport through a law offering to naturalise the descendants of Sephardic Jews who had been forced to leave the Iberian peninsula centuries earlier. All of a sudden top officials in Portugal were arguing to UK counterparts in OFSI, the Treasury and the Foreign Office that the sale framework would have to adhere to EU law given Abramovich's citizenship of the country.

While lawyers for Abramovich quickly rejected that assertion, staff at OFSI and the Treasury were said to have been sent into something of a spin. Less than six days out from the deadline for the sale's completion, here was another major setback.

For several fraught hours as legal teams representing each interested party scrambled for answers in double-quick time, Abramovich's camp harboured renewed and genuine fears that at the eleventh hour the sale could collapse, and over an order of process that should have long since been handled. As the time ticked by and no update was forthcoming, lawyers for Abramovich and the prospective owners were all in agreement that Brexit nullified any requirement to follow EU law, irrespective of the issue of the Portuguese passport.

Officials at OFSI and the Treasury were still determined to include Portugal, however, leaving all parties to continue to sweat on the outcome of the Portuguese review. Palpable internal relief all round met the Portuguese government's confirmation on the evening of Wednesday 25 May that, from their perspective, the sale could proceed.

Portugal released a confirmatory statement the following morning, publicly explaining the result of a process that many legal experts still felt had been entirely unnecessary due to Brexit. 'Portugal gave authorisation, this Wednesday night, to the sale of Chelsea Football Club,' read a Portuguese government statement.

> The two responsible national authorities – Ministry of Foreign Affairs and Ministry of Finance – have given the green light to the request received on behalf of Roman Abramovich for a humanitarian derogation, allowing the English club to be transacted. The Portuguese authorisation follows the guarantee given by the British authorities that the proceeds from the sale will be used for humanitarian purposes, not directly or indirectly benefiting the owner of the club, who is on the European Union sanctions list. The national position has the agreement of the European Commission.

Finally, with no time to spare whatsoever, the Chelsea sale was ready to be carried out. Under normal circumstances a week would be the minimum timeframe required to complete a transaction of such size and complexity: Chelsea were left with less than five days to rubber-stamp everything, or risk total ruin.

By 27 May, though, both Abramovich and his camp and, entirely separately, Penrose and his colleagues were all quietly excited about the pending foundation and its potential as an overwhelming force for humanitarian good. The reason for such high spirits was contained within the details of the Chelsea sale licence. The Treasury documents granting the Chelsea sale were never made public but were issued on 24 May and updated on 25 and 27 May.

Abramovich's camp have always maintained that the official government document stated that the proceeds of the Chelsea sale 'shall be donated to set up and fund a new charitable foundation for exclusively humanitarian purposes supporting all victims of the conflict in Ukraine, and its consequences'.

The deed of undertaking signed by Abramovich and Tenenbaum, acting as director for Fordstam, the sanctioned company that would receive the sale funds, mirrored the statement made in the government document on the aims for the foundation, the Russian-Israeli billionaire's team asserted. Abramovich staff insist that the deed of undertaking read:

> The foundation will be established as a charity to provide immediate relief and long-term support to victims of conflict anywhere in the world, through the provision of grant financing (or any other support deemed suitable). The initial focus of this foundation will be on Ukraine and those affected by this conflict, but given the size of funding from the sale of the club, it is likely to expand into supporting victims of conflict worldwide.

This all chimed entirely with Abramovich's initial pledges all the way back on 2 March, for the proceeds of the sale to be used as aid for all victims of the war in Ukraine. As the final, fraught few days of a whirlwind sale process played out, however, the geographic specifics of exactly where the foundation would concentrate its humanitarian work would turn into a row all of its own. From an organisation primed to create a paradigm shift in humanitarian aid, all that followed was a sequence of bitter recriminations, that would rumble on for years.

CHAPTER THIRTEEN

BLUECO IS THE COLOUR

Boehly regarded his consortium being named Chelsea's preferred bidder as just another step on the journey – not due to any indifference but rather thanks to his awareness of the magnitude of the task still ahead in order to become the Blues' new owners. So when the call had come from Chelsea's executive and the selling team to inform Boehly and Clearlake that they had been chosen ahead of all other bidders, there was no celebration, just a few words of appreciation and thanks, due respect and reverence to the process up to that point – and then an immediate refocus on what was to follow.

From Bruce Buck and Marina Granovskaia's perspective, however, the moment they and Raine selected the Boehly–Clearlake consortium as the preferred option, everything changed. From Roman Abramovich putting Chelsea up for sale publicly on 2 March right up until the phone call to Boehly–Clearlake to install them as preferred bidders on 29 April, the power dynamic had been entirely on the side of the selling group. Even in the unique scenario of the first ever distressed sale of such an elite sports organisation, the Chelsea executive and Raine Group still held sway.

But from 280 expressions of interest, via fifty serious bids, now

the sellers were left with one consortium. For weeks, Buck, Granovskaia, Joe Ravitch and his partner Colin Neville had been inundated with calls from desperate bidders determined to find any
edge, now there were no more calls – only hard negotiating on the
very specific, ultra-detailed terms of the sale contract itself. And if
the Boehly–Clearlake group were suddenly to walk away from the
table, if some course of events, however unlikely, would lead them
to wash their hands of the entire process, Chelsea's future could
still be plunged back into doubt. Similarly, if the Boehly–Clearlake
group were to make an egregious late demand, Chelsea and Raine
would have precious little option to refuse.

Under the circumstances of a deal with no external pressures and
no enforced deadlines, the sellers always retain the prerogative to
walk away at any stage, either to call the entire thing off or to return
to a previously interested party and try to resume negotiations.
Even though the disappointed final bidders Broughton and Pagliuca had vowed they would step into the breach should any snags
arise, Chelsea and Raine were acutely aware that time was not on
their side to that effect.

The selling representatives and the buyers now had less than a
month to strike the terms of the deal, sign the contracts – and then
satisfy the requirements and regulations of a slew of government
departments, official authorities and organisational hierarchies.
Buck and Granovskaia had always known how the dynamics would
shift, but facing up to that reversal of power was something else entirely: the Chelsea pair knew they had to tread extremely carefully
in order to secure the very best deal, one that would satisfy the government, accrue the largest possible donation for the foundation
and safeguard the club's future and also its fans.

Buck had casually mentioned in passing to civil servants early on in the process that some slack on the deadline for the deal would be bound to ease the process enormously, at which point he was met immediately with a firm response that no extensions would even be considered. The deadline was 31 May or bust, literally, as the government seemed prepared to let Chelsea fail should that hard cut-off point not be met.

Almost the very moment the Boehly–Clearlake consortium had been handed preferred bidder status, all parties still involved in brokering the sale convened once more at Stamford Bridge, this time determined to work around the clock until contracts were not just drafted and thrashed out but also signed. While publicly Sir Jim Ratcliffe was still agitating to be recruited into the Chelsea sale process, behind the scenes, the bidding phase was well and truly over. Instead, the key players in the Boehly–Clearlake consortium settled in for gruelling sessions with the selling delegation, lawyers accompanying both sides in what became day and night summits with more than twenty people sat around a boardroom table, painstakingly examining the draft agreement documents line by line.

The round-the-clock negotiations stretched a full seven days and more, as all involved stuck to their task with impressive focus, up to and sometimes beyond twenty hours a day. Meals were either taken on the run in brief comfort breaks or foregone. And what should have been a chance to sleep at night became chance only to return home or to a hotel for little more than a nap, followed by a shower, a change of clothes and a quick hop back to Stamford Bridge.

The time pressure, the sleep deprivation and the rising stressors across the board meant that tensions were always heightened, even though all parties were extremely motivated to rattle through in one week what ought to have been carried out across the space of at least a fortnight. Chelsea's men's fixture list was at least one element where pressure was eased rather than raised in that most crucial of weeks, though, given the Blues were twice on the road, at Manchester United and then Everton. While Thomas Tuchel and his team's fortunes were dented by the 1–1 draw at Old Trafford with United on 28 April and, worse, the 1–0 defeat by Everton at Goodison Park three days later, the hefty group of people thrashing out the Chelsea sale documents were relieved not to have to conduct those negotiations while also tiptoeing around one or even two home matches.

• • •

The palpable relief was etched all over Todd Boehly's face, the fatigue and stresses of the marathon contract negotiations writ large as he posed for perhaps his first picture as pending Chelsea owner. As the clocked ticked past 11 p.m. on Friday 6 May 2022 outside Stamford Bridge, three Blues supporters bumped into Boehly and part of his delegation that had been thrashing out the terms of their purchase of the club. Shattered but happy, Boehly and his colleagues had been able to end the week by striking terms on the deal to end all deals.

Chelsea fan Darren Lavery and friends had just been out for dinner when they happened upon Boehly, who was accompanied by his Eldridge co-founder and general counsel Duncan Bagshaw and Adams Miller, another lawyer from his investment firm. Former Chancellor and Boehly–Clearlake bid adviser George Osborne was there too, and the group happily posed for a picture, with Boehly himself taking the time for a quick chat with Lavery and his pals.

The relief on Boehly's face caught on camera in that snap, which would quickly find its way onto social media, told the full story. The terms of the deal had been signed and sealed between Abramovich and his representatives, Raine and the buyers. That raft of regulatory agreements with a host of other agencies would still await, but here at least was one of the most pivotal pieces slotted into the jigsaw, and in a perfect fit. For one more day at least, the constant threat of a deal tanking and Chelsea slipping into receivership had been averted, which allowed Boehly, casually dressed in zip-through hoodie, chinos and trainers, a moment's pause before redoubling efforts to drive the deal across every final line.

The significance of that picture stretched well beyond simply representing the first shot of Boehly as the impending new Chelsea owner too; it also acted as the sum total of his celebration at completing terms on the record £4.25 billion transaction. No big bash, no celebratory dinner, not even a moment of quiet contemplation – just a picture with some rightly excited supporters, and then Boehly and partners jumped straight back into the mountain of work that still lay in store.

In a picture with a stranger, though, lay a fleeting parallel with the very start of the Roman Abramovich era. Some 226 months earlier, Abramovich and his colleagues had fallen about in hysterics when a member of the public had asked for a picture but specifically of just himself in front of Stamford Bridge. After Abramovich had posed with the member of the public, the ultra-polite tourist had then asked if the group could take one of him on his own in front of the stadium. Back in July 2003, that stranger had no idea he had bagged himself one of the first pictures with Chelsea's new owner.

In the nineteen-year gap between members of the public grabbing spur-of-the-moment pictures with Chelsea owners from two eras, the pace of change had been as relentless at Stamford Bridge as it had in the wider world. Chelsea had lifted twenty-one trophies, while mobile phones had come on in lightyears, from the 2007 launch of the first iPhone to everyone having a micro-PC in their pocket. So when Chelsea fan Lavery asked for that picture on 6 May 2022, there was no confusion or comedy mix-up: he knew exactly who he was asking and why. From one snapshot of hope and excitement at the start of a new era to another – but this time the evidence would be instantly uploaded to social media.

• • •

That same night, once all the terms had been agreed and all the contracts signed, Joe Ravitch and Colin Neville led their ten Raine Group colleagues out onto the middle of the pitch at Stamford Bridge. Exhausted, exhilarated, wired and ultimately winning, Ravitch, Neville and company had just brokered the biggest sports team sale in history. Even though the governmental and regulatory approvals were still required, Ravitch and Neville felt the magnitude of the deal, and the moment of its completion, deserved to be duly noted.

The dozen Raine staff gathered together for a selfie with a difference on the Stamford Bridge turf in the deserted ground late at night, marking the occasion and immediately wondering quite what set of unprecedented events would be waiting around the next corner. It is the floodlights and stadium glare set against the pitch black that somehow contrast and combine to hand night matches an extra magical edge, not just in football but in sports the world over. Perhaps it is the metaphoric feeling of hope generated by beams of light bursting out of the darkness, or maybe it is just the mundane realisation that making the effort to get out to watch your team in the cold, often wet, of night deserves greater than usual reward.

Whether for the poetry or the prose, standing under stadium lights will for ever invoke the strongest of feelings and responses.

And so it proved for Ravitch, Neville and the rest of the Raine crew, who found themselves unusually emotional amid a setting to remember. While they soaked up the atmosphere, and the quiet, they all knew they had just emerged from the most challenging elements of the deal of a lifetime. While big issues had still to be ironed out, Raine's most vital role was complete. In a matter of weeks, all things being equal, the Boehly–Clearlake group would own Chelsea, and they would be the ones with the keys to the Stamford Bridge kingdom, making the decisions on exactly who could wander out to the middle of that pitch and take a late-night selfie. In the middle of the night on 6 May 2022, however, it was the investment bankers from Raine who had the privilege of marking their place in sporting administrative history with a snapshot of their own, and definitely one to frame for the office.

• • •

In the small hours of Sunday 7 May, Chelsea published official confirmation of the Boehly–Clearlake deal on the club's website. After a week of non-stop negotiating, no one involved wanted to wait any longer to disseminate the breakthrough. The statement catalogued Boehly, Clearlake Capital, Mark Walter and Hansjörg Wyss as the partners who would buy the Blues from Abramovich, in that record £4.25 billion deal. Later that morning, supporters waking up and hoping for a win over Wolves in the Premier League clash at Stamford Bridge were handed an immediate scrap of good news when clocking the statement.

If the shock announcement of Abramovich's sale had caught the Chelsea fans cold at that fifth-round FA Cup tie at Luton on the night of 2 March, this anticipated breakthrough generated both relief for a club finally in the grip of a transfer of ownership and further wistful sadness at the necessary end of such a glittering era.

'Chelsea Football Club can confirm that terms have been agreed for a new ownership group, led by Todd Boehly, Clearlake Capital, Mark Walter and Hansjörg Wyss, to acquire the club,' read the Chelsea statement.

Of the total investment being made, £2.5 billion will be applied to purchase the shares in the club, and such proceeds will be deposited into a frozen UK bank account with the intention to donate 100 per cent to charitable causes as confirmed by Roman Abramovich. UK government approval will be required for the proceeds to be transferred from the frozen UK bank account. In addition the proposed new owners will commit £1.75 billion in further investment for the benefit of the club. This includes investments in Stamford Bridge, the academy, the women's team and Kingsmeadow and continued funding for the Chelsea Foundation. The sale is expected to be complete in late May subject to all necessary regulatory approvals. More details will be provided at that time.

Confirmation of the Boehly–Clearlake deal transformed the Stamford Bridge atmosphere that afternoon, and the addition of bright sunshine helped foster a feeling more readily associated with the start of a season than the Blues' reality of inching towards the campaign's close. Refreshed and reinvigorated by a good night's sleep at last, Boehly was in the stands and looking far more energised than he had in that social media snap from the night before. Dressed casually again, but this time with a crisper cut to his cloth, he had donned a pair of aviator sunglasses and drank in the Premier League atmosphere while sipping a cup of coffee.

Tuchel's side had slipped into a sticky patch of results, with two defeats, one draw and one win in their previous four league matches, but the buoyant mood appeared to rub off on the hosts, and especially Romelu Lukaku, making his first league start in three months. The Belgium hitman scored twice before the hour for his first Chelsea goals of the calendar year – and after an indifferent run, here, to sit alongside the hope of incoming owners, was a potential upturn in form for the club's £97.5 million record signing.

Just when Chelsea were primed to turn their dominance into total control, however, the hosts slipped off the pace and let Wolves back into the match. Francisco Trincão conjured a fine goal to halve the visitors' deficit, and then at the death, England defender Conor Coady headed in an added-time equaliser. The 2–2 draw denied Chelsea the chance to seal their top-four finish and Champions League qualification, but the point gained did keep them on course to end up in third place.

After the match, Tuchel welcomed the 'good news' of the ownership deal, then revealed he had been encouraged by record recruit Lukaku's performance, insisting the Belgium striker would be a pivotal player for the long term. Finally able to take a ninety-minute breather and enjoy the match, Boehly for his part had been spotted alongside his legal colleagues from Eldridge, then later talking with a smiling Chelsea chairman Bruce Buck. Having relished the turbulent nature of the match, though, Boehly was quickly back to work alongside his other bid partners as the daunting task of signing off government and regulatory approvals came squarely into view.

• • •

While Abramovich's staff and Chelsea's top executives moved straight from negotiating the deal contracts with Boehly–Clearlake to interacting with the government and other official bodies, the chiefs of the buying consortium mirrored those processes. For the Clearlake duo particularly, the overriding feeling remained that the stakes could not be raised any higher: completing the deal documents with the sellers in some respects only ushered in an even more delicate and difficult process. Settling on the mechanisms by which the Boehly–Clearlake consortium would actually pay the funds for Chelsea proved a tricky task for all involved, and the Chelsea buyers were sympathetic to the Treasury and OFSI's trials and tribulations of determining exactly which method would be best employed. Potentially as long as a week's grace would be required to ensure that the funds could be moved safely before the 31 May deadline, which left just a fortnight for Boehly–Clearlake to pass the Premier League's owners' and directors' tests, for the government to draw up and ratify a new licence that would allow the sale mechanism to be carried out and for approvals from the likes of the EU to be secured too.

The pace of the entire process had been so relentless that even some of the world's brightest and best business people were at the end of their tether, with individuals who had built their careers on their ability to deliver results feeling they had been pushed to the limit. Ministers, civil servants and lawyers at both the Treasury and OFSI were in exactly the same boat, and so by the time the latest temporary licence was being negotiated, people on all sides were under huge duress. Staff at Clearlake found themselves embroiled in a host of situations across that tense, dramatic fortnight where, even after all the crises that had been averted along the way, it appeared that the entire sale process was on the brink of failing. People from all sides of the process were exhibiting signs of those who had gone through heavy trauma.

Representatives of the Boehly–Clearlake consortium were left to gain even higher levels of respect for the likes of Granovskaia and Buck, whom they both considered to have stepped in on a number of occasions to find solutions that headed off potential disasters at the pass. The influence and expertise of Simon Robey and George Osborne also came to the fore once more, with both acting with cool heads that helped keep the atmosphere cordial and respectful even amid the greatest of pressures.

The Boehly–Clearlake attitude to all these talks and negotiations was to be as helpful and available as they could. All the key players stayed in London for as much of the time as possible, and in most cases that meant almost the entire month of May. The buyers' flexibility and openness on the detail and procedure took a level of pressure off the shoulders of OFSI and the Treasury, with key figures in the government able to approach the many and varied problems that arose with a level of confidence in the aims and objectives of the Boehly–Clearlake consortium.

The buyers' unstinting resolve to remain open to suggestion was rooted in the genuine fear that at any point the entire edifice could collapse, at which point Chelsea would sink into receivership and the sale would be off – not postponed or delayed but cancelled. Given all parties were having to feel their way through the process of carrying out the transaction under the auspices of the sanctions, some on the Boehly–Clearlake bid team felt that there would be no way back for Chelsea from falling into administration during this crucial window.

Precious few clubs can fight back to the elite end of sport after folding under normal circumstances, but allied to the clear financial challenges, in Chelsea's unique scenario, the mechanism of lifting a sanctioned club out of administration could well have proved beyond the wit of all concerned. The only way out was through, and the buying group simply made themselves as amenable as possible in a bid to make it to the other end as quickly as they could.

• • •

Once documents were signed with the Premier League, the UK government, the Portuguese government and therefore the EU, the Boehly–Clearlake consortium ratified the final paperwork with Chelsea on the evening of 27 May. Just four days shy of the government's cut-off point for completion, there was no time to lose as all the representatives who had spent so much time in the process added their signatures to the last official documents. The next morning, on 28 May, the club released a statement to confirm that, barring government announcements, the Chelsea sale was over. 'Chelsea Football Club can confirm that a final and definitive agreement was entered into last night to sell the club to the Todd Boehly–Clearlake Capital consortium,' read the briefest of club statements. The new owners would run the club under the umbrella holding company name of BlueCo, with supporters citing spotting information lodged with Companies House as one of the ways in which Chelsea's sea change at the top was starting to sink in.

Pleased and relieved that the sale process was at an end, and hopeful that Boehly–Clearlake would prove suitable guardians of the club, Abramovich marked the end of his nineteen years of Chelsea ownership with a statement of his own. 'As I hand over Chelsea to its new custodians, I would like to wish them the best of success, both on and off the pitch,' said the departing owner. 'It has been an honour of a lifetime to be a part of this club – I would like to thank all the club's past and current players, staff and of course fans for these incredible years.'

If he had retired from frontline business when he bought Chelsea in 2003 and then promptly transformed both the Blues and British football, here, Abramovich was in effect hanging up his metaphorical ownership boots. Bruce Buck came away from Stamford Bridge after those final documents were signed on 27 May still beset by mixed feelings. The long-serving Chelsea chairman knew only too well that there was no choice in the matter over the club's sale and that he and the other executives had carried out Abramovich's wishes across a fraught and relentless process. But even amid the wider context of the stark realities of the war and its gruesome consequences, there was still space to lament the end of an era.

Boehly again found himself with precious little chance to reflect or even raise a glass to winning the race for Chelsea and meeting all the political and legislative requirements. Applying his usual approach to the business world, he simply shifted his focus to what was next, and that just so happened to be a pivotal summer of building and preparing.

The Clearlake representatives were struck by a deep appreciation of the magnitude of the task they had inherited in being passed the custodianship of a club founded all the way back in 1905. Eghbali and Feliciano considered that Abramovich could be regarded as perhaps the most influential figure in the entirety of the club's rich history, and the owner who had forced a paradigm shift in the entire sport. The Clearlake organisation considered the challenge of following Abramovich as akin to that of trying to step into the shoes of Babe Ruth in the world of baseball, and with such a deep respect for the outgoing leadership, the determination was to show their admiration and gratitude by creating a new era of lasting stability and success.

· · ·

One day shy of the 31 May deadline, when Chelsea's temporary operating licence would expire, the UK government issued a 'unilateral declaration' that finally signalled the end of the Stamford Bridge club's sale. The 371-word statement allowed Chelsea to breathe again, and for the Boehly–Clearlake era to begin in earnest. The technical language underscored the depth of detail the government deemed necessary, both to allow the sale to be transacted under Abramovich's sanctions and to continue their determined efforts to ensure that the funds would not somehow be misappropriated.

'If the transaction is licensed and takes place, all proceeds from the sale will be held in a bank account in the United Kingdom, which will be frozen in accordance with the Russia Regulations,' read the government declaration.

The United Kingdom will ensure that Roman Abramovich does not benefit from the sale of Chelsea Football Club in any way, and that the proceeds of such a sale are used for humanitarian purposes in Ukraine. Accordingly, the Treasury will not issue a licence which enables any part of the proceeds from a sale to be used in a way which would directly or indirectly benefit Roman Abramovich or any other designated person. Furthermore, the Treasury will only issue a licence which ensures that such proceeds are used for exclusively humanitarian purposes in Ukraine.

The United Kingdom will work closely with the Portuguese government and the European Commission when considering an
application for such a licence and the destination of the proceeds.

The document that was published was left unattributed, where-
as the version that was sent to all parties involved in the sale was
signed by the MP John Glen, the Economic Secretary to the Treasury. While the publication of the document sparked relief and hope
among all Chelsea fans for the future, and no little reflection on the
official, cast-iron end of the Abramovich era, the specific wording
raised another new problem, not with the sale or the transaction
process but instead with plans for the independent humanitarian
aid foundation.

The government's unilateral declaration pledged that the humanitarian foundation would only be given the green light under the
specific terms that 'proceeds are used for exclusively humanitarian
purposes in Ukraine'. With the deployment of one two-letter prepo-
sition, the government had laid out a barrier that would remain immovable for years to come. Abramovich's camp had always insisted
that the government's own document that licensed the Chelsea sale,
issued on 24 May and updated on 25 and 27 May, had not specified
that the foundation must only deploy funds within Ukraine, instead
citing simply that the foundation would support 'all victims of the
conflict in Ukraine, and its consequences'. The deed of undertaking for the foundation, signed by both Abramovich and Eugene
Tenenbaum, as a director of Chelsea holding company Fordstam,
was said to have stated: 'The initial focus of this foundation will be
on Ukraine and those affected by this conflict, but given the size of
funding from the sale of the club, it is likely to expand into supporting victims of conflict worldwide.'

The difference was semantic, but stark, and there was no error in the government's 30 May unilateral declaration: the Tory administration was determined that the proceeds from the Chelsea sale would only be spent within Ukraine. The government considered this was the only means to ensure with absolute certainty that Abramovich would not benefit in any way from the Chelsea sale, as per the sanctions regulations, and particularly that none of the sale proceeds could possibly find their way back to him through potentially circuitous routes.

Such intimations had stung Mike Penrose, the former head of Unicef UK, who was poised to launch the humanitarian foundation on receipt of the green light. Penrose felt his thirty-year humanitarianism career marked him out as more than trustworthy enough to ensure the money be deployed correctly, but he also saw precious little merit or efficacy in consigning the £2.5 billion funds to being spent exclusively in Ukraine – especially during the conflict. The sheer scale of the funds meant the foundation could transform global aid, but only if the government would allow the independent body to apportion funding wherever required.

Abramovich and his staff were stunned by what quickly developed into an entrenched impasse with the government. He had stated from the outset that he wanted the funds to be put to the best and most humanitarian use. After all, he had been exploring a significant humanitarian donation since 2021, and ever since the outbreak of war he believed the need for such a move had vastly increased.

However, no amount of dialogue, meetings or discussions between Abramovich and his staff, the UK government and Penrose could lead to a thawing of the position on either side. The £2.5 billion proceeds of the Chelsea sale were quickly deposited into the frozen Fordstam account at Barclays Bank, and a new licence would be required for the money to be released and the foundation to be incorporated. The account holding the Chelsea sale money might have been frozen, but the atmosphere between Abramovich's camp and the UK government was icier still.

• • •

The first call that Boehly fielded on Chelsea after his consortium had bought the club came from representatives of Romelu Lukaku, insisting that the Belgium striker would not stay at Stamford Bridge under any circumstances. The Eldridge Industries boss had always known that a baptism of fire would await the new Chelsea owners, and when the call on Lukaku came, on day one in the Stamford Bridge hotseat, the Boehly–Clearlake group was plunged straight into the very thick of the Blues' most challenging operating issues.

Chelsea's £97.5 million club record signing from the previous summer, Lukaku had mustered just eight goals in twenty-six Premier League appearances in an underwhelming start to his second career stint with the Blues. Viewed as the missing piece of the jigsaw that could elevate the 2021 Chelsea Champions League winners into serious Premier League contenders, Lukaku had instead spent the season at Stamford Bridge struggling for form and riling Tuchel with the perceived hot and cold nature of his attitude. Even though Lukaku had drawn angry protests from Inter Milan supporters when he quit the Serie A club for Chelsea a year earlier, the Belgium striker was still set on a return to the Nerazzurri. By the end of June, a season-long loan deal with Inter had been brokered and announced, but the immediacy and decisiveness of Lukaku's insistence he would not stay at Chelsea had left the new owners on notice about the speed and ferocity of the football administration world they suddenly inhabited.

Any and all breathing space evaporated as the new ownership group had to negotiate both the summer transfer window and the pre-season tour to Los Angeles, where a number of logistical problems beset the men's first team and left manager Tuchel short on patience. Back at Stamford Bridge, the new owners also found themselves having to handle a far wider turnover of senior staff than initially anticipated. When all the terms on the sale had been signed on 7 May, the Boehly–Clearlake bosses had fully expected to have Bruce Buck, Marina Granovskaia and Petr Čech on board for the following season.

The initial plan was to transition across with the senior executive set-up from the Abramovich era, to retain as much continuity and market understanding as possible, before easing through any potential changes in the fullness of time. During the final three weeks of May, however, senior government figures had expressed in no uncertain terms behind the scenes in private conversations that there were those in the Westminster corridors of power who might potentially look particularly unfavourably on a change of Chelsea ownership that did not conduct a complete cleaning of house at the top of the structure. As Boehly, Eghbali and Feliciano began to get to grips with the challenges of Premier League ownership, they were confronted by a host of hands-on realities that required rapid, decisive responses. As Boehly and Eghbali dug into the details of talks with Buck, Granovskaia and Čech, looking closely at the composition of their executive team for the summer of 2022, football's light-speed pace of change was in full effect once again.

CHAPTER FOURTEEN

WHAT NEXT?

The Boehly–Clearlake consortium had been led to the realisation across the course of May that the fittings, as well as the fixtures, would have to be changed at Chelsea. The best-case scenario was for a protracted handover in which Roman Abramovich's top Chelsea executive team would remain in place and help achieve a smooth transition from one era to another.

Instead, as May turned to June in 2022, Todd Boehly and Behdad Eghbali hardly had their feet under the Stamford Bridge boardroom table as co-controlling owners when they felt they had to make sweeping personnel changes. If the whisperings from an establishment level had suggested, discreetly but firmly, that the new Chelsea owners carry out a full changing of the guard, the consortium felt the prudent course was to follow the hints.

By the tail-end of May, extended talks between the new owners and director Marina Granovskaia and chairman Bruce Buck had failed to discover any suitable middle-ground option for the influential, experienced pair to stay at the Stamford Bridge helm. On 20 June, Chelsea announced that Buck would end his nineteen years as Blues chairman by the end of the month. 'Now is the right time to step down and let new ownership build on the strong foundations we have in place,' said Buck, who would at least continue with the club in a senior advisory role. 'The owners have a compelling vision for Chelsea's future, and I look forward to helping them achieve it in this new role alongside our incredible staff, players, coaches and supporters. I am proud to have helped Chelsea realise great success on the pitch and make a positive impact in the community.'

Ever-present in the Abramovich era, Buck had numbered among a small nucleus of existing Chelsea supporters who had joined the Stamford Bridge set-up when the club had been bought from Ken Bates in July 2003. Buck's desire to remain as Chelsea chairman after Abramovich's sale had carried bearing in the sale process, and the Boehly–Clearlake consortium had been supportive of that plan. The gradual change of tack across May and into June, driven largely by what were understood to be perceptions in government about relationships with prior ownership, had changed the situation not just for the executives but also for the club and its owners. Now the Blues needed a new chairman, on a far quicker timescale than ever anticipated. The upshot of quick deliberations among the consortium was that Boehly should fill the breach. Two days after the public release of Buck's impending departure, the hastily coordinated switch was completed, with Chelsea confirming Boehly's installation as the new Stamford Bridge chairman.

'As custodians of Chelsea FC, we now begin executing our long-term vision and plan for the club, creating an outstanding experience for its passionate, loyal fans and continuing to challenge for top honours in line with Chelsea FC's decorated history,' said Boehly in a statement on 22 June. 'Working together, side by side, we are firmly committed to winning, both on and off the pitch. For us, that effort has begun.'

At the same time, Chelsea announced the exit of Granovskaia, another figure who had been part of the Abramovich era from start to finish. The senior director had been open to staying at Chelsea in the long term after the change of ownership but had wanted to wait to see the composition of any new role in the Boehly–Clearlake set-up. As her own talks had progressed with the new owners, she had ended up offering to stay on across the summer's crucial transfer window and continue to direct the club's transfer operations, but the club's options were limited. In the end, neither party could quite thrash out how a new-look relationship might work out in practice, despite strong determination on both sides in principle. Granovskaia pledged to remain available to help with transfers across the summer window, but this had morphed instead into an ad hoc arrangement.

As the sale process had unfolded, technical director Čech had been one of the key figures in helping managers Thomas Tuchel and Emma Hayes support the players to maintain a steadfast focus amid all the worries, fears and distractions. Čech was left particularly proud of Chelsea's men's team for finishing third and securing Champions League qualification, allied to reaching both domestic cup finals and running Real Madrid all the way in Europe. The former Blues goalkeeper had worked tirelessly to help keep the men's squad sufficiently motivated, calm and tight-knit in order to put fears for the club's very future to one side and deliver on the field. Hayes's women's team, meanwhile, had retained their WSL title and swiped the Women's FA Cup crown too, in another remarkable show of strength. The performance of the first teams was crucial to Chelsea managing to secure the highest possible sale price, and both the men and the women managed to deliver under the greatest of pressures.

As the Boehly–Clearlake consortium heads were settling into their new Stamford Bridge surroundings, Čech took it upon himself to make the decision to relinquish his role and leave the club. In the end, the fact that he had only ever experienced a Chelsea owned and run by Roman Abramovich settled his decision to leave: Čech felt the new owners deserved the right to shape the club their way, and given his long association with the existing practices, he thought stepping away would be to everyone's benefit.

Čech's departure was confirmed in a club press release on 27 June in which he said:

It has been a huge privilege to perform this role at Chelsea for the past three years. With the club under new ownership, I feel now is the right time for me to step aside. I am pleased that the club is now in an excellent position with the new owners, and I am confident of its future success both on and off the pitch.

Boehly wished Čech well for the future, saying, 'Petr is an important member of the Chelsea family. We understand his decision to step away and thank him for his contributions as an advisor and his commitment to the club and to our community. We wish him the best.'

As three of the most senior pillars in Abramovich's final off-field structure at Chelsea, Granovskaia, Buck and Čech would in effect be leaving together, further cementing the end of an era and also leaving a significant void that the new ownership group had to find a way to fill, and fast.

For Buck, the immediate transition from Abramovich to Boehly–Clearlake had also been underscored by the relentlessness of the never-ending football cycle. The transfer window opened in early

June and the new owners had no time to waste to rebuild a squad that had been dented by the three months under sanctions when no players could be bought or sold and no new contracts negotiated or awarded. When Buck talked with the new owners about the specifics of an adapted role, he could not quite square away where or how exactly he would fit. Like Čech, he fully accepted that the new owners had the entire right and justification to take the club in a new direction.

And so, after nineteen years and as many major trophies, with countless experiences that money could not buy, from turning from supporter to chairman, to being on hand when the Blues twice lifted the Champions League trophy, Buck packed up the contents of his Stamford Bridge office into several boxes and walked them down to the entrance. He backed up his car, loaded his belongings and, for the last time, completed the short drive home from work. Buck could not help but reminisce as he completed that commute for the final time, for a role that had always been so much more than just a job. The mixed emotions washed over him again, the sadness and the memories of a lifetime, but overall, just as Granovskaia and Čech found themselves feeling too, Buck had relished his role at Chelsea so much that he simply did not want it to end.

Buck had always held onto the two Chelsea season tickets he had first bought back in 1989, keeping the same seats unbroken through all that time. In the immediate aftermath of leaving the Blues, he opted not to return as a supporter in the short term, as he adapted to life after his chairmanship. By February 2025, he still had the season tickets, and although he still had not returned to attend a match, he remained totally confident that that day would not be far away.

•   •   •

From the moment Boehly stepped into the Chelsea hotseat, the clock was ticking on the start of the new season. That summer was just as breathless for the new Chelsea chairman as the sale process had been, and he spent it criss-crossing Europe to meet agents, build contacts and strike deals for new recruits – because he had to step into the breach as interim sporting director. Chelsea had a clutch of options for their long-term sporting directors, but gardening leave thwarted them at every turn, so whichever direction they took, there would be a protracted wait for off-field reinforcements.

Allied to fighting fires like pre-season tour training facilities that were not up to scratch, Boehly and Clearlake quickly opened the coffers to refresh the Blues squad. Some £225 million was shelled out by the September close of that window, the headline arrivals being England wing Raheem Sterling, Leicester centre-back Wesley Fofana, Brighton full-back Marc Cucurella, Napoli defender Kalidou Koulibaly and Barcelona striker Pierre-Emerick Aubameyang. Spain speedster Cucurella had arrived on a six-year contract while highly regarded defender Fofana was handed seven years. Boehly's long-term contract plan would not gain widespread media coverage until Mykhailo Mudryk signed an eight-and-a-half-year deal in January 2023, but extended contracts were on the table from the off in the Boehly–Clearlake set-up.

The long-mooted theory is that the extended deals would allow Chelsea to make big outlays and still meet Premier League spending limits, with a player's transfer fee spread across the length of their contract, or amortised, when analysed for the league regulations. The reported £55 million spent on Cucurella would break down to slightly north of £9.1 million per season across his six-year deal, while the £70 million for Fofana would level out at £10 million for each of his seven-year Chelsea commitment. The commentary across Chelsea's new ownership has claimed Boehly and Clearlake attempted to disrupt the market with something of a transfer spending loophole. But when it came to long-term contracts, Boehly and Eghbali had not even been aiming to capitalise chiefly on amortisation. In a commitment to structuring the best player contracts for the club, they were drawing from broad business experiences across the varied industries in which they were invested, including music.

In the music industry, if an artist signed a four-album deal with a record label, after two albums it would be common for both parties to start talks exploring whether the existing arrangements could be extended; as Boehly had observed, a four-album deal would only truly hold good for two albums. While amortisation became a fringe benefit, Boehly and Eghbali had initially been looking for ways to create stability in the Chelsea squad and continuity for the club's future. The new Chelsea owners quickly became of the mind that in a player's five-year contract, after three years, that player will most likely start to seek talks on a new deal, as well as receiving subtle overtures from rival clubs. So a five-year contract in effect becomes almost a three-year deal, a seven-year contract a five-year commitment, and so on.

Chelsea had just been stung by Toni Rüdiger joining Real Madrid on a free transfer and Andreas Christensen heading to Barcelona for nothing too, with both players' Blues contracts expiring while the club was sanctioned and the previous regime powerless to offer new deals. The new Stamford Bridge owners were determined not to fall prey to a similar situation in future.

The 2022–23 season kicked off with the transfer window still open and Chelsea immersed in a large number of ins and outs, many on loan. Boehly had relished the Premier League opening 1–0 win at Everton on 6 August for its milestone nature, but he found himself fully exposed to all the fire and fury of the English top flight just one weekend later. Whatever the trials and tribulations of running an elite football club, the transfixing nature of the role was laid bare when Chelsea hosted city rivals Tottenham at a rocking Stamford Bridge. Summer signings Cucurella and Koulibaly combined, as the latter volleyed home to put the Blues 1–0 up before Pierre-Emile Højbjerg levelled for the visitors.

Boehly marvelled at the derby day intensity as Chelsea railed against Rodrigo Bentancur going unpunished for a challenge on Kai Havertz. Managers Thomas Tuchel and Antonio Conte were both booked for clashing on the touchline over the incident, as neither team tried to hide their sporting hatred of the other. Reece James thought he had won the game for the Blues when latching onto Sterling's pass and finding the net, which led Tuchel to sprint past Conte in an inflammatory celebration on the touchline. But Harry Kane headed in from Ivan Perišić's corner after seven minutes of added time to swipe Spurs a controversial 2–2 draw, and one that sparked further fury.

Chelsea were incensed that Cristian Romero was not punished for pulling down Cucurella by his hair as the hosts had defended a corner. From the very next corner, Spurs levelled, and at the final whistle there was bedlam on the pitch as the two managers' customary post-match handshake turned overly aggressive. Walking past each other and hardly making eye contact despite shaking hands, neither man refused to let go, and an immediate fracas saw both benches pile in. Referee Anthony Taylor sent off both men once tempers had returned to something approaching level. In the post-match press conference, Tuchel admitted feeling that it might be prudent for Taylor not to referee Chelsea again, in an unsubtle reference to long-running grievances held by Blues supporters against the official.

Beyond the aggravation in the clash and the frustration of the result, Boehly looked on knowing fully that this was why he had been so determined that his candidacy for the club had to prove successful. Although he had fallen in love with football before any other sport, his upbringing in the US meant he had not so often been exposed to the raw, visceral nature of something like a London derby. As he tried to regain his composure and gather his bearings after the final whistle of that pulsating 2–2 draw, Boehly was left with the overwhelming sense of vindication for having chased down the Chelsea ownership – and the overriding desire to install the Blues at the game's very summit for the long term.

• • •

The end of Roman Abramovich's Chelsea ownership took on an abstract air for the Russian-Israeli billionaire, such was his enforced detachment from the sale process. The UK government sanctions against him meant that his staff had to represent him in the Chelsea sale, so he was always several steps removed from the entire saga. As soon as Russia had invaded Ukraine at the end of February, however, he had dropped all focus on Chelsea and transferred his full efforts towards attempting to facilitate peace talks between the two sides.

As the conflict raged on, while the Boehly–Clearlake consortium were trying to find their bearings and their feet at Stamford Bridge, Abramovich continued his discreet mission trying to help foster peace talks, looking also for other initiatives that might ease certain elements of the war or its repercussions. The chances of a peace accord slowly receded after the early hopes of the Istanbul Communiqué of late March, but several pressing problems occurred across the second half of 2022 in which Abramovich was prepared to lend whatever support he could.

Russia's blockade of Ukrainian ports had stopped almost all grain exports, which not only applied a chokehold within the country itself but also threatened to lead to a world food shortage given the sheer amount of product shipped out in times of peace. Sanctions were preventing grain and fertiliser being exported from Russia at the same time, leading to even greater concerns about food shortages and rising prices.

By early July, the situation had become so entrenched that only extended sit-down talks, again in Istanbul and hosted by President Erdoğan, would stand any chance of Russia and Ukraine reaching some kind of neutrality zone or pact that could see the resumption of grain exports.

Again, Abramovich made himself available for any facilitative function required, and he was once more thought to have been influential in helping foster key meetings that would ultimately steer towards central summit negotiations in Istanbul. Several rounds of talks in Turkey came and went across a number of weeks before finally, on 22 July, both Russia and Ukraine signed the Black Sea grain deal that would lead to the resumption of vital exports. António Guterres, the UN Secretary General, hailed the agreement as 'a beacon of hope on the Black Sea' that would 'bridge the global food supply gap and reduce the pressure on food prices'.

President Erdoğan, again the host of key talks between the warring nations, called again for further efforts towards peace, while acknowledging that the grain deal was a significant and vital breakthrough. 'This joint step we're taking in Istanbul together with Russia and Ukraine will be a new turning point that will revive hopes for peace, this is my sincere hope,' he said.

Abramovich continued going about his new business, which was focused predominantly on ways in which he could aid the wider work towards peace, however entrenched the war was becoming. Beyond frustrations that the Chelsea sale funds continued to languish in the frozen UK bank account and did not look any closer to being freed in order to launch the humanitarian aid foundation, Abramovich's considerations of Britain were relatively rare.

But then, without prior notice or warning, on 23 August, the details of the UK's sanctions designation against him were altered markedly. As there was no communication with the Abramovich camp from any government officials, or any other body for that matter, no explanation for the changes was forthcoming. The statement of reasons in the official public documentation of the UK sanctions against Abramovich was condensed, with a number of detailed allegations removed, including many of the claims that Abramovich had always vehemently rejected.

While the revised sanctions designation still branded Abramovich a 'pro-Kremlin oligarch' associated with Vladimir Putin, it no longer alleged that Abramovich's association with the Russian President was a close relationship dating back decades. Allegations that he had received tax breaks via that claimed association to Putin, bought and sold shares at favourable rates and received preferential treatment regarding contracts around the 2018 FIFA World Cup were all removed too. Also among the varied claims that had been removed was the allegation that Evraz PLC, in which Abramovich was invested, was 'potentially supplying steel to the Russian military which may have been used in the production of tanks'. Abramovich and his representatives have always maintained that this allegation was entirely false.

Unable to decipher any particular rhyme or reason to the significant updating of the sanctions designation, after a fashion Abramovich and his staff turned their attentions to more pressing matters, though they continued to ruminate on quite why any of the alterations were considered necessary at all, especially as the most important element had not changed – that he was still sanctioned by the UK government.

A number of independent UK sanctions law experts have interpreted the amendment to the statement of reasons as the UK government potentially attempting to strengthen their position against any possible legal challenge against or even judicial review of the sanctioning of Abramovich. Several top specialists consulted on the matter all offered the same analysis: that the removal of such allegations from the official UK statement of reasons does not mean that the UK government no longer holds those assertions; rather, that such allegations could carry an extremely difficult – and also potentially unnecessary – burden of proof. Those same independent UK sanctions experts interpreted the changes as of potential reputational benefit to Abramovich, but with clear limits as his status did not change materially given that UK sanctions were still imposed.

By September 2022, Abramovich had far more pressing matters, in the shape of yet more back-channelling and discreet facilitating. This time, there were no logistics to try to thrash out for potential peace talks, but the stakes were just as high and the climate equally delicate. Negotiations for a prisoner swap between Russia and Ukraine had appeared to make progress across September, to the point where a trade seemed a genuine possibility. A deal had somehow been puzzled together across a number of months, which involved some work behind the scenes from Abramovich, allied to vital influence and no little statecraft from Saudi Arabia, understood to have been accomplished with the express backing of the crown prince, Mohammed bin Salman. In total, ten foreign prisoners were due to be released and some 215 Ukrainian fighters were in line to be swapped for fifty-five Russian soldiers and the pro-Kremlin Ukrainian politician Viktor Medvedchuk.

Among the foreign prisoners were five British citizens who had been captured by Russia while fighting as privateers in Ukraine, explicitly against UK government warnings. After months of the British citizens being imprisoned, often moved and sometimes beaten heavily, they would later claim, eventually plans were put in place for their release. And so, on 21 September 2022, Abramovich and several of his staff travelled to Rostov, eventually arriving at an abandoned airport that was to be the venue for the release of the five British prisoners and the five other foreigners. Representatives from Saudi Arabia and Russian military personnel were on hand; all present then simply had to wait for the arrival of the prisoners.

Several trucks eventually rolled onto the tarmac and the ten prisoners, handcuffed and with bags over their heads, were walked into a building and sat together for yet another wait. Some twenty-four hours earlier, the five men had been handcuffed, their heads covered with the bags and they had been moved. After months of detainment in terrifying and grisly conditions, they all feared they were being moved in order to be executed. Stunned and confused to find themselves at an airport, though still scared, all the five men could do was wait while all the relevant delegations attempted to finalise the deal that would allow them to be set free.

The final paperwork that was required to be ratified in order for the men to be released was only signed in effect on the steps of the

Saudi aeroplane that was waiting to fly the prisoners from Russia to Riyadh. The Saudi government had agreed to facilitate the men's departure as part of the release deal. While all the paperwork was being signed, a Saudi medical team examined the prisoners, making sure they were physically fit to fly. As soon as representatives from all sides agreed everything was in order, the men were led onto the plane.

John Harding, Shaun Pinner, Aiden Aslin, Dylan Healy and Andrew Hill could hardly gain any kind of handle on what was happening, but quickly the plane was up in the air, bound for Saudi Arabia, with Abramovich on board as well. The men were quick to thank their rescuers, and amid the conversation, Pinner remarked, 'You look like Roman Abramovich,' to which the former Chelsea owner replied, 'That's because I am him, sir.' The snap laughter from the entire group only cemented the relief and gratitude that those five men felt on their new-found freedom and safety. The freed prisoners of war travelled to Riyadh before being examined by more Saudi medics and then put on a flight to Heathrow to go home.

Back in the safety of the UK, Harding told *The Sun* how the five men had been stunned when they realised it was actually Abramovich on their flight. 'He's well respected by Ukrainians and massively by us now too, he's done a hell of a lot for us and we couldn't thank him enough. He was a sound bloke, a really lovely guy. We absolutely love him and I'm so grateful for his efforts.'

• • •

The more the new Chelsea owners chased stability and direction, the more they felt the club required comprehensive change. Manager Thomas Tuchel never really recovered his standing after airing his frustrations around the chaotic pre-season tour in the US, and his desire to be left largely to his own coaching devices did not endear the no-nonsense German to the new hierarchy. Where the Abramovich set-up, which had required coaches to operate with a fair amount of autonomy, had suited Tuchel perfectly, the Boehly–Clearlake regime demanded far more contact time as the project was lifted off the ground. These extra meetings drove Tuchel to distraction, which in turn agitated the owners. The net result proved that after a 100-day review of the operation, Tuchel was sacked. Damaging Premier League defeats at Leeds and Southampton had inflamed the situation and then a 1–0 loss to lowly Dinamo Zagreb proved the catalyst for change.

No expense was spared as the Boehly–Clearlake leadership geared up to appoint their first manager, with a reported £21 million release fee required to prise Graham Potter away from Brighton. Recruited on a five-year contract, Chelsea wanted the upwardly mobile Potter to grow with the club. On 8 September, Potter was at Chelsea's Cobham training ground to sign the paperwork and seal his switch to the Blues. Boehly and Eghbali were in attendance too, excited and energised by the coup. Tentative plans had been drawn up for an unveiling press conference late that afternoon, but as the day developed news was breaking that Queen Elizabeth II's health was in a grave condition. Any press conference plans were dismissed when the monarch's death was confirmed later that day, and the cancellation of the country's sporting programme that weekend meant Potter's Stamford Bridge arrival had to be handled in an extremely low-key manner.

Potter's installation caused a near immediate upturn in form, however, as the Blues put together a nine-game unbeaten run, which included five wins in a row and six in total. A makeover of a sharp haircut, beard trim and stylish wardrobe additions, which had Potter learning a new term in 'glow-up', appeared to indicate the ex-Brighton boss was growing into the magnitude and status of the Chelsea job. When the new-manager momentum wore off, though, and that beard trim started to grow out, Potter could not sustain the required level and results plummeted markedly, especially after the domestic break for the World Cup in Qatar. Two wins in twelve matches dragged Potter to the brink, and that was after the Blues had spent £320 million on a raft of new players in the January 2023 transfer window.

Argentina's World Cup-winning midfielder Enzo Fernández topped the money charts at £106 million, while Mykhailo Mudryk, signed from under Arsenal's noses, was not far behind at £89 million. Andrey Santos, Noni Madueke, Benoît Badiashile, David Datro Fofana and Malo Gusto were all signed permanently, with João Félix arriving on loan. The influx meant there were more players than first team changing room berths, forcing a nucleus of players to change in an overspill room.

When Chelsea sealed the Mudryk deal, thwarting rivals Arsenal for the Ukraine winger with an eleventh-hour swoop, suddenly the plan of amortisation for transfer fees became wider knowledge. The new owners continued to consider the strategy as just one part of the challenge to ensure that Chelsea could recover from the wide-ranging impact of the sanctions that had affected everything from the playing squad through to operations personnel, sporting and technical management.

Boehly and Clearlake felt they had further future-proofed the club by recruiting Paul Winstanley and Laurence Stewart as co-sporting directors, meanwhile, but less than two months after that ship-steadying move, Potter became the second Blues manager to be sacked in the season. In early April 2023, just seven months into his five-year contract, Potter was removed from the Blues hot-seat, having failed to keep up with the pace of change at Stamford Bridge or to impose his full will on the set-up. Assistant Bruno Saltor would take charge of Chelsea for four days, before Frank Lampard was drafted in for a second managerial stint, this time an interim role until the end of the season. The Blues would have four different managers in one season for the first time in their history, and Lampard's return also failed to hit the mark. Chelsea won just once and lost eight times in their eleven matches under Lampard's caretaker stewardship, slumping to a twelfth-place Premier League finish, their lowest finish in the league since 1993–94.

Chelsea's owners were still trying to bed in an all-new set-up off the field at the same time as constantly seeking the right blend on it. Former Tottenham manager Mauricio Pochettino was recruited to bring some much-craved stability to the coaching outlook and he was backed to the hilt again in terms of big-money new arrivals. By the close of the summer transfer window, Chelsea's transfer outlay under the Boehly–Clearlake ownership, which does not account for monies recouped, was reported to have hit £1 billion, spent on twenty-six players. Moises Caicedo from Brighton topped the summer 2023 money list at £115 million, with Southampton's Romeo Lavia commanding a £58 million fee and Manchester City's Cole Palmer £40 million among twelve recruits requiring significant deals.

The recruitment had finally started to take tactical shape, and then it bore tentative fruit too, with Palmer the major success story, lighting up Stamford Bridge and firing twenty-two Premier League goals in the process. Losing the League Cup final to Liverpool 1–0 after extra time and then the FA Cup semi-final 1–0 to Manchester City perhaps represented significant sliding-doors moments. Win a trophy and Pochettino could have secured himself a second season at the helm, but instead he had to battle through to the end of the term with doubts lingering on his future. Five league wins in a row to close the season had some wondering if Pochettino had finally mastered the Chelsea squad dynamics, and others if the late rally was too little, too late. A sixth-place Premier League finish was a vast improvement on the previous year's lowly twelfth but still not good enough for Chelsea, nor for an ownership group with designs on consistently elite results and competition finishes.

Pochettino had also never truly committed to Chelsea in the long term, appearing to weigh up continually whether he considered the Blues job something of a marriage of convenience. Blues fans felt he had never warmed up to them fully, never quite acknowledging the crowd in the way supporters so craved and then backing that up with lukewarm sentiments in media interviews. Throw in the fact that he had on several occasions waxed lyrical about his continued strong relationship with Tottenham owner Daniel Levy, and Chelsea fans, beyond the club's ownership, saw their patience and perhaps even their trust eroded.

Chelsea eventually opted to unseat Pochettino after one season at the helm, with the overriding principles behind that decision rooted in the owners' continued desire to see the men's side managed by a coach who would commit fully to the Blues and grow their career along with a developing squad.

•   •   •

While Chelsea's new owners hurtled through the necessary Stamford Bridge overhaul at breakneck speed, comfortable with change and relishing the constant challenges, the proposed humanitarian aid foundation meant to capitalise on the club sale proceeds remained at complete odds, in stasis, mothballed and gathering dust. After various deductions and reserved monies, the Chelsea sale proceeds amounted to a mammoth £2.35 billion. Perhaps the only repercussion of the Chelsea sale where nothing had actually changed, a sum of money that could change the face of global humanitarian aid for ever was left stuck in the frozen UK bank account into which it had cleared when ownership of the Stamford Bridge club was transferred from Roman Abramovich to the Boehly–Clearlake consortium.

Every time Mike Penrose, the former Unicef UK chief lined up to lead the foundation, would check in with government contacts to chase the latest situation, he would be either stonewalled entirely or passed from pillar to post. He could never decide whether he preferred the silent treatment or the *Yes Minister* merry-go-round. Abramovich and his team thought the government had signed terms to the effect that the proceeds should go towards 'exclusively humanitarian purposes supporting all victims of the conflict in Ukraine, and its consequences'.

The foundation's deed of undertaking, referenced in the Chelsea sale licence document, was said to state that the body should provide 'immediate relief and long-term support to victims of conflict anywhere in the world'. The sticking point came when the UK government had issued its 30 May 2022 unilateral declaration that insisted 'the Treasury will only issue a licence which ensures that such proceeds are used for exclusively humanitarian purposes in Ukraine'. The discrepancy in language threw up an impasse that had somehow proved insurmountable, right the way into early 2025.

By January 2024, Peter Ricketts, the chair of the House of Lords' European affairs committee, was lambasting the failure to free the money in an excoriating report. 'It is incomprehensible that two years after the deal between Abramovich and the government was struck, it has still not been implemented,' he wrote in the report, which proved damning for all sides.

> The unfulfilled promise made by Mr Abramovich at the time of the sale of Chelsea FC reflects poorly on him and the government for not pushing for a more binding commitment. We urge the government to use all available legal levers to solve the impasse rapidly so that Ukraine can receive much needed, promised, and long overdue relief.

Abramovich's position, of course, was that he had only ever signed an agreement stating that the sale proceeds would be used to aid all victims of the Ukraine conflict and its consequences, as well as other global conflicts, with no exact geographical constraints. This was on the advice of Penrose and his humanitarian aid colleagues who were primed to join the foundation's board, who all insisted that to limit any aid inside Ukraine would fail to strike at the highest need, given, as just one example, the spread of refugees across Europe.

Ricketts was David Cameron's former national security adviser, and the ex-Prime Minister turned Foreign Secretary, by now sitting in the House of Lords, had stood up behind the scenes as one of the few politicians who appeared determined to mobilise towards a solution that could free up the funds and launch the foundation. Ignored or evaded previously, at the start of 2024 when that Lords report was issued, Penrose had found himself being helped where at all possible by Cameron and his staff. Try as both sides might, however, that impasse could still not be shifted, and once the momentum was again lost and the issue began to drift once more.

By the end of January 2025, the sale proceeds were still frozen and the entire enterprise of the foundation still in limbo. By that stage, Penrose had heard nothing from the UK government for the best part of six months and was beginning to fear the project may never see the light of day. As Penrose made tricky journeys across Ukraine, experiencing first-hand the fatigue of the people who had lost countless friends and loved ones to nearly three years of war, with high food prices, unstable electricity and constant threat, his anger at what he felt were simply bureaucratic problems thwarting the foundation had receded, to be replaced by emotions teetering closer to the brink of resignation.

Penrose was in Ukraine at the end of January 2025 helping Ridne, a local project aimed at providing the logistics and wherewithal for Ukrainian companies to boost food production in the country while also creating strong export markets. Hopes were high at that point that a superior-quality vegetable oil product was close to being ready to export to the UK for sale in major supermarkets. Expectations for that game-changing humanitarian aid foundation were still regrettably low, though Penrose still hoped that Keir Starmer's Labour government might eventually be able to take a fresh look at the problem, if the in-tray ever cleared sufficiently.

•　　•　　•

Where Chelsea's men's set-up proved in regular flux, the women just kept on winning. Emma Hayes steered the Blues to a third consecutive Women's Super League and FA Cup double in 2022–23, in another remarkable achievement. The Women's Champions League crown remained just out of reach, however, as this time Hayes's side crashed out at the semi-final stage. The change in ownership caused few issues for Hayes, but in November 2023, she announced she would leave the Blues at the end of that season for a new challenge. The speculation ran and ran that she would take up the role of manager of United States Women, and in due course that would be confirmed. One last tilt at the only trophy to elude Hayes in her glittering Blues tenure remained, but as with the season before, her side fell at the Champions League semi-final hurdle. Chelsea failed to lift either domestic cup, adding an extra layer of frustration, but the Blues did drive on and win their fifth WSL title in a row.

The record fifth-straight league crown was secured thanks to a 6–0 thrashing of Manchester United on 18 May 2024, to beat Manchester City to the title on goal difference as the top flight went right down to the wire. As the Blues ran riot to send Hayes off in style, her twelve-year Chelsea stint was capped at seven league titles, five FA Cups, two League Cups and one Champions League final appearance.

'I'm just so relieved it's over,' said Hayes.

The hardest thing to do is five in a row because people take their eye off the ball. My legacy is winning while building a team for the future. I can't say it's my most enjoyable but it's definitely been the toughest, without doubt, and for that reason probably the sweetest. I am full with a ton of different emotions, knowing it is the end and I won't be with this team or these fans again – but they are always in my heart. I have given everything I've got, and now I am ready for my next adventure.

And ready Hayes proved, guiding the USA to Olympic gold in Paris that very summer, beating Brazil in the final as she switched seamlessly into perhaps the biggest job in the world in women's football.

From the moment Hayes had arrived at Chelsea in 2012, the visionary coach had struck up a special working relationship with owner Abramovich. In 2003, when Abramovich had bought the Blues, the women's team were housed under the umbrella of the club's charitable foundation, in an era of precious few advocates for the women's game. Determined to set new standards and opportunities, by Abramovich's second year of ownership the women's team were incorporated fully to the club. Greater funds were invested, the squad was moved to train at Cobham and a dedicated stadium was provided, in moves that were all ahead of the general curve for the women's game in the UK.

Abramovich had considered that Hayes had always matched his own vision for the women's team and the club's investment, and that the combination provided the platform for remarkable success. At the advent of the war in early 2022, Abramovich had hoped that Hayes would be able to lead Chelsea's women forward, perhaps even in a greater leadership role with the club. But as Hayes stepped away and into a new challenge, he was left as impressed as ever with her demeanour, leadership and drive.

Chelsea were able to move from strength to strength even in light of Hayes's departure, however, with Boehly–Clearlake recruiting decorated coach Sonia Bompastor as the new manager on 29 May 2024. Bompastor was recruited to continue Chelsea's quest for that maiden Champions League title, the one accolade that had eluded Hayes. By mid-February 2025, the Blues were unbeaten in all competitions, winning thirteen of fourteen league matches to open up a seven-point lead at the top of the table. A League Cup final, an FA Cup quarter-final and an all-important Champions League quarter-final were all in the offing too.

Hefty squad investment had still been common for the women's team across the new owners' tenure, notably in setting a new British record fee of £384,000 to recruit Levante striker Mayra Ramirez in January 2024. The recruitment went up another notch in January 2025 however, as Chelsea set a new world-record transfer fee with the £900,000 capture of USA defender Naomi Girma from San Diego, widely considered one of the globe's top talents. As Chelsea's women drew breath on an almost flawless first half of Bompastor's first campaign at the helm, and even more world-class faces came through the doors of specialist ground Kingsmeadow, the new-look women's team remained as potent as ever.

Bompastor's side would storm on to sweep a stunning domestic treble, powering through the entire league season unbeaten. Hopes were again soaring that the Blues' women could break their Champions League duck, only for Barcelona to swat them aside in the semi-finals. Just when Chelsea looked prepared to take that next step, the Catalan giants floored them 4–1 in both legs, for a chastening 8–2 aggregate thumping. Despite the blow, Chelsea's treble-winning exploits still pointed towards yet more success ahead.

• • •

The Chelsea sale process left a lasting impression on all involved, not least the thwarted bidders. Sir Jim Ratcliffe refused to let the football bug go, and just six months after the Blues had been sold he was in early negotiations on a possible deal for Manchester United. The divided loyalties he had talked about when attempting to mount his last-ditch bid outside the sale process for Chelsea no longer applied: born in Manchester, this was the club he had supported as a child.

Qatari billionaire Sheikh Jassim bin Hamad al-Thani was the main competition and for months the frontrunner to buy United from the Glazer family. Sheikh Jassim's superior financial muscle meant he was only ever interested in a complete takeover, and he was thought to have offered north of £5 billion with the expectation that such a blockbuster fee would seal the deal. Instead, the Glazers demanded even more money for the Old Trafford club, which sources close to Sheikh Jassim told reporters in October 2023 represented a 'fanciful and outlandish valuation'. Sheikh Jassim duly walked away from any deal, leaving Ratcliffe in the clear; the INEOS boss did go on to invest in United but bought only a 27.7 per cent stake as the terms shifted greatly for both sellers and buyers. Ratcliffe assumed control of the football operations after his investment was confirmed in early 2024, but by February 2025, the club was beset by mounting problems, including slipping to the bottom half of the Premier League table, new manager Ruben Amorim struggling to make sense of a muddled squad and a tired-looking Old Trafford in increasing need of renovation work.

The Ricketts family had been left to reflect on their turbulent, eventually withdrawn bid for the Blues, lamenting what might have been but still relishing the process. Tom Ricketts's long-term fandom of Chelsea meant that the Blues were the only football club he would have wanted to buy, and that stance has been reflected in the fact the family has not even considered another Premier League investment. Tom and Laura Ricketts found themselves back in London in June 2023, at the London Stadium for the MLB international matches with the Chicago Cubs. Watching their baseball team play at the home of West Ham appears as close to any Premier League operation as they are now likely to come.

Martin Broughton had spent the week after the sale process ended racking his brains to see if his bid team could have done anything differently that might have tipped the process in their favour.

In the end, he and his partners were left of a mind that in presenting their authentic selves they had delivered their best possible pitch, and they simply had to respect the Boehly–Clearlake success. Josh Harris and David Blitzer, who had provided the bulk of the capital for the Broughton bid, shifted sporting tack in July 2023, buying the Washington Commanders NFL franchise for a new sports team record fee of $6.05 billion, eclipsing the Chelsea sale price.

Leaving Chelsea had a lasting effect on the Blues' former executive team too, with Bruce Buck choosing not to make a quick return as a fan while he took stock of the nineteen years under Abramovich. For Marina Granovskaia, however, the sale process was not even over before she had to deal with another major concern. On 22 May 2022, Granovskaia received what she would later allege in court was a threatening email from football agent Saif Alrubie, seeking a £300,000 payment he believed he was owed from Kurt Zouma's £29.1 million move from Chelsea to West Ham in August 2021.

A saga that would last more than two years ensued, as a worried Granovskaia quickly passed the email to Chelsea's security team as a matter of protocol, who then in turn contacted the police. Alrubie would be charged with one count of sending an electronic communication with the intent to cause distress, and the case eventually went all the way to trial at Southwark Crown Court, though it would not be heard until late April 2024.

Granovskaia told the court how she felt 'physically threatened' by the email, but Alrubie insisted the threats were only ever of a legal nature. Prosecutors had claimed in the trial that part of Alrubie's contentious email had intimated Granovskaia might 'suffer the same fate' as Kia Joorabchian, another prominent football agent. This was taken by Granovskaia as a reference to Joorabchian's claims in a separate incident that he had been accosted by a group of men demanding payment on Alrubie's behalf. The night before Joorabchian was due to give evidence, however, he flew to the US without informing the police, and in the end never testified in court.

Alrubie was eventually acquitted of the charge, at which point he quickly went on the offensive, revealing his anger that the case had ever reached court at all. He had insisted in his court testimony that threatening Granovskaia physically would have been a 'suicide mission' given her senior position at Chelsea and among Abramovich's staff.

Granovskaia issued a rare statement after the court case, in which she laid bare the impact on her across the preceding two years. 'Coming to court to give evidence in the Crown's case against Mr Alrubie was an extremely difficult decision,' said Granovskaia in late April 2024.

> I am an intensely private person, but I was willing to do my part to ensure that no one else – particularly no woman – was ever made to feel as I did upon receiving his email, a feeling this trial has revived. I was also minded to testify as I received messages of support from colleagues and associates in football following news of Mr Alrubie's arrest, including some who have had dealings with him over the years. There are things I miss about football: my colleagues and counterparts, including some wonderful and decent agents; the players; the spirit of Chelsea; and, of course, winning trophies. One thing I do not miss is the difficult and ugly side of football.

It was a statement designed to put the matter to bed, even though the outcome did not match Granovskaia's assessment of the situation. Alrubie had other ideas, however, and quickly pursued a multi-million-pound lawsuit against Chelsea. Though he dropped that case in November 2024, at that point he insisted he was still pursuing Granovskaia personally for recompense regarding the Zouma transfer. By early 2025 there had seemingly been no end to the matter, leaving Granovskaia in the dark and clearly wanting to put the entire episode behind her.

While Buck still needed more time before returning to Stamford Bridge for a Chelsea match, Granovskaia was faster to feel ready for her first game of the new era and duly attended the Blues' 2–1 win over Newcastle on 27 October 2024, even posting pictures on Instagram and joking that she was not tall enough to see the goals. As for a return to the business of football, perhaps another executive role, Granovskaia had not entirely ruled out the prospect, but her statement from April 2024 and the end of the Alrubie trial still stood, and she had no great desire to be exposed anew to the sport's dark underbelly.

Petr Čech's decision to relinquish his technical directorship at the end of the Abramovich era had allowed him the time to realise another childhood dream: to play ice hockey professionally. Growing up, the Czech Republic goalkeeper had first dreamed of a hockey career and had never let that slide fully from his mind, despite his glittering successes in football. When he retired from playing in 2019, he had enjoyed low-key netminding stints with Guildford Phoenix. After leaving his director role at Chelsea in 2022, though, he stepped up to the third tier of the British game with Chelmsford Chieftains and then Oxford Stars. But it was with Belfast Giants that, aged forty-one, Čech made his pro ice hockey debut, in November 2023; an opportunity he thought had passed him by was suddenly ticked off the bucket list.

As his step back from football allowed him more time, Čech was also studying for a PhD, with an MBA already in the bag. He still knew that eventually the right time would come for him to make a return to football, and he harboured a strong feeling that it might just come in the shape of a fresh challenge in coaching. Beyond all his playing accolades at Chelsea, however, the Champions League triumph, a Europa League win, the five Premier League titles, four FA Cups and three League Cups, Čech would for ever remain overwhelmingly proud of the Blues' response to the club being sanctioned.

When the pressure, chaos and threats hit their peak, Čech was able to play his part in ensuring the men's team kept their heads and their collective spirit, then qualified for the next season's Champions League. Where it would have been so easy for the Chelsea executives to make promises that could not be kept, or for the players to lose their focus amid genuine fears for their futures, instead the Stamford Bridge collective shone through and delivered what was required. When Čech left Chelsea for the second time, in June 2022 at the end of his directorship, he did so with his head held high, his primary objectives crucial to the club's very future achieved, and with a legacy more than preserved.

• • •

Back at the sharp end of the new Chelsea era, in the wake of Mauricio Pochettino's Stamford Bridge departure in May 2024, the Boehly–Clearlake ownership group were still convinced that a young, upwardly mobile manager could spearhead the Blues' drive towards sustained success. The search to replace Pochettino proved comprehensive but swift, then ended squarely with Enzo Maresca. The Leicester boss was recruited for his unfussy, decisive style, whether that be a low-key handling of public issues like the media or a tactical approach that would always retain the same base principles but that could be flexed in order to maximise resources. His apprenticeship in the Manchester City set-up, working with and being quietly mentored by Pep Guardiola, was also valued by Chelsea, who saw a coach ready to apply and also bid to develop those best-in-class lessons.

Pochettino had left Chelsea formally on 21 May 2024, while Maresca was appointed on 3 June but would not officially start work until 1 July. The club and its new manager would be in constant contact across Maresca's summer holiday, though, as the former West Brom and Fiorentina creative midfielder took a vital opportunity to recharge, having steered Leicester to promotion back to the Premier League from the Championship before leaving the Foxes for the Blues.

Another transfer window led to further squad flux at Chelsea, but the evidence of the owners' craved stability was starting to creep through. Pedro Neto's £54 million switch from Wolves, João Félix's £45.5 million permanent signing from Atletico Madrid and Maresca's £30 million raid of Leicester for midfielder Kiernan Dewsbury-Hall were among the headline-grabbers as twelve new recruits came through the door. The balance came in the shape of ten players departing, not least Romelu Lukaku finally being found a permanent move, to Napoli for £25 million to reunite with his ex-Inter Milan coach Antonio Conte.

The transfers that generated the most intense response from fans were the protracted £36 million sale of academy graduate turned England midfielder Conor Gallagher to Atletico Madrid, with Dewsbury-Hall recruited from his own home club of Leicester in his stead. The deals, and a host of others for many Premier League clubs that summer, had in part materialised due to new profit and sustainability regulations (PSR) that meant that fees received for selling homegrown stars would be regarded as pure profit.

The continued tightening of spending regulations by the Premier League, in a bid to drive the English top flight towards a more measured transfer strategy, was well intentioned – but the unintended knock-on effect was that Premier League clubs realised selling academy graduates could stretch their buying power, albeit at a clear price of offloading potential home favourites. As the relentless drive for any edge continued to grip the division, few clubs were immune to the notion of letting homegrown stars – developed and honed in many cases, like Gallagher's, from primary school age – move on to pastures new to create other squad opportunities. While many clubs capitalised on a potential fringe benefit that also harboured sizeable risk, not least in terms of upsetting a fan base, the pervasive view behind the scenes at Premier League clubs was that, eventually, top-flight chiefs would have to rethink the policy. A number of clubs from the outset wanted the Premier League to find a way of incentivising the odd prudent player sale that could also protect an academy graduate's chances of making the grade with their boyhood side.

The advent of Maresca's managerial tenure brought tentative improvement to the Blues across the first half of his maiden Stamford Bridge campaign. A 6–2 win at Wolves offered early hope, while a five-match winning run in all competitions cemented a solid start. Eight victories in succession across November and into mid-December raised hopes and expectations, only for three wins in eleven matches to temper that progress by the latter half of February 2025.

A fluctuating season eventually ended on a major upswing for the Blues, however, as Maresca steered his side to a fourth-place

Premier League finish for crucial Champions League qualification. Another significant bonus proved the Europa Conference League final, where Chelsea sealed their first men's silverware of the new ownership.

On 28 May in Poland, Chelsea slipped an early goal down against Spain's Real Betis, taking that setback into half-time and fearing the worst. After the interval, however, the Blues returned refocused, with star man Cole Palmer orchestrating a total turnaround. Palmer laid on two goals as the Blues strode to a 4–1 triumph, thanks to efforts from Enzo Fernández, Nicolas Jackson, Jadon Sancho and Moises Caicedo. Another season of change had been capped with a finish that had many of a Chelsea persuasion eyeing another upward curve.

Even after almost three years at the Chelsea helm, the Boehly–Clearlake ownership group were only just beginning to find space to breathe, having been driving non-stop to impose new processes, systems and structures, especially off the field, from the day they had taken control of the Stamford Bridge club. For the first time in his Chelsea tenure, Boehly found that he could take a step back and take stock. The opportunity for perspective left Boehly convinced Chelsea were indeed on the right track and prepared to capitalise on all the hard groundwork that had been completed. And with a team of trusted experts in place across the leadership structure, down through to the first team set-up, Boehly was able to adopt a more hands-off approach.

From the outbreak of war on 24 February 2022, Chelsea had been turned upside down and the club's very future threatened on countless occasions, but in just ninety-five fraught days, 280 would-be suitors had been whittled down to one group, focused, driven and, ultimately, deep-pocketed enough to receive the Stamford Bridge baton from Abramovich, and strive to take the club forward in the manner in which he had always intended. Just like the sale process itself, the extended beginnings of the Boehly–Clearlake era had been turbulent, but as the first quarter of 2025 unfolded, Stamford Bridge had clarity, stability and passion from a leadership group heavily invested in and driven towards winning the top trophies, not just in a quick fix but instead for the long haul.

EPILOGUE

Water taxis strain against the torrent, dodging container ships hauling goods from Asia to Europe and back again. Roman Abramovich looks out across the Bosphorus and takes stock. 'From one life… to another,' he says, speaking in the immaculate house of one of his friends, in an exclusive neighbourhood of Turkey's largest city. At the crossroads of east and west, Abramovich talks endings and beginnings.

His time as Chelsea chief ended officially on 30 May 2022, when Boehly, Eghbali and Feliciano's consortium took Stamford Bridge control. His new beginning ultimately came almost four months earlier, however, the moment Russia invaded Ukraine. Less than twelve hours after the war began, Abramovich started his efforts towards peace, in a back-channelling role that would last almost two years.

Above the lip of the 31km strait cutting two continents apart, luxurious properties with direct access to the water skirt the riverbanks. Higher still, on the street, black minivans housing security personnel fringe the pavement. Fatih Sultan Mehmet Bridge sits in a haze in the distance. Barbed wire adorns eight-foot walls flanking solid steel entry doors, giving way to a modern house of understated comfort.

Leaning his arms on the table hewn from reclaimed wood, Abramovich flicks between two photos in his phone's camera roll. The two lives in those consecutive pictures: the ending and beginning. First, that 200-year-old tree, felled by high winds on Abramovich's estate in the south of France. Then, tanks deployed in the war. The two images, just twenty-four hours apart. The first taken the day before the Ukraine war started – the second the day the conflict broke out.

From east to west, Asia to Europe, beloved Chelsea owner to 'kleptocrat', according to the UK government and 2022 Foreign Secretary Liz Truss, 'complicit' in Putin's war in Ukraine. Britain and the EU had continued their sanctions against Abramovich and still considered him as effectively an enemy of peace. But in the very same city where he is adamant a deal to end the war was almost sealed in late March 2022, Abramovich reasserts his hopes for a lasting resolution.

'Perhaps one day we can get back to a similar situation to the one at the end of March 2022,' says Abramovich. 'We all hope for that. But everything becomes a new normal, people have to adapt to a new everyday life and learn how to live it.'

The speed of the Bosphorus, churning from the Black Sea to the Sea of Marmara, only reinforces the impermanence that has always surrounded one of football's most enigmatic figures. Intensely private, a natural introvert, Abramovich has never before spoken so openly. Over the course of several meetings, starting on those Bosphorus banks, he would chart the dramatic change from Premier League powerbroker to putative pariah.

He did not seek sympathy nor launch any defence, instead displaying an ability to pivot his energies from one passion project to another. Those who know Abramovich best say the speed with which he shifted focus from Chelsea to trying to aid efforts towards a resolution in the war was typical of his character, in both business and life.

Small wins along Abramovich's involvement in the early negotiations saw thousands of people evacuated through humanitarian corridors, and hostages freed just when they had feared execution. In his old life, Abramovich might have celebrated with abandon the most crucial of Chelsea goals. He and his closest companions remember unexpectedly wild reactions when the Blues claimed their maiden Champions League glory in Munich in 2012, for example. Now that almost indescribable, visceral feeling of celebrating a vital Chelsea goal has been replaced by the wide-eyed elation and relief of playing even the smallest part in helping people affected by the conflict.

Abramovich is more than smart enough to parallel the Bosphorus with the crossroads still ahead of him. Perhaps the sight of this surging, pan-continental expanse is enough to elicit a rare moment of reflection.

'There is an old expression from the Soviet Union, "Don't complain about being poor or about being in prison,"' he says. 'We had fifty good years, and now, something else.'

MAYFAIR, LONDON, FEBRUARY 2025

Todd Boehly sits in his immaculate but understated office, explaining why he believes he and his partners won the race to buy Chelsea some two and a half years earlier – before setting out the Blues owners' steadfast ambitions for the Stamford Bridge club's future.

Leaning forward, he drums his fingers momentarily on the coffee table, then delivers a succinct, insightful rundown on the crux of the ninety-five days that changed Chelsea, and also his and his fellow owners' lives, for ever.

Three black and white photos adorn the wall of Boehly's office, one for each of his sporting investments and passions: an arty shot of Dodger Stadium, a reflective snap of LeBron James in LA Lakers action, and a yesteryear picture of Chelsea locked in a mud-soaked rough-and-tumble encounter. Boehly cuts a relaxed but focused figure, matching his casual but impeccably turned-out attire.

To win the right to take Chelsea forward into a new era was, in part, to find a way to convince Roman Abramovich, via his most trusted and long-serving advisers, that the Boehly–Clearlake consortium were the clear first among the billionaire equals of their many and varied rival bidders. All the Chelsea bids that were taken to the final stages of the enforced sale process were considered sufficiently sophisticated, capable and well-funded to have kept the Stamford Bridge club as an elite-level going concern. One key task for Boehly, his partners Mark Walter and Hansjörg Wyss, allied to Clearlake Capital and their co-founders Behdad Eghbali and José E. Feliciano, was to harness the requisite emotional intelligence to prove they could uphold Abramovich's winning Chelsea legacy. Another was to convince the UK government they could also diverge from the previous ownership just enough to ease the Blues away from the spectre of Russia's illegal invasion of Ukraine.

The bidding phases of the Chelsea sale absolutely required that Boehly, Clearlake and partners pulled out all the stops in pivotal pitch meetings with Blues chairman Bruce Buck, director Marina Granovskaia and Raine Group heads Joe Ravitch and Colin Neville. At the end of a gruelling process, ultimately, Boehly, Clearlake,

Walter and Wyss had sold themselves better than any of their rivals. Abramovich and his cohort had selected the Boehly–Clearlake group as the best fit to take Chelsea forward, with Buck and Granovskaia both regarding their consortium as bearing the closest synergy in terms of swift, decisive action combined with robust investment.

Those black and white pictures on Boehly's London office wall are no accident: Chelsea has been placed in the exact same category as the Lakers and the Dodgers. And where Boehly and Walter's Dodgers investment is concerned, the measured, patient drive for success has paid the inarguable dividend of World Series triumphs in both 2020 and 2024. The second World Series win led to a victory parade that left Boehly only ever more determined to bring that kind of celebration to Chelsea on his consortium's watch.

'If you look at our ambitions for the Dodgers and for the Lakers, you're here to win, and it's our business to win; and we're doing everything we can do to win,' said Boehly.

In European football, you're on your edge every second, because when you go down 1–0 it's almost like you got kicked in the teeth. So it's unlike any other sport because the goals are so few and far between that there's nothing more satisfying than scoring a goal, and there's nothing more painful than conceding a goal. When you're losing, I've never had the minutes go faster, and when you're winning, I've never had the minutes go slower. That experience, I didn't know it in my soul like I now know it. And I know it because I care so much.

You can understand something intellectually, but you don't really feel it and know it until you've gone through it emotionally. We didn't get a parade with the Dodgers in 2020, because of

Covid. But when you see a 300,000-person parade, and the whole town comes out, you see how much the team matters to the town. That will be something that sticks with me for ever, and now, the players have seen it, and felt it, and they want it again. So our goal with Chelsea is also to win silverware, because we know, and I know, how much it means to the fans. It makes you appreciate again that sport makes people happy, especially when you win, and Chelsea's supposed to win. But I really believe that sustained success is an investment, and no matter what business I'm in, or any industry, there are no shortcuts.

ABU DHABI, JANUARY 2025

Peppa the corgi blinks into the winter sun as Roman Abramovich considers whether he felt any vindication when proof was beamed around the world of his efforts towards facilitating peace talks between Russia and Ukraine. Waves from the Arabian Gulf break gently onto the beach in the distance as Abramovich surveys the scene from an outdoor seating area in a residence tucked into a quiet, gated Abu Dhabi community. 'There is an old Russian saying, "The dogs bark but the caravan keeps moving," and that fits here,' says Abramovich when we meet for the second time, in early 2025.

As relaxed, affable and engaging as in our first meeting a year prior, Abramovich was also still under the yoke of UK sanctions. Phlegmatic and accepting of the UK government's sanctions against him, Abramovich's old Russian adage explained that he had never much worried what people say about him, and that was extremely unlikely to change.

When he had put down all thoughts of Chelsea in early March 2022 in order to try to help set up peace talks between Russia and Ukraine, however, pockets of the international political community adopted an at-best sceptical stance towards his involvement. When footage of him attending summit talks in Istanbul aimed at brokering peace in Ukraine was broadcast around the world at the end of March 2022, the questioning of efforts receded. 'Whatever I do, people will always accuse me of some kind of agenda,' he explained calmly. 'In the end, I have done what I have done simply to try to help.'

Still ignoring outside comment, Abramovich has adjusted to both life under sanctions and life after Chelsea. Mightily relieved that the club that he doted on for nineteen years was sold as a going concern and avoided ruin, Abramovich still wonders if, one day, he might be able to return to Stamford Bridge just once more. Amid a swirl of uncertainty in many areas, however, one thing is clear: there will never be another Chelsea for Abramovich, and never another football club stewardship. 'Perhaps one day there would be a situation where I could attend a match and say a proper goodbye, but nothing more than that,' he said, when asked about Chelsea and the future.

I don't have any interest in any role in a football club, certainly not a professional role. There might be something where I could help with academies and youngsters, giving greater opportunities to people from difficult backgrounds, if there were an initiative that could make a difference. But as for ownership or a professional role at a club, I am done with that in this lifetime.